Back From War

FINDING HOPE & UNDERSTANDING IN LIFE AFTER COMBAT

Introduction by
General Tommy R. Franks
Former Commander-in-Chief
United States Central Command
★★★★

Once in a while a book on war comes along that knocks your socks off. This is one of those truly great books, packed with authenticity and truth. Lee Alley and Wade Stevenson not only tell it like it is, but also like it was. It is factual and forthright. *Back From War: Finding Hope & Understanding In Life After Combat* hits you in the gut with realism. Even today, our many veterans who find post-war experiences troubling, might benefit and find solace from this incredible read.

I met Lieutenant Lee Alley in October 1967, my first day at Binh Phuoc, Vietnam. Our first meeting, there in our barracks, was a casual one. Lee was wearing a green towel around his waist and shower clogs on his feet, I in my GI shorts.

In short order our friendship solidified; we came together, brothers-in-arms, sharing combat experiences of the most horrible kind. Brought together in extreme circumstances, we witnessed heartbreaking losses—our fellow soldiers, civilians and our buddies. The times called for sympathy and comfort; we relied on one another for strength, courage and persistence.

An unbreakable bond was formed back then, one that has endured throughout the years. Lee Alley is a true patriot and a bona-fide American hero! He led his troops with honor and distinction and is a living legend in the 5th/60th 9th Infantry Division.

I respect him and stand in awe of his heroism. Lee represents the best of America. It is my honor to call him "Friend," and to heartily recommend, to all, this outstanding book.

— Tommy Franks

Back From War

Finding Hope & Understanding In Life After Combat

1ST LT. LEE ALLEY
WITH
WADE STEVENSON

$16.95 US • $21.95 Canada
Copyright ©2007 by Lee Alley

ISBN-10: 0-9767329-4-7
ISBN-13: 978-0-9767329-4-5

Trade Paperback, First Edition 2007

Library of Congress Control Number: 2007925161

Printed in the United States of America

Back From War: Finding Hope & Understanding In Life After Combat is published by:

Exceptional Publishing, a division of The King Consortium
Robert King, Publisher
2760 Ellesmere Drive
Midlothian, VA 23113
804.794.0347

Production Credits:
Editor: Barbara Teel
Layout and Production: Ben Teel
Publisher's Editor: John Pine
Maps drawn by Erika Haroldson
Cover Design: MeyerNewYork@aol.com
Photo Credit: Getty Images/Stone/Mark Andrews
Index written by Deborah Patton
Back Cover Design: Riddick Advertising

Lee Alley may be contacted via e-mail at: lee@leealley.us

This book may be ordered by mail from the publisher or downloaded in PDF format at www.backfromwar.com.

DEDICATION

We dedicate this book to all veterans who have answered their nation's call to duty. Every veteran has paid a price for the freedom we enjoy. That price regrettably often comes in the form of wounds of war. Many of the physical wounds are evident. However, the psychological wounds which others may carry are not as easily identified—yet they hurt just as much. Then there are those who paid the ultimate price with their lives. My heart aches for all families thus affected by war.

With this, special dedications go to the men of the 5th Battalion, 60th Infantry of the 9th Infantry Division. I ate, slept, cried, laughed, bled, and served proudly with these men. It was my special once-in-a-lifetime opportunity to be a member of that proud unit, to enjoy such outstanding cohesion, esprit de corps and pride in comradery.

Little did I know as I trained for war that I would be dropped into the middle of such an outstanding group of individuals. My commanding officers set the standard of leadership I strove to achieve: Captain Steve Siegfried (Sieg), now a retired Major General; Captain Hector Villarreal (Capt 'V'), retired Lieutenant Colonel; Colonel William Steele, retired Major General; Coloncl Eric Antilla (retired and now deceased). I owe these men so much!

I still think of them as my commanders. I would follow each and every one of them again, anywhere.

My peers and fellow lieutenants: Tommy Franks, Mike Schlee, John Sweet, Jim Sharp, Bo Whitworth, and Alec Wade—we were as close as a band of brothers in combat could ever be, and remain so today.

The men I was honored to command were the best ever! I don't remember ever trying to command them. I simply strove to live up to the high standards they deserved in a commanding officer. Some 35 years later when asked for a quote to be placed on a placard in the Veterans Park, Casper, Wyoming, I answered as honestly as I could, and from my heart, "Anyone spouting the demise of our American youth's patriotism and devotion to God and country never had the honor of commanding those like I did in combat."

Truly, it was an honor to be associated with the men of the 5th/60th. You hold a special place in my heart. I love you one and all.

This is your book.

*During the final process
of putting this book together,
my dear friend and co-author Wade,
fondly called "Wilson,"
passed away.
Without him
this book would still be
just a dream.*

Thanks Wilson . . .

— Lee Alley

CONTENTS

CONTENTS CONT.

PART FOUR - SECURE THE AREA & CLOSE DOWN

PREFACE

Initially when thinking about writing this book, I had no intention of telling another war story. However, the Vietnam section is included for two reasons. First: The events described actually happened as told and are true. They appear simply to provide background information as to what led to some of the problems I've had in readjusting to civilian life after my war experiences. And, secondly: I hope that in relating them in this manner, it will give credibility and a face to the men of the 5th Battalion, 60th Infantry, 9th Infantry Division. They are the world's finest guys. I have been honored and privileged to know them. And they and their organizations produced some of our country's greatest military leaders.

Thus the primary purpose of this book is to provide examples of some of the problems returning veterans, who perhaps like me, may have had to face and struggle with. Hopefully it might yield some aid in helping them to regain a sense of comfort and relief from their troubling war experiences.

As I talk to groups around the country or share my stories with other veterans, a common, recurring question is always present: "Why weren't you sharing this twenty years ago?"

Simple answer: " I couldn't."

Hence this book. I don't want our young veterans of today to return home and be held hostage to nightmarish war memories. I'm hoping maybe this book will help with that.

If one veteran, regardless of the war or conflict: WWII, Korea, Vietnam, Persian Gulf, Desert Storm, Afghanistan, Kosovo, Iraq, any and all conflicts—even if just one veteran, a veteran's family member, or loved one reads this and says, "Hey, maybe I'm okay after all," or "Maybe my son," or "Maybe so and so's husband is okay,"—then this book is a success.

I thank you.

— Lee

Acknowledgments

I would like to thank my family, my loves, my life. First my wife of 34 years, Ellen. Her support for all veterans and me has been steadfast. She has opened her home and her heart to the men of the 5th/60th. By taking an active role in the Military Reunions, she has earned the title of First Lady of the 5th/60th.

My daughter Kresta has always been one of my best friends. I could not have finished this book without her typing skills and computer knowledge. She is a better softball coach, fisherman, and golfer than me. I just try to keep up.

Bo is the son everyone hopes for. I am so proud of him. His testimony in the book is heartfelt and greatly appreciated. Everyone needs some person in his life who believes you can do no wrong. I have that in my son. I try to live my life so as not to let him down.

Wade Stevenson, my co-author, was such a special person. His ability to take my words and have them suddenly make sense was overwhelming. With his sincere and concerted caring I didn't just get a co-author. I found someone who cares for veterans as I do. I found all of this and more in Wade. Thank you "Mr. Wilson."

Hector Villarreal, lovingly known as Captain 'V', thank you! Without your push, not so subtle, this book never would have taken shape. You made me believe we could take a heartbroken father's words from "The Letter" and build a cornerstone around which others could rally. "The Letter" spawned this book. Capt. V, you are a true leader of men.

General Tommy Franks' often seemingly small gestures can be life-changing. A lunch at Malio's Restaurant in Tampa Bay when he introduced me as a war hero, a personal invitation to attend the coming out party of his great book, *American Soldier*, in New York City, and having me stand and be recognized as he spoke to a packed house in Denver, CO. This made me believe my service was honorable. And, I, too, have something to say thanks for: Thank you for all of your support, Tommy. And thank you for the use of your Jeep in Tan An.

To all of you who have contributed: I always heard writing a book is difficult, and now I know that to be true. The book, *Back From War: Finding Hope & Understanding In Life After Combat,* has presented real challenges, and the biggest of which was how to use the writings sent in by you, the contributors. I was deeply touched and honored you would take the time to open your heart and soul and put those most sensitive of emotions on paper and share them with me. Wade Stevenson, the co-author, and I hung on every word—then the problems began.

How do we fit all the testimonials into the theme and limited length of the book I have in mind? We used some of the stories as presented, but we necessarily had to omit some; others were edited for length, and some, with your concurrence and help, were expanded. However with all of this never—never, not with even one single word—is there the intent of showing partiality, or to diminish in any way the superbly well-presented, obvious pride of authorship and heartfelt sincerity in your submissions.

Rather, having to work within the confines with which we are restricted, the main thesis and keeping the end result solidly in mind, unfortunately and sadly, some material had to be edited and excised.

For all who have contributed to this effort in any manner, Wade and I thank you from the bottom of our hearts. As with most things in life, we achieve not always on our own. Never has this been truer than with the writing of this book. We have listed each of you as best we can recollect, and have recorded your names below.

If *anyone* has been omitted, we beg your forgiveness, as the omission is due strictly to error—and is not intentional.

It has been our pleasure to have known, served and worked with you. We pray God's richest blessings, a long, happy and healthy life for you and yours.

Thank you:

Alan Kisling, Barb & Ben Teel, Bo Alley, Carl Hernandez, Charlene Busk, Charles P. (the Von) Ryan, Curtis Hatterman, Dennis Garms, Dick Prahl, Daniel and Tammy Berg, Donnie and Judy Race, Dorothy Jane Stevenson, Ed Scarborough, Ellen Alley, Eric Reckard, Erika Haroldson, Erin Barnett, Hector Villarreal, Howard and Betty Enghelm, J.A. Coutant, James M. Cronan Sr., Jim Maves, Jim Miller, Joe Milbrodt, John Chepes, Joseph Kozloski, Justin Walker, Keith Nolan, Kevin Robinett, MD., Kim Cooper Findling, Kresta Alley, Larry Nixon, Linda Lang, Linda Tiffany, Louis 'Tex' Balas, Malcolm McConnell, Mark Koons, Mark Slama, Misty Woodall Costner, Reverend Ron McCants, Rita Slama, Sam Bailey, Sam Taylor, Thomas O'Brien, and William Metzler.

We most sincerely thank all of you
for your understanding and support.
Any errors are ours.

Lee Alley & Wade Stevenson ·
December 1, 2005
Wheatland, Wyoming

Please refer to
Glossary of Terms
for definition and explanation
of acronyms and
military terms.

PROLOGUE

I can't see them, but I know they're out there. And they know we are here. Creepy feeling.

I can actually *feel* their close proximity. Now and then, when the breeze is just so, I'm certain I can smell them. It hasn't taken me long to develop a sense of their malodorous fragrance. Apart from their distinct body odors—which are bad enough—they reek of Nuoc Mam, the fermented drippings of rotted fish, which they pour over their rice. The smell would make a buzzard puke. But who knows? Maybe we smell as gross to them.

In the lingering daylight after digging our foxholes we briefly strip, revealing prune-like shriveled skin and waterlogged wrinkled feet, and attempt to dry our clothing. There won't be time for every-thing to completely dry, but *any* relief is surely welcome. It's warm this Saturday night in mid-November 1967, although muggy with high humidity. Won't be long 'till Thanksgiving—back home. Won't be hot and muggy in Wyoming.

Everything's still damp after our earlier helicopter drop here from Landing Zone Brown where we'd been virtually pinned down in waist-high canal water for over 12 hours. I know my men are tired, worn, and battle-weary. And although now prepared and in a high-defense readiness posture knowing another battle is imminent, it feels good, at least for the moment, to stretch out on dry land and to have left the smell of battle. Here the gentle breeze off the river is · pleasant; the air smells sweet and fresh. I'm enjoying this slight, but tenuous feeling of normalcy.

It's around 2300. Full moon—a Hunter's Moon—and few clouds. Privates First Class White and Lopez stationed at Listening Post (LP2) hear movement of someone wading towards them in the canal. White yells, "Camon Ty! Chieu Hoi!" (Halt—Give up!) The enemy ducks and White riddles his body and blows his face away with a short burst from his M-60 automatic.

An eerie and nervous hour and a half of silence follow. From a distance but suddenly getting closer I can hear the singsong chants of the VC encroaching through the bamboo and brush. God, there must be at least a hundred of them—and there are thirty-five of us. They yell with vehemence and a curdling hatred, *"GI you die! We get you tonight!"* I feel tingling chill bumps on my arms and the hair on the back of my neck rising. I hear the unmistakable "thump" of a mortar round leaving a tube and yell, *"Incoming mortars!"* The night erupts in a cataclysmic explosion of mortars, tracers, claymores, grenades and rifle shots. The air is filled with bullets, smoke, gunpowder, and explosives.

My men are being killed. Goddammit! I can see them being hit! I scream at the top of my lungs, *"Get down, get down!"*

My shouts wake me and I realize my long-time haunt has once again returned. I am chilled, downright cold, but also covered in sweat. And I'm actually trembling. I find I'm gasping for breath; my throat is dry and it's hard for me to swallow. Finally I'm able to pull some air into my lungs. Still shaking I look at the red digital numbers of the clock showing 01:30 in the morning. This is about the time the full-fledged attack at Fire Support Base Cudgel began *that* November night. Yet another strange coincidence?

Christ, here I've been feeling good and thankful for not having dreamt about Vietnam in over a month. But the memories and dreams always return to torment me. I just cannot seem to shake my 'Nam experiences. The recollections are *always* there—sometimes held at a distance by forcing them away with thoughts of other, more pleasant things—but seems like they're never far away. Standing poised like a silent evil sentinel lurking, *always there,* and especially in the darkness of night.

It's taking me a long time trying to readjust and return to a "normal" life. But optimistically, even with the dreams and nightmare memories, I tell myself, *I think I'm doing better.* And I have learned to live with the humor some of my friends seem to find whenever I still jump at a loud, close noise, a sonic boom, Fourth of July fireworks, or if I brace when there's a sudden unexpected movement either toward me or near me. They just don't understand. But, thank God, my wife seems to understand.

By now I am wide-awake and turn to look at my life-long soul mate. I'm glad I didn't wake her this time—disturb her sleep again as I have so many times in the past.

I touch her skin and smell her hair, and a calmness seems to return and quietly settle over me.

I leave my sweat-dampened pillow and sheets and get out of

bed. I roll the logs in the fireplace that warm the night's chill and provide a soft, comforting glow in our bedroom. I look again at my wife. My heart's love, my wife of five years who also loves me. She cares for me, and I know it. She seems to understand things difficult for me to discuss when others would not. We met at the University of Wyoming in Laramie through a mutual friend, Jim Cundall. Jim's also a Vietnam vet. I sometimes talk to him and feel comfortable doing so.

I once more poke the logs in the fireplace and think *life is now good.* I've graduated from the university, taught school, and settled into a life I love as a partner with my father-in-law on a cattle ranch near Laramie.

Some days I truly believe I am solid. Yeah, solid. Very few know I was in Vietnam—and I like that. The few who know of my war history are also vets. Makes me feel good that some come to me, confide in me, and ask for my advice.

My message to them is always the same, firm and simple—*quit living in the past!* Shake it loose! Vietnam is a world away. Dammit, that was then. This is now! I resolutely swore to separate myself from all of that the moment the plane I flew back to the USA on went wheels-up, leaving the tarmac runway at Tan Son Nhut Air Force Base in July of 1968.

Damn right. Easily said—not easily done. Even with my staunch resolve to put it all behind me, there are nights I can't sleep. Yeah. Always, the nighttime is the worst.

I again see vivid pictures of my troops being shot, mortar rounds landing in our trenches, heads blown off, bodies exploded and shredded to pieces. My nostrils clog with the stench of war and the coppery smell of blood. In these recurring dreams I can feel myself tremble and seem completely helpless. It's as if I'm standing someplace far off seeing the battles—replay after replay. And I can't stop them! Sometimes it seems as if I am back there again but in a drugged, hazy, slow-motion and otherworldly dimension. I can see myself as clearly as if it were happening this instant. I'm struggling and dragging my wounded comrades through the mud and water, enemy shots are plunking all around us. I'm angry and frustrated, but even with adrenaline running high I begin to feel tired and then suddenly beyond exhaustion. Now in pain I realize I have been

3

wounded. Swearing and shouting I continue to drag and pull the wounded to safety. These images, sights, sounds and sharp pungent smells of war come to me with a stinging freshness, a brilliant clarity and dread. The scenes now flash through my head as if someone has put a camera in fast-forward motion.

I get a drink of water and watch the red, yellow and orange flames dance on the logs that I've stirred to new life. The red numerals show 02:30 on the clock. I can't go back to bed.

Sitting in my recliner, I extend the footrest and stare at the fire.

Nine years since I left Vietnam. Nine years of mostly keeping all this inside and refusing to talk. Doubt anyone would understand anyhow. And, I always think: *Why should I burden others with my problems?*

But sometimes I wonder how I can appear so strong on the outside, while having to hold myself to stop from trembling? Seems I just can't talk about these things—*I can't share them with anyone.*

Back home Wyoming newspapers hail me as a returning hero: "Recommended for the Congressional Medal of Honor, Lieutenant Alley is one of the most decorated soldiers ever to come out of the state of Wyoming. Twice wounded by enemy action, he was awarded two Purple Hearts (the extremely proud and respected medal established by General George Washington in 1782). For his extraordinary heroism and valorous actions Lieutenant Alley received the Distinguished Service Cross, two Silver Stars, one Bronze Star, two Air Medals and numerous other high military honors, medals and awards."

Flames from the fireplace seem to hypnotize me as I sit here in a state of quandary.

What possesses me? Why can't I forget these things? What has led me to this personal and troubled dichotomy, and why can't I shake it? Perhaps even more importantly—*what am I going to do about it—Jesus,what can I do about it?*

There is a destiny that
makes us brothers:

None goes his
way alone:

All that we send into
the lives of others

Comes back into
our own.

— Edwin Markham

*Some people live a lifetime and wonder
if they have made a difference in the world.
Our veterans don't have that problem.*

Ronald W. Reagan

*Commander-in-Chief
and Fortieth President
of the United States*

PART ONE

THE ADVENTURES OF WAR

CHAPTER 1

THE BATTALION 500

VIETNAM Binh Phuoc Base Camp, October 1967

Unlike other outfits, our days off are never scheduled. If down-time activity finds us in Base Camp we might sit around shirtless, but always still hot and sweaty, in our tents or under whatever very limited shade is available. In between swatting mosquitoes and flies that had previously clustered and dined at the now burning, horrible-smelling latrine 'Honey Buckets'—the smoke/odors of which will sometimes graciously and gently breeze in our direction—we listen to Armed Forces Network Radio. The AFN plays popular songs of the time. We groove to Sonny and Cher's *And the Beat Goes On*, Dionne Warwick's *I Say A Little Prayer For You,* Tom Jones' *I'll Never Fall In Love Again,* and others.

But even then, first and foremost we are cleaning, oiling, and with sore fumbling fingers wet with sweat and oil, (and now and then some well-chosen curse words) we stretch, pull and struggle to reset springs and restraining clips while reassembling our M-60s and M-16s. We then wipe each individual round clean and tap it down into the magazines to make sure the weapons won't jam whenever we might be in a tight spot and place them on full auto. We check, double and triple-check our weapons and munitions. That is *always Top Priority.* Then we go over to the motor pool and work on our M113 tracks, or APCs, Armored Personnel Carriers.

Our tracks literally are both life-saving and damnable uncomfortable rides. They carry the commander in the hull center, the driver in hull, left front, and up to 11 passengers. The vehicle has a large rear ramp with an entry door on the left side and a roof hatch over the passenger compartment. With their engines roaring and their tracks clanking, they can travel at teeth-jarring speeds up to 40 miles-per-hour on maximum level roads, and 3.5 mph in water. Basically they are armored boxes (aluminum armor) on tracks and are fitted with .50 caliber machine guns capable of firing 2,000 rounds. The outer camouflaged surface where we most always ride gets hot enough in the scorching sun to burn and blister skin, and the black clouds of emitted diesel exhaust are choking. But we weren't promised plush reclinable captain's chairs and air conditioning. Our tracks have saved countless lives—they take good care of us, and we take good care of them.

A major part of Recon's effectiveness is our ability to move fast with no equipment malfunctions. When we're engaged in enemy activity, either under fire or returning fire and a weapon jams, misfires, or a track stalls, the stateside manufacturer's guarantee or warranty is about as worthless as a limp dick in a Tan An five-dollar-a-pop whorehouse. Our equipment has *gotta be—always gotta be*—in perfect working order!

I take pride in our record as a reaction force. From the time I get the call to roll 'till the last of 10 armored personnel carriers clears the compound gate, not a second over five minutes has passed—day or night. When activity is relaxed and time allows it, we make practice patrols near Base Camp. These patrols are in areas where I feel enemy contact is not likely. These help newbies (newcomers) adapt to my method of operation and how we operate as a unit. The newbies are paired with seasoned men who do the majority of the teaching as to how proper positions and maneuvers should be executed. We operate in five groups with each having its own team leader. There's the point, left flank, right flank, command, and trail.

As each individual's responsibility has its own distinct function, a breakdown or interruption of needed support from any one position weakens the entire element. For this and other reasons I try not to show any favoritism to any one element. However, I gotta say a great personal respect always goes with the guys walking point, the ones out front. The courage these men show daily is a monumental tribute to the guts and glory, the truly magnificent bravery of the American fighting man.

The unknown and always first danger to the point is ever present. His keen eye and sharp instincts are honed to perfection. He's got to be alert and look for any and everything: slightly disturbed grass could indicate a camouflaged punji pit—a hole dug then filled with sharpened bamboo knives covered with human excrement. In the steamy jungle, flesh torn and injected with such filth means instant infection and eventual gangrene. A piece of bamboo from the not quite matching tree could hold the triggered hand grenade which, when tripped, will mercilessly strip off the flesh of anyone within the blast area. The rustling of leaves low to the ground, a startled bird in flight, any number of signals alert point to the possibility of an enemy lying in ambush.

On one of those rare, not a lot of hot activity going on kinda days, I am ordered to Battalion Headquarters at 0900 for specific operational instructions.

"Lieutenant Alley," the Colonel says, "I've been looking over our record and find we have been credited with 498 enemy kills. We need to get around and over that 500 count. Can you and Recon help with this?"

I don't hesitate in responding, "Yes sir. I know of an area where I suspect enemy movements have taken place. If we get there early enough we might have some contact."

The Colonel looks me in the eyes. "Will you do that?"

"Yes sir." I snap to attention, salute and do an about face taking my leave.

I return to my tent never thinking twice about our mission. I call the men together. They are immediately in formation. Five rows.

It's hotter'n hell. Everyone is sweating, but they stand at attention waiting for 'the word.'

I stare at 'Double L' Willson. I call him 'Double L' 'cause there are two Sergeant Wilsons in my unit—single and double 'L' name spellings. Double 'L' is the absolute best point man in the country. I also concentrate on Sergeant Teague, and Sergeant Miller, a newbie, who comprise my main force of point. These men, in fact all my men, are true experts at their work. They stand motionless, quiet for a moment or two and occasionally glance at me. They seem lost in thought, waiting for me to announce the assignment.

I learned early that if I explain a situation, tell the what and why, and lay things exactly on the line, I always get good results.

I look closely at my men. God, but they're good. I explain the mission and they ready themselves for inspection.

I move to the left front row and stop, facing my point man, Sergeant Miller. As I take his M-16 he subtly smiles at me. The bolt

11

glides back effortlessly. I slide my thumb into the chamber then look down the barrel. The bright sun damn near blinds me. The barrel is spotlessly clean. I knew it would be. He did, too. I hand him his weapon back and pat his canteen; it's full. I adjust his ammo belt while looking him in the eye. He stares back resolutely. We both know there is a solid mutual respect for one another.

"Are you ready, soldier?" I ask.

Miller nods in the affirmative again, displaying his almost indistinguishable smile. He is and will always be ready. I know I am blessed and extremely fortunate to have men of his caliber in our ranks. They just flat-assed don't come any better!

I move on to the next man, equally satisfied he is locked and loaded and in top form. However, I inspect each one thoroughly, confirming his readiness. This mission is no less important than any of the others. Every man and his equipment must be prepared and ready—no errors.

After inspection, it's around 1030 hours. In intense heat with their surfaces all but sizzling we mount our tracks and head out of the gates for 'The Nuts,' or 'The Testicles,' depending on who is saying it, to the site I have in mind. This is an open area where the Song Van Co River makes its way to the South China Sea and forms two distinct symmetrical loops in the shape of testicles. It's nearing the dry season. Damn, it's been a long, wet and miserable monsoon.

As our 10 tracks roll down the road, rusty orange trail dust accompanied by the black smoke and acrid odors of the burnt diesel fuel mushrooms up and envelopes us. All APCs and the three to five of us riding on top of each of the bouncing, hot, camouflaged tracks are covered in the choking clouds.

We near the area where I said we might make contact and I order the tracks to leave the road and enter rice fields. Anticipation and anxiety mount. Always do with these missions. You don't know what to expect. Up ahead there's a tree line and in that area are several Vietnamese hootches, which I suspect might be Viet Cong controlled. Now and then there have been reports of occasional sniper fire around here. We approach the tree line, stop and dismount, leaving a driver and a gunner on each of the vehicles, which then move in to circle and enclose the entire area.

On my order Double L enters the tree line and sets up security so the rest of us can enter. His radio silently signals an 'all clear' to me. This is done by depressing his talk/send button on his radio, but saying nothing. There's absolutely no sound, conversation or otherwise on his end to betray his location. However, his pressing that button emits a static squawk which I receive on my radio.

I deploy my men and we begin a very slow, nearly silent patrol toward the cluster of hootches. The trees buzz loud with insects, sweat trails down my back, it also runs into and stings my eyes. Suddenly up front there's some movement!

Everyone hits the ground dead still. No shots fired. Turns out it was two black pajama-clothed people dashing from one hootch to another.

"Surround the hootch," I whisper into the radio.

"What now, sir? Shall we fire?" someone comes back.

"No. We don't fire until we know who they are. I don't want any innocent people killed. Double L, you and your point team work toward the hootch. We'll keep you covered."

"Yes sir," Double L responded, and his team begins to move forward. Just before they are set to enter the door, which is the only entry/egress, there comes a loud crashing sound from the side of the hootch. Two men come flying out, each carrying an M-1 carbine rifle and trying to zero in on targets. Presumably suspecting they can't get out the door, they simply burst through the wall made of palm tree leaves, branches and sticks.

The air is shattered by the sound of machine gun fire as point opens up on the two men. There's some momentary screaming, and then all becomes quiet. No one moves.

Double L breaks the silence on the radio. "I got 'em, sir. I got 'em. Come on up!"

"No!" I reply, "all maintain position. There may be more." Slowly Westphal, my radioman, and I work our way toward Double L. As we draw near I smell the rotted mildewed materials of the hootch then view the two prone bodies of the dead Viet Cong—just exactly, I reflect, as the Colonel ordered. I look down at their riddled bodies. I try to avoid the vivid sight and strong smell of their odoriferous, unclean bodies and their fresh spilled blood, still seeping. A strange knot seems to form in my gut. After canvassing the rest of the area without further encounters, we search their bodies and take their weapons.

On the radio, I report back to Battalion, "Sir, this is Romeo 6. We have two dead Victor Charlies. Will secure area and patrol further to see if there are any other potential problems. If not will return to base. Over?"

The radio crackles with excitement. "Good work Romeo 6. I'll radio Brigade Headquarters right away. As soon as you secure the area come on back. Job well done."

Shortly afterward we remount our tracks and on the hot, dusty, return ride I remove my steel pot and with the grease pencil I carry in the liner, add two more single marks on the back to the long rows already there following the letters, VC KIA: //. Jesus! Is this possible?

Still, mostly, seems like the tension is lessened. What the hell. It's about time for a beer.

The completion of this particular mission is just one of the many memories I have of my year in Vietnam. It has been with me from the moment it happened and has, many times over, caused me to stop, pause in remorse, and think. Of course it's a war and they are the enemy. You get them whenever and wherever you can. And by God certain, the same—vice-versa! Don't *even think* that if they had the chance they wouldn't hesitate to blow my ass away in a micro-millisecond. There can be no question about that. But I, many times since, have pondered, wrestled with and agonized over a hard personal question: "How can I, Lee Alley, back then a normal everyday kind of untested young Wyoming man, so easily have become a hired killer?" I had no qualms then at all about any of this, or other similar missions. It's like there had developed a side of me that has no value or respect for human life. I casually thought, *Well, what the hell? If we need two more kills, no sweat, I'll rack 'em up. That's my job.*

My guys and I had a reputation. If something like the mission described above was needed, they called on the 35 hand-selected Recon men. We got the job done. I was damn proud of them, then and now, and damn proud to lead them!

But that was way back then—decades ago—an ocean and worlds away in wartime and in a war zone. Today I find I'm not so sure that all of that was right. I sometimes am remorseful and troubled with reflections. I hope there might be a person reading this now who understands. I wish I did.

Yeah. Yeah I know. Ten-four.

That was then—this is now—and the beat goes on . . .

CHAPTER 2

INDIAN COUNTRY
THE BATTLE OF FIRE BASE CUDGEL

There's been some tight-lipped scuttlebutt of a possible large
engagement floating around the past couple of days. Suspicions
confirmed today, November 16, 1967, when all the officers are
called to Battalion Headquarters for a special briefing.

We're going into a large battalion-sized operation in an area
called the Cai Lay region. Someone has given the area the name
Indian Country. Guess that's because anytime we've gone there it's
always been a 'bad news-oh shit' kind of happening.

Evidently there's a sizeable buildup of regular North Vietnamese
activity in that area. Unusual for such a large gathering of North
Vietnamese rather than Viet Cong. We are given up-to-date Intel
information and other briefings and then as a battalion load up in
trucks here at Binh Phuoc. We go to Dong Tan where we spend an
anxious night. At first light the morning clouds hang like a shroud
over the area giving us a gray and forbidding dawning with an
indifferent beginning. But soon a blood red sunrise breaks through
and a strong upper wind clears the heavens to a bright almost
cloudless day. An indifferent beginning, but the day will end violently.

As usual, it's hot and humid. We're supposed to air mobile to
our objective and land at LZ (Landing Zone) Brown.

We board the HU-1B Helicopter, nicknamed Huey, filing past
the now familiar to me M-60 machine gunner strapped in on his
fixed mount next to the right-hand side. He gives me a quick, not
mandatory salute, and a smile, which I promptly return and pat him
on his back. There's another, new guy I think, on the opposite side.
We squeeze in with bulky gear and weapons as tight as we can. Five
sit on the back sling bench. Several others and I sit on the floor. I'm
at the door's edge with my legs hanging out of the copter. I want to

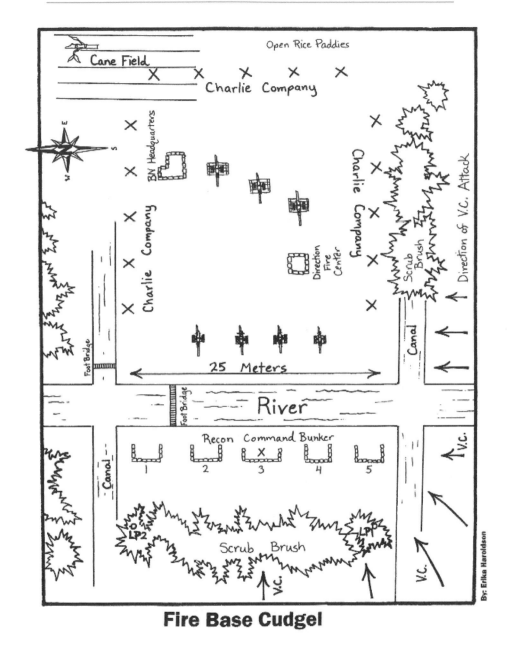

Fire Base Cudgel

get as good an aerial view as possible of the area we'll be working. I look up on the inside of the helicopter and note we've been aboard this particular chopper several times before. On the right side there's a hand-painted sign attached to the low overhead of the green-gray quilted mat above the gunner. It reads, "They can run, but they'll just die tired."

I like the Huey despite its loud 'whomp whomp' sound caused by the tip of the advancing rotor blade, which breaks the speed of sound creating the small sonic boom. Guess we just get used to that. It's a little cramped but each bird carries seven of us with full gear. Huey is a great combat and Medevac workhorse.

I always get the early order for Recon to load up first and we do. This is normal. My 35 men and I are extremely mobile. Because of our size we're fast and move around a lot; we're easy to get in and easy to extract. Usually after we make first contact the other companies follow us in. That doesn't happen today.

We no sooner get loaded than the radio cracks, "We have changed operations. The Viet Cong are damn sure in there—big time. We've spotted them by air. However, this is a much larger force than we expected—it's too big for your 35 men to go into. We're going to send the companies in first."

So we unload and Companies A, B, and C climb into the helicopters and are air-mobiled into LZ Brown. We're annoyed with the change but know it's for the best so we sit as patiently as possible on the hot tarmac waiting our turn. The blood that was pumping with excitement before now overheats under a scorching sun. And for damn sure we're not thankful for and don't want *any downward breeze* at this particular moment and setting.

The postponement exposes us to the daily ritual burning of the latrine honey buckets. Every camp has large yellow drums spaced about 10 feet apart at locations, that will hopefully carry the odor and smoke away from all personnel and human activity. But sometimes the wind and heavy chopper flights will disturb the upper black, smoky trails and bring them low to the ground. Those occasions make *everyone* exposed wish he or she were somewhere else, maybe like being nearer some nice smelling sulfur pits, the grossest of rotted pulp areas, or the stinkiest of animal stockyards. The smell is far worse than exploded cordite and literally takes your breath away. I don't believe an adequate description exists for the 'Honey Bucket' content elimination process with its accompanying odors.

The camp's latrine barrels are collected by hired villagers and dumped into the huge yellow drums where the contents are set ablaze and burnt by gasoline. Today's nonstop chopper operations have made sure the entire area will have more than just brief whiffs.

The sweltering tarmac with heat waves shimmering becomes more torrid and, if it's possible, the horrible honey bucket odors even more repulsive; however, everyone is glued to the radios listening to the fast developing action. The helicopters and all three companies are under immediate fire as they go in. All Landing Zones are *hot.* This will be the biggest battle we have experienced.

"Recon, load up," comes the call, "you're going in. *Now!*"

We hurry aboard, strap in and moments later we're again told to unload. This goes on and off all day. We're up, we're down, and we're antsy as hell! They aren't sure exactly how my 35 men will fit into a battalion-sized operation where *everyone* is already in heavy contact.

The LZ area was so hot that within minutes of unloading Company C, their commander is critically wounded, and the company is without its leader. Captain Russell, one of the more tested veteran captains, is working in Headquarters and is a short-timer with only days and minutes left in-country; he is rushed in to assume command of C Company.

My friend Captain Siegfried most ably commands B Company. Both of his RTOs were shot out from under him—William Metzler is wounded by a shot through the neck—and Max Zurcher is severely wounded in the chest. Metzler will later return to his unit, Zurcher won't come back. It has become apparent that the enemy is heavily concentrating fire, zeroing in on our commanders and those close to them.

All three companies are soon pinned down tight and cannot move. Once more my radio squawks and I am told to load up. This time it's definitely a *Go!* The adrenaline once again surges.

We are to be dropped into a more rear position to see if we can flank the enemy, embedded in a tree line. We *finally* go into battle— and we're past ready!

The LZ remains extremely hot and our helicopter takes hits. There are numerous 'thunk' sounds as bullets slam into the body of the craft. It kinda reminds me of the back-home sound of Wyoming's large hailstones smacking our tin roofs. As we sit nervously, mostly bouncing around from the rough flight, waiting for touchdown, we see the inside green-gray quilted panels jerk as they mostly absorb the spent remnants of penetrating small arms fire. When ground fire strikes the steel parts of the copter there are loud clanging sounds and then the zinging ricocheting off echoes. We're gonna have to disembark fast!

Although a clear day, we're still in the wet season. A forest of three to four-foot reeds stand tall in a field full of water. We bail out, impact the ground and hunker down. We lie on our bellies. The reeds are probably two or three feet over our heads. This, added to the approximate six inches of water we lie in, make us fairly invisible to the enemy in the tree line. Good and bad with this.

We're taking heavy fire, but as they can't see where we are, the bullets go over our heads. So far. That's the good. The bad is because we're sucking, eating and breathing mud with having to stay down so low, and we can't poke our heads up to determine directions—where the shots are coming from—or where'n the hell we should be going. In this position and angle we can't see from Jack Shit to six inches in front of us because it's all solid reeds. Mixed blessings I guess—but I think to myself—*damn soggy, stinking reeds and mud*!

I motion and my RTO, Westphal, crawls up beside me. I radio the Battalion CO, who is overhead in a helicopter, well off in the distance. I report all my men are accounted for and okay and tell him our situation.

He responds, "You are within one hundred and fifty meters of a tree line. Go a little bit left."

Not worth a shit do I like this! It's one of those occasions when you can't even hope to escape, or much less start planning for a long retirement by relying on your training, wits, past experiences, or a tight sphincter. Although at the moment, there can be no question about the tight sphincter part. I have no fuckin' idea where the enemy is, or even where *we are.* The firepower passing over our heads reminds me a little of some of Wyoming's calmer wind gusts—a steady roar! We continue to low crawl through the reeds unable to see and guided only by the directions from the Command Helicopter flying overhead. We crawl about 100 meters. I know we are getting closer to the unseen enemy as the sharp, distinct clatter of the VC AK-47 firing over our heads is becoming louder and louder.

"Romeo 6," the radio squawks, "change in mission! We are

going to turn you around. One of our helicopter gunships has just been shot down. It's maxed out with machine guns and armament. The VC are trying hard to get to it."

We are ordered to proceed to the site and protect the helicopter.

This sounds great to me 'cause I'm more than anxious to turn the hell around and haul ass out of here! Our movements are again directed from the air, and we soon crawl into a four-foot and deeper canal and take up defensive positions. From here we see the downed helicopter and can provide enough deterrent so the Vietnamese can't get to it.

Any overt movement by us is going to be pretty much impossible. The rest of the Battalion are in similar situations, whether in canals, or dug down in the tree line.

I decide it's definitely going to be one of the longest nights of my life. We squiggle down to our necks in the dirty, smelly water for protection from the intense firing overhead.

It doesn't take us long to discover that the canal swarms with mosquitoes. One slap of a hand kills dozens, but there must be millions. Any body area not covered or doused with repellent is soon covered in welts. The canal also has an overburdened population of leeches. The friendly rascals, once attached to your body, quickly bloat to the size of a hot dog. You get rid of the boogers only by dousing with insect repellent, or a burn from a glowing cigarette, which damn sure can't be done here. Some tear the leeches off because they can't stand the thought of the ungodly things feasting on their blood. Others give up the fight and resign themselves to the thought of getting rid of them come daylight. Exhaustion begins to creep in. Men try to doze curled up with arms hooked over and around washed-out tree roots, or by whatever means necessary to keep their heads above water.

Finally, after three forevers, there are faint light signs of the new day approaching. We stay put as there is an eerie gray luminescence in the area. Swamp devils hover close to the surface of the canals and river waters then merge into the miasma of a scattered low blanket of fog. Tendrils of fog curl and twist around the tree line. Outlines are vague and forbidding. There's an abnormal stillness. And then a hazy copper-colored sun breaks through and the fog quickly disappears. The deafening roar of yesterday's battle and now total silence sparks interest. There's nothing but complete quiet.

The Viet Cong and North Vietnamese are peculiar warriors. They will give us fierce battles all night long and for days on end, but suddenly they'll break contact and promptly leave. Just like that. Gone!

Our radios break the morning's silence with their first loud squawks and shrill static screeches. Everyone who has been pinned down for an entire day now begins to stir and move. As a unit we leave the canal and Doc assists in removing leeches, then quickly douses the areas with alcohol and treats the welted skin. We enter the tree line, the same from which we previously received intense small arms fire. Our searches soon reveal nothing but spent ammunition and bunkers that comprised their well-designed defense positions.

We'd landed smack-dab in the middle of a giant hornet's nest, and overnight the hornets have evaporated into thin air.

We hook up with B Company, which had also been in the canals, and complete a sweep of the area, and then we sit down to eat a breakfast of C-rats. Later B Company moves on in search of 'Charlie,' and we proceed from tree line to tree line in search of the enemy. As Recon is the smallest and most mobile unit, the helicopters pick us up on Eagle-type operations and bounce us in and out of the tree lines, rice/reed fields, canals and so on, where we attempt to make enemy contact. Today we are picked up and dropped five times. Each time we board and are airborne again it's a big relief. When we are dropped, the 'pucker factor' ratchets tight. 'Charlie' is here somewhere; we all damn well know that—it's just a matter of time.

By mid-afternoon new orders arrive. We are going to stop the Eagle flights and be airlifted into a defensive position where we will link up with the Bandidos of C Company. The two units will provide perimeter security for a hastily put together artillery position and battalion field headquarters. It's being called Fire Support Base Cudgel.

Because the terrain we've been operating in for the last two days is accessible only by air, the seven 105 Howitzers of the 2/4th Artillery had to be flown in, slung beneath the bellies of the huge dragonfly helicopters.

As dry ground is limited, three of the seven guns are placed on large aluminum firing pads which were also flown in. From the air the firing platforms look like shiny lily pads topped off with the three Howitzers.

We are dropped approximately 100 meters from where the artillery is set up and then slog through a knee-deep muddy reed field to the newly established base.

My 35 Recon troops and I undoubtedly look like misfits. We're covered in mud from head-to-toe. Each step is dead slow; we're dragging ass. Eyes are glazed because of lack of sleep and near-total exhaustion as we, finally, step on dry ground!

The Artillery Battery is busy setting up guns, placing sandbags, and digging bunkers. They all look spiffy. Clean, and can you believe it, some even in starched, creased fatigues! As we slowly swagger our way past them I can damn near hear them thinking out loud: *"So, these are the Recon guys who are our protectors? You gotta be shittin' us!"*

Doesn't take long to find Colonel Steele, and a Defense Plan for the evening is promptly drawn up. C Company will secure three-fourths of the perimeter, north, south and east. There's a small footbridge across the river, which is nothing more than a log with a makeshift handrail. An individual can use it to cross, but any equipment, extra ammunition, or other bulky items must be floated over the water on air mattresses. My Recon has the assignment. We'll be the first line of defense. Because of the close proximity of the artillery to the river, the western perimeter must be located across the river, and thus separated from the main unit—far more vulnerable, but necessary.

Extra ammunition and C-Rations come via a resupply helicopter, which was waiting for us at the Fire Base. As we go through the supplies we find three entrenching tools and a bundle of sandbags. What the hell? Hardly enough for the 35 of us who have to dig in. Doc complains the medical supplies are sorely lacking and someone comments there isn't enough ammo to replace what we've already used. But we'll have to make do.

I know my men are exhausted, battle-weary and worn, but we are in an extremely hostile situation and everyone must be alert. We cross the river and I check out the area to be defended. It is unspoiled by war, pristine in fact. Green grass and palm trees. I assign positions to the five groups; each group will have their own bunker. Sharing the three tools we learn the ground is hard-packed and like chiseling holes out of rock; we use the small amount of extracted dirt to fill the sandbags, and dig in near the small lateral canals. We soon have shallow bunkers dug and shit—wouldn't you know it—water immediately begins to seep into them.

I look at the river and see my medic, Coutant, buck-assed naked taking a swim.

"Dammit, Doc, get your pants on, this isn't a picnic. We've still got work to do!" Damn fool sometimes acts like a kid—hmm—he's only 19.

Afterwards we attempt to grab as much rest as we can. It's great to be back on dry land! The sun is still high and feels good. The humidity is still oppressive—always is—but there's a refreshing breeze heavy with the odor of the sweet-smelling green grass. The river separating us from C Company and the artillery battery is swift-flowing and clear. It all seems rather serene. Yeah, it all seems rather serene, yet somehow hostile. Something's up. I've got this feeling . . .

As the setting sun sinks below the horizon delivering a thickening twilight, I send out two Listening Posts, LP1 west and north on an incoming canal, and LP2 south and west on another canal.

By 2200 the LP's have belly-crawled into position. Don Westphal is with me and has my battalion radio. Private First Class Dean has my platoon radio and Jerry Stepp, my forward observer, also has a radio and will assist with the execution of air strikes and artillery or whatever else I may need. Once everyone is in place I receive radio squelches, no voice contact, to confirm that all are ready, locked and loaded. We settle in for the night. Nights are bad. The VC love the night. No one really sleeps. The air is thick with anticipation.

Suddenly the silence is broken by a single burst of machine gun fire, and then silence again.

"LP1, this is Romeo 6. What happened?" I whisper into the radio.

"They're probing the perimeter. We had three Vietnamese approach. Killed one. Have his body here. Pretty sure we hit the others, but can't find them. Your orders? Over."

"Don't move, I'm coming out." I leave the bunker and crawl into the jungle. Indeed they have a body and it isn't in the common pajamas, shorts or sandals of the Viet Cong. The uniform is of a force we haven't seen in a long time. These guys are well armed and trained. They're skilled in fighting and *Damn, it's gonna be another long night!*

I relocate LP1 because that location has been compromised. Then I crawl back to my bunker. Again, an abnormal silence envelopes the area. *It's way too still! Way too quiet!* The only sounds are those of mosquitoes and other insects constantly buzzing and biting.

And then at 0130 all hell breaks loose.

The first sound is the unmistakable thunk of mortars being dropped into the tubes. We're under a fierce mortar attack. God, they're close and the exploding mortars turn the night into day. All five of my positions are taking hits, or near hits. "Maintain! Maintain your positions!" I yell into the radio. "There won't be a ground attack. This mortar is so heavy if we can get through it we'll be okay. Take protection under your flak jackets. Cover as best you can. Maintain and get through this attack. We'll be all right."

The mortar attack continues and is so fierce I'm confident there can be no ground attack. To do so would be suicidal. They'd be killing their own people.

But, I'll be goddamn! Here come the sons-a-bitches. They're screaming at us using their nauseating singsong chant, *"GI you die now! You die tonight GI!"*

From the sounds around us it must be an overwhelming force— in the hundreds—and there are only 35 of us. Some of them charge toward me then pause, stop and pull their wounded back into the night. I hear screaming from others more forward and near our perimeter being slaughtered by their own mortar explosions. Crazy bastards!

"Maintain," I again shout into my radio. Remembering we are already short on ammunition, I add, "Make every round count!"

Seems only seconds till our bunkers are being overrun and we have casualties. We're gonna have to retreat to the edge of the river where we had earlier crossed on a small footbridge. Man, they're right on top of us! It's obvious we can't use the bridge to cross back over now because we would be too high and in the line of fire. I shout to my men, "Get to the river if you can swim across and if you can't swim, figure out some other way to get across. Leave one man in each bunker to provide cover. Go! Do not leave any wounded behind!"

As I finish giving the order, I turn and see my radio operator Westphal stand up right next to me and get shot in the neck. I zero in on and kill the person who shot him. Blood rains. "Take him to the river!" I shout to Jerry Stepp who weighs maybe 135 pounds soaking wet. Westphal weighs over 200. Adrenaline pumping high, Stepp picks up Westphal with ease and races to the river, hands him to the men there and returns to our bunker.

Just as Stepp returns the ground around us explodes in gunfire and my other radio operator, Dean, is seriously wounded. Stepp opens up his machine gun and wipes out the men who shot Dean, plus several others.

Things are accelerating and happening too fast. Just too damn many of them and too few of us. We can't maintain.

The strong smell of gunpowder hangs heavy in the air, as do the sounds of explosions and screams of the wounded. My ears ring with them. I grab the radio and yell, "Everyone to the river. Go! Now!"

I turn to Stepp, "We gotta get Dean to the river." Dean is another very large man. We drag him to the water's edge where I tell Stepp and the others, "Help get the wounded across hand-over-hand as you hold on to the bridge, and then get yourself across. Leave your weapons for me and I'll cover you." I collect the available weaponry the troops entering the water won't be able to use and return to my bunker. Quick count: I have four M-16s and 10 or 12 hand grenades. This will be used as a last stand position. I no longer have radio capability.

I take a quick look back at the river and my men. I'm proud of them. *They operate and act as if this entire scenario has been planned and practiced. Despite the urgency and seriousness of the moment they show no panic, but act with calm and caring for the wounded. It's going smoothly—and as fast as possible, but it's very, very slow—too slow! Everyone will soon be exposed to the Vietnamese. It'll be like shooting fish in a barrel, and my men will be the fish. They'll be cut to ribbons. No one will escape! I gotta stay and protect them.*

Decision made. I'm not thinking hero stuff or self-sacrifice. *I know only that I have to give protection to my men* until everyone is across the river and joined up with C Company.

By now the Vietnamese ground attack is ginning up to full force. The mortars have let up and it's just basically gonna be a full frontal attack. Sons-a-bitches are still screaming their sing-song *"GI you die! Tonight you die, GI!"* God, I hate the sound of that!

I can smell the blood of Westphal and Dean. *For Chrissakes I'm lying in puddles of it!* I see death all around me. Suddenly I get a roaring inside my head that drowns out all other noise. I tell myself, *Okay, now's the time, it's do or die. Let's get to it!* With hands soaked in my comrades' blood I pick up a rifle and flip the fire selector lever to "Auto" with my thumb, rise up out of my bunker and once again witness the extreme power of the M-16. The uniforms of the Vietnamese in the front line are shredded into pieces as the enemy comes screaming *"Caca dau,"* (I kill you) racing toward me. Their splattering blood and disintegrating body parts seem to fly out from them and the vividness seems magnified a thousand times— but in slow motion—extremely slow motion. Those in back hit the dirt or fall on top of their now lifeless comrades in front of them just as my rifle signals empty with a 'click-click.'

I must be running on pure adrenaline. I have absolutely no fear. I later learn I've been wounded, but I don't know it and feel no pain. I grab another M-16 and again see the ripping flesh of the second wave of those coming toward me. I continue until I hear the 'click-click' again, and then grab another rifle, and then another until they're all empty. I do a quick reconnoiter to the river and confirm all my men are across.

Good! I also pick up a remaining weapon or two and a few more grenades. In seconds I'm back in my bunker and now it's hand grenade time. *Gotta make these babies count.* The bastards are so close I'll just roll the first grenade over the top of my bunker's edge. With the explosion I feel and see more blood and body parts shower down on top of me in the bunker. I do this again and again. Now, I'm down to my last grenade. I pull the pin, hold on to it longer than the others, then let go. I duck for the detonation and am soon in the river swimming to the other side with everything I've got. I hear the enemy shouting at my back and then bullets begin to plunk around me as if it is raining. The VC are in our bunkers and in addition to firing at me take aim at my Recon men and those of Company C on the far side of the river, who immediately unload nonstop return barrages of fire.

When I reach shore I don't stop but go on to the nearest artillery piece and yell, "You gotta use Beehives! Lower your guns, they're in our bunkers. Gotta use Beehives and fire lower!"

I run to the next position and search for some kind of communication. I find a PRC-25 radio and get on the Battalion frequency. "This is Romeo 6. Bring smoke! We need gunships! Bad! We need artillery and we need Spooky's Gatling guns—big time! Where's Spooky?"

Gunships appear almost magically and immediately. I'm back at the river and among the troops looking for my men. *Damn!* I can't account for them all. Still missing troops! *Where are they? Goddammit, where are they?*

I'm talking to the gunships instructing them to strafe the area I've just left. "Spooky, drop a flare so I can guide your and the gunship's fire. Okay, good! One hundred meters north from the flare the Vietnamese are thick. They're everywhere in there!"

Someone grabs my leg and shouts, "Lieutenant Alley, you gotta get down—you're running around like you have a protective shield around you—get down!"

From in back of me I hear a sudden shout, "Cease fire, cease fire! There are GIs in the river!" I dive into the river. There are a couple of artillery guys ahead of me. One of my wounded men has been placed on an air mattress and is being pulled across by Sammy Davis. Bill Murray and I take the remaining two GIs across. As we get them up on the shore the backs of their flak jackets look like porcupines with all the Beehive steel fragments sticking out. I look at them, blink back tears and choke out, "Simmons and Holloway—you're alive!"

"Medevacs, we need Medevacs!" I shout into the radio.

"Can't get them in just now," comes the instant response. "There's too much fire. They'll be with you ASAP."

The gunships, in wave after wave, continue strafing. They devastate everything on the other side of the river. Return fire from the Vietnamese instantly fades to insignificance—and then suddenly it's all over. The silence of the gunfire and battle seems deafening.

The Medevacs are here within seconds. They're some of the

bravest men I know. With each mission they risk their lives, sometimes several times daily, to help our wounded. There's no question that without the expert care and attention from these outstanding and devoted people, many of our men would not live beyond the day. The most seriously injured are loaded first. Stretchers soon fill each helicopter. And other Medevac flights come rushing in.

Abruptly I'm gripped in a bear hug and there's Colonel Steele. I wonder, *"What the hell?"*

He says, "Lieutenant Alley, the last thing I heard coming from your radio was some Vietnamese shouting, 'GI, you die!' I just knew you had to have been killed."

"Sir, it's no surprise you could hear them. At that point they were in my bunker."

Doc, the same carefree kid splashing and swimming around in the river a short while ago, is now the trained, devoted soldier performing his usual standard and normal miracles of tending to those suffering. I help load and look closely at each wounded soldier carried aboard the helicopters. My men. Twenty-four of them are being Medevacced out, some seriously hurt. Some may return. Some, I fear, will not survive. I say a prayer for each as I grip their hands or pat them on their shoulders. Thirty-five men and now—eight of us left. *But I'm missing three! Where are they?*

Finally, a glowing full orange sun begins its slow climb and ephemeral patterns appear against an azure sky.

I look around and say to my remaining men, "Grab a pot and your rifle, we're going back across the river." We cross over the footbridge this time.

Stark evidence of the battle is extremely fresh everywhere. There are nauseating scenes and odors of globs of blood, intestines, chunks of flesh, and other splattered and small body parts scattered about. Those smells inexorably mix with that of the still-smoldering greenery of the now stripped bare palm trees, the ashen areas of burnt grass, weed and clumps of bushes.

The Beehives, ordinance and all other explosive activity, theirs and ours, have stripped the entire area and set fire to the remnants. What seemed virgin, pristine and refreshing before is now unrecognizable as the same place. It has been reduced to an odorous, scorched and sickening area.

However, very few Vietnamese bodies remain. They, even under intensive fire, have cleaned up the battlefield.

"They gotta be here!" We keep searching for our three men.

Finally we find them. Brownotter and Scott first, and then McGarvey. The three LP men we are missing. Seems like all my remaining strength drains from me as I stand, shaking and weak and look down at them through tear-dimmed eyes. *Goddammit! My men. My buddies. Great guys with all their futures ahead of them. And they've sacrificed all of that in this battle for their country. Thousands of miles from home!*

We carry our three dead back across the river.

I've lost all track of time. Colonel Steele comes over to where I'm sitting. He squats down and nudges me, "Get your troops ready, Recon. I'm getting you out of here." Although we move slowly from exhaustion and wounds, it now doesn't take long for just the eight of us to board up and move out.

Once in Dong Tam we are guided to a deuce and a half. We crawl up in the back where we ride in silence the rest of the way back toward Binh Phuoc.

As the truck bumps along the road I sit by myself, motionless. Feel like I'm numb. Totally numb. Other than feeling lost in a kind of deep infinite sadness there seems to be a complete void of human emotions about me. With hooded, and barely open eyes, I stare ahead intently, blankly, at nothing.

I take notice and come around at the feel of a slight, tentative tap on my shoulder.

With effort I focus on and see my Vietnamese interpreter, Sergeant Trang. He's crawled over extremely close to me. He looks at me in a reserved, humble and sort of strange way.

His eyes are the color of black olives, moist with tears, and glistening.

"Di wee," he whispers, calling me 'Lieutenant' in his Vietnamese language. "Di wee," he whispers again and once more lightly, feather-like, pats me on my shoulder.

"Di wee. You saved us, Di wee! Ga-mug!" (Thank you!)

Early morning the next day Colonel Steele approached me and said, "I know you are troubled and concerned about your lost and wounded men. All of us in Battalion feel the terrible loss and pain. However, Lee, your hurt and grief is, of course, the greatest. Knowing you as we do, everyone knows that.

"I've made arrangements for you to have my command helicopter for the day. Here's a list of the medical sites where our wounded have been taken. Take as much time as you want to see and be with your men. Maybe that'll help some." With obvious emotion, he patted my shoulder and said, "I wish I could do more."

Sergeant Miller accompanies me. We visit each of our wounded comrades and return to base camp late at night.

Colonel Steele made many significant and commendable impressions on me as my commander in Vietnam. But that day the singular act of his caring for me and my Recon men, and showing his caring in that personal manner, elevated him to a position of the highest honor and respect I can have for an individual. That high pedestal of honor and respect where I placed him back then has remained solid with me throughout my lifetime.

A CERTIFIED TRUE EXTRACT COPY

Headquarters
5TH BATTALION (MECH), 60TH INFANTRY
**9TH INFANTRY DIVISION
APO U.S. FORCES 96373

AVDE-IJ-O   25 November 1967

SUBJECT: Combat After Action Report for Reconnaissance Platoon
5th Battalion (M), 60th Infantry in Defense of FB/PB
CUDGEL on 18 November 1967

TO: Commanding Officer
5th Battalion (Mech), 60th Infantry
9th Infantry Division
APO U.S. Forces 96373
1. Date of Operation: 18 November 1967.
2. Location: Dinh Tuong Province.
3. Command Headquarters: 5th Battalion (Mech),
60th Infantry.
4. Reporting Officer: 1LT Lee B. Alley.
5. Organization: RCN Platoon, 5th Battalion
(Mech), and 60th Infantry.
6. Friendly Forces:
        A.   3rd Bde conducts airmobile search and destroy
operations, saturation patrolling, eagle flights, and establishes blocks
and screens as required in Base Area 470 to locate and destroy VC
forces, their supporting elements, and base installations commencing
160830 Nov 67.
        B.   2nd Battalion, 60th Infantry conducts search and
destroy operations in zone to the west of the Battalion sector of
responsibility.
        C.   3rd Battalion, 47th Infantry conducts search
and destroy operations in zone south of the Battalion sector of
responsibility until 19 Nov 67, and secures FS/PB CUDGEL initially.

D. 3rd Battalion, 39th Infantry continues current mission.

E. 7th Infantry Division (ARVN) conducts operations east of the Battalion sector of responsibility.

F. One platoon of an armed Helicopter Company conducts armed reconnaissance north of the Battalion sector of responsibility.

G. 7th USAF provides CAS.

H. 2-4 Arty DS 3rd Bde.

7. Intelligence: No hard intelligence prior to the Battalion's employment to the Cai Lay area. However, intelligence trends indicated the following enemy units had been reported in the Operations area.

A. 261 MF Bn.

B. 263 MF Bn.

C. 514 Prov Bn.

D. 212 Sapper Co.

E. 458 Co.

F. 460 Co.

G. 462 Co.

H. 464 Co.

Statements also documented units would evade rather than fight U.S. units.

8. Mission: Reconnaissance Platoon of 5-60, OPCON to C/5/60, to provide security for the western portion of fire support base CUDGEL commencing 171500H Nov 67.

9 Execution: On the afternoon of 17 November 1967, the Reconnaissance Platoon was airlifted into fire base CUDGEL (XS034519). At which time I, as Recon Platoon Leader, received a briefing from the C/5/60 Company Commander, Captain Russell. My platoon was to cross the river and set up security for the defense of the western flank of Fire Base CUDGEL.

LEE B. ALLEY
1ST LT, USA
Recon Platoon Leader

Editor's footnote: In the beautiful, historical city of Casper, Wyoming's Veterans Park, there is a proud, patriotic placard which shows Lieutenant Lee Alley being presented one of the U.S. Army's highest military awards by General Creighton Abrams, Commander of the Vietnamese Military Assistance Command and later Chief of Staff of the U.S. Army.

The placard stands beside an impressive memorial in a solitary, peaceful place in the park where a respectful calmness and serenity prevail. Together, the placard and memorial captures a full range of emotions, and many who visit the site leave reverently, with tear-brimmed eyes.

Both the placard and memorial are a dedicated reminder of the Battle of Fire Support Base Cudgel. They silently pay solemn tribute to our heroic veterans who fought and died in that battle—they gave their all in their service to our country. God bless them.

And, may God bless all of our veterans.

CHAPTER 3

REBUILDING RECON

It's November 22. Tomorrow's Thanksgiving. Only four days since Cudgel. My Recon platoon has been rebuilt. Just four days since that bloodbath, and once again 35 of us are now standing by to be picked up at 0700. We'll be dropped back into expected VC territory. Time over here rarely stands idle.

Another 'Pick-Up and Drop,' Eagle-type of operation. We'll be dropped into an area, and if no contact is made during the first thirty-to-forty minutes, we're picked up and dropped into a new area. This'll go on all day—not my favorite mission.

As always, the spare few minutes before lift-off are our own. I look into the eyes of my men. Many new. Only four days, but their stares are already familiar to me. They are the same, but also not the same. Their actions and reactions like those before them replicate. Some pray, some joke, some are thinking of home, and some'll take a quick piss. So many things seem to be the same. Yet, to me and the other seven remaining from the old Recon, everything is different.

I'm no longer the 'FNG,' Fuckin' New Guy. I have over 100 days of hardened combat behind me. The Battle of Fire Support Base Cudgel was less than a week ago. Recon is rebuilt and back in action. A lot of new faces.

I look at my new RTO radioman and think of Don Westphal. Don's in a hospital somewhere. I hope and pray he's recovering well. Westphal. What a great soldier and friend. I miss you pal.

My thoughts flash back to a month ago and I feel a smile suddenly form.

Westphal, my radio man. RTOs carry the PRC-25 radio (many, of course, call it 'prick') with a four-foot antenna which signals to the enemy—shoot me first. He always stands next to the commanding officer. It's not the best job. That person is always a target, but Don never complained and was always there. I picture him in my mind and smile again. Crazy nut! Damn near got me demoted, but his actions were never really a surprise to me, and they were always best intended.

Like many other units, Recon has a mascot. In our case we adopted a stray mutt that we call 'Dammit.' I'm sure the name developed because he just would not listen.

"Dammit, come here! Dammit get down! Dammit get outta that!" Gotta be the dumbest dog in Southeast Asia. He mainly just hangs around our camp, but excited and with tail wagging and body contortions he's always a welcome sight when we come in from patrols. He invariably seems happy to see us; he likes everyone, and in a comforting way somehow represents a small connection to home. I'm reminded of our old family dog, Poncho. Sometimes Dammit rides with us on the tracks, but for obvious reasons, he's never allowed to go on patrol.

That day this past October was fairly routine. We once more cordoned off a tree line with our tracks, using them as a blocking force. We dismounted and began our patrol. The point element just entered the tree line when an explosion shattered the silence. In combat your ears quickly become attuned to various sounds and this was definitely a hand grenade. I got a sick feeling, as I feared a booby trap.

The radio crackled—"Medic! Medic, we need Doc!"

"Roger," I replied, "secure the area. We're coming in. Who's down?"

"Dammit! And it's bad!" came a concerned reply.

"Yeah, I was certain that was a grenade, and I know it's bad. But who's down?" I repeated.

"Dammit is. He jumped off the track, ran into the tree line, and set off a booby trap."

I looked at Don Westphal. He'd turned white. "What's the matter?" I asked.

" I just called in a Medevac for a dog!"

Seemed like he had no sooner said that than I hear the familiar whomp-whomp of a helicopter.

"Recon 6, this is Greyhound 1-7 inbound with Medevac—pop smoke. Roger, I see purple smoke. Am touching down."

As the helicopter hovered one to two feet off the ground for immediate extraction, the point element ran from the trees and gently placed the dog on the helicopter.

"You gotta be shittin' me!" yelled the pilot. "You call me into a combat mission for a fuckin' dog? Who the hell's in charge? I want his name—he's going down!" And with that the helicopter lifts and is gone with my name written on a note in the pilot's flight jacket pocket.

Everyone just stands around looking at me, afraid to speak.

"What the hell was that all about?" I ask. "Am I going to be court-martialed?"

"Seemed to me like it was the right thing to do," someone said quietly.

"Bummer," said another.

Three weeks later I receive a call on the radio. "Romeo 6, this is Greyhound 8. I'm inbound to your position. Meet at landing strip."

Aww shit, this is it. Goodbye Recon. I walk out to the back gate to meet the helicopter. As the rotors die down, out steps the pilot carrying Dammit who has a cast on both back legs. "You guys are in the field everyday—he seemed important to you—the least we could do. Good luck, soldier."

He turned around, climbed back aboard and flew off, and we have Dammit back!

Thanks, Greyhound 8—wherever you are.

From somewhere off in the distance I hear the sound of a helicopter drawing near and am brought back around in thought. I smile with the fading memory—*and, hey, Westphal, my friend, God bless you and keep you wherever you are. Wish you could know I'm thinking of you.*

The echoes of the helicopter off in the distance draw nearer. My radio squawks.

"This is Greyhound 3. I'm inbound."

I continue to look obliquely at my men, the old timers and the newbies. Outwardly I smile, but silently and heartbreakingly I grieve the absence of the 27 who are not here. *I've been damn lucky with all my men. Been blessed to have them. They don't and won't ever come any better!*

The helicopter touches down and we load up—Recon rolls again.

But soon my men will be rolling on without me.

CHAPTER 4

NUMBER TEN GI

Much to my dissatisfaction and chagrin, my six-month line-duty was over, and I was pulled from my Recon and assigned duties as an Assistant S-3, Operations Officer in Battalion Headquarters. As if it were yesterday, I remember the day I had to leave. Be damned if I didn't actually have tears in my eyes when I left Recon. I've since discovered it's not that unusual an occurrence for men who have been in the heat of battle practically daily and then suddenly transferred out.

Guess maybe it's like an addiction. Sort of. You do become the warrior you have studied and trained extensively, day and night for months and months and months, to become. And if you are well trained and good, you become successful, and dammit, you know it and feel good about it. There's an accompanying sense of accomplishment and resolute pride. In my case I seemed to revel and actually felt comfortable in the role—there've been occasions when I believe I was born to be a warrior. I believe at one time I looked forward to the suspense, personal uncertainties, risks, hazards, the tempting of chance, or perhaps luck. The actual, gut-level—hey, there ain't no replay with this; the placing of my life on line.

There's this hard to explain feeling. You get pumped and adrenaline triggers a high. There is in fact a feeling, a mixture of things: anticipation, uncertainty, adventure, thrills, excitement and, yes, fear, too, but an ambient sort of fear. Not the raw pure kind that fuels panic, but maybe something more like a speculative gambler-chance kind of thing. An almost pleasant, challenging frisson of the creeps. Scalp tingles, a curious restlessness, and internal alarms build and demand release.

Today it's just dry, dull, boring duty, and I miss my men. But this afternoon the Colonel calls for an immediate staff meeting.

"What's up, Lee?" A fellow lieutenant buddy, Terry, asks me.

"I just had a call from Brigade. Something hot's supposed to be cooking, but I'll let the Colonel fill you in. We better get in there."

"Gentlemen," Colonel Antilla began, "Brigade headquarters called and some of their best Intel believes Brigade headquarters could get hit hard tonight. As a precaution we have been directed to send two full companies and our command group to Tan An for security.

"Captain Norton, your B Company will go and provide night patrol outside Tan An to see if you can pick up any early movement. You will be briefed on patrol locations and size at Brigade. Captain White, your Company C will go to reinforce what perimeter defense is available. You also will receive further information at Brigade. Lieutenants Alley, Schlee and Sweet, you will accompany me, as we will establish our own operations headquarters. It's now 1430. If there are no questions we will roll in 45 minutes. That's all, thank you." As everyone was leaving Terry again calls me to the side. "Hey, Lee. You took the call. What are we in for?"

"Terry, with the type of intelligence we get you never know for sure. These boys are pretty reliable, but between you and me I believe it's a bunch of bullshit. Those Brigade desk jockeys who have never seen any action are so damned freaked they always panic. Problem is *we're the ones* who have to sit up all night baby-sitting the general."

The 15-mile trip from Binh Phuoc to Tan An is fairly routine. Although a short distance, the trip nearly always takes about 45 minutes as much of it must be made via rice fields for fear of the land mines the VC continually plant in the road.

Upon arriving at Brigade headquarters, all the officers assemble in the heavily sandbagged briefing room. As expected, Company B is prepped on the night patrol locations and then make last-minute inspections of the troops and weapons. After that they'll wait for the cover of darkness to move out. Company C meets with the security force and they decide it will be best to split up the perimeter defense.

Though nothing is said aloud, there are general mumblings and obvious feelings we would all be better off if the Brigade boys would just go to bed and let us handle everything.

Life at Brigade level is far different from ours. For the most part the men put in eight-hour days and can spend the rest of their time in the Officers' or EM clubs. They are generally free to wander downtown in search of a change of pace to break up the boredom of rear-area duty. As far as combat goes, it is something they read about or watch on the TV news.

At any rate, the Brigade is on Red Alert, which means nothing moves in or out of the perimeter after dark. Rigid SOP under these circumstances are that you shoot first and ask questions later.

Once B Company has set up operation, the remaining assignments are handed out. Lieutenant Schlee will be on reserve tonight. I take first watch and will be relieved at 2000 hours by Lieutenant Sweet.

I settle easily into my radio duty and begin receiving calls as security is established. The radio cracks as Bravo 6 reports all patrols have positioned into their first locations. Nothing else other than boredom going on so I decide to get back into Sherlock Holmes' *The Sign of the Four* book until my relief arrives. Been trying to finish reading the damn thing for months. Maybe years.

Lieutenant Sweet arrives and relieves me at 2000. I summarize the evening's happenings, which takes maybe two seconds, and point out all patrol locations on the operations map.

"Well, guy," Sweet said, "you're off 'till morning unless we get some action. Whazzup?"

"Hey," I reply, "you know for us grunts an officer's club is a luxury we don't but rarely get to enjoy. I'm meeting Oscar over there for a few drinks. If you need me send someone over."

Haven't been in an officer's club in months! You can bet your sweet ass, wherever she might be, I'm hyped up and good to go. *Just let me at 'em! Booze, broads, great music!*

I open the club door and wilt.

There are two local male lieutenants, a barkeep, and Oscar in the quieter-than-a-crypt club. That's all!

"Christ, Oscar, where is everybody? Where's the girls? Why's the jukebox dead? What the hell kinda joint is this?"

"Hey, the quiet ain't no big thing! As if you haven't heard, Lee, this outfit's on Red Alert. Might be attacked any minute."

"Yeah, well that may be, but I can't *even remember* the last time I had this kind of opportunity and don't know when I might *ever* get back. Dammit! Ain't at all like I'd hoped for, Oscar. Think I'll just haul off and get shit-faced drunk.

"Barkeep, please bring us a twelve-year-old bottle of your finest Chivas Regal Scotch."

One drink follows another and our conversations range from past missions to our present situation and the chickenshit Brigade boys here who are always crying wolf.

As frequently happens, the demon firewater inevitably turns our robust thoughts and conversation to women. Damn! I can't *even* remember last when . . .

"Hey, bartender, where can we find a couple of women? Young, cute and cultured, healthy and pure, athletically inclined, educated, vivacious, personable, and immensely talented . . . Hmm." I pause and think. "Well, maybe on second thought, where can we find a couple of horny broads?"

"Sorry guys, but there won't be a touchdown, or any scores, tonight. Everything's closed up tighter'n a drum."

"I can't believe this! I been savin' up—really no choice—but I've been lookin' forward to this for months! Someone told me there's a damn good whorehouse downtown . . . C'mon, Oscar. Let's go!"

Oscar's game. We strut out the door and leave the pansy-asses to their BFD Red Alert.

I know a lieutenant here who owes me a favor. With that and some sincere pleading (more like begging), Oscar and I are able to obtain a jeep and driver. So, filled to the brim with lust, steam coming out our ears, the remaining contents of our bottle of Scotch, our trusty .45 pistols—and a driver scared spitless—we bullshit our way out of the main gate by saying we're part of the security force and have to join the patrols *now!*

Still, the driver refuses to go any further unless we promise he won't have to wait for us. I tell him, "Okay, just drop and go." I have absolutely no idea where my thinking is at this moment. Well—maybe I do.

He makes a slow, squeaky U-turn as Oscar and I bail out at our destination. We bump into one another, stagger around, and eventually straighten up to see his taillights fade out of sight in seconds. Okay, here we are. Illegally in town during the highest possible Red Alert status, both drunker'n a brewer's fart and no possible transportation back to the base. Are we worried?

Hell no! Delighted with our success of arrival we exchange hi-fives, sit on the front porch of the whorehouse, and once more attack our bonny bottle of Scotch.

"Hey, Lee. Don't you find it strange these Vietnamese gals don't like to kiss?"

"Nah. But to tell you the truth guess I never really thought about it a lot. That's okay with me."

"Yeah, huh? Boy, we're different!" he says with a smile. "Things like that grab my attention right up front. They can sometimes occupy my mind for hours on end."

With that bit of intelligent conversation over with we sit idle for about three seconds. Believe it was me who started humming a tune and then it doesn't take long for us to decide on a song we just damn right well know we'll do a great job on by harmonizing, "Home on the Range." Reminds me of the great Gene Autry, the high plains, and back home in Wyoming. Can't say for sure—maybe it's our harmonizing quality, damn we sing good; maybe it's the melody or the lyrics—but I'm certain there's something about our singing that'd bring tears to most any person's eyes. Reluctantly, though, got to admit that while I think I'm doin' pretty good with the singing, seem to recall Oscar sounded kind of flat with his part. Bet he's never been out West in God's country so he probably can't really get the feeling.

We're just getting wound up and into it pretty good when we see a small dim light approach and our singing is curtly and most rudely interrupted by the stern voice of the Madam.

"Choi oi! You, klazy GIs! Get hell out of here! VC everywhere. They shoot you in head and cut off you nuts. Di di mou! Di di mou!"

"Wait, wait, wait. Chotto mottie Mama-San," Oscar countered. "We came here for two girls and we're not leaving 'till we have them!"

With a rash of Vietnamese, which I assume to be a good ass-chewing, she grudgingly opens the door only to begin again in rapid-fire broken English. "You, GI, you numbah 10! You the worst and smella likea drunk! Come here get Mama-San in trouble plenty!"

"Calm down. Take it easy, Mama-San. The sooner you get two of your girls down here boom-boom and the quicker you get rid of us."

Oscar explained that rather well I thought. Gotta try and

remember to congratulate him later.

She hurries out and we promptly belt down a couple more healthy shots of Chivas. With the last swallow I start to get a red flashing warning signal in my drunken thought process. 'Over limit—Over limit!' Damn. In red, too!

Mama-San soon returns with two girls. They look all right, but then, too, I'm shit-faced, damn near knee-walkin' drunk. "Okay, GI, thirty P. And you be boom-boom, damn quick. VC everywhere. You get Mama-San plenty trouble."

"Thirty P like hell," I say. "Here's fifteen. Take it or leave it. C'mon, Oscar, let's get 'em upstairs!"

At the first landing the girls, holding our hands, lead us into different bedrooms. Mine closes the door and I lean against the post of the single bed and stare down at the soiled linen. *Hmm.* All of a sudden I'm not so sure about things. It's dirty and rumpled from the girl's earlier activities with a customer. My stomach kinda lurches. *Not a good sign,* I think.

I try to gain some composure and balance from the excess Scotch, and my eyes wander around the room, which I seem to note strangely and all of a sudden appears to tilt and turn just slightly. A bed, simple dresser, and bamboo chair furnishes the room.

My gaze continues toward the door where the Vietnamese girl, obviously nude beneath her partially opened robe, is silhouetted by the single candle on the dresser. Her long dark hair frames her simple face and hangs down to her waist.

She puts on a mock-sexy voice and exhibits herself—mostly crotch. "You like, GI? Hurry. Mama-San say foopy-tan. You dinky dau huh? VC outside—you and friend better leave plenty quick!"

"Hey, little lady," I say using my suddenly developed Wyoming rugged and invincible tone, "you just let me worry about the VC. You know what I came here for so let's get with it—boom-boom—foopy-tan!" (Whatever the hell that means?)

She removes her robe and lets it fall to the floor. *Damn! Look at that. Naked as a newborn magpie!* She slowly walks towards me, arms outstretched and wearing only a sensuous smile. The thick, sweet smell of incense mixed with the strong musky female odor of her body overwhelms me. *And—oh shit—oh dear!* The room now doesn't just tilt and turn slightly, it's beginning to spin, faster and faster. *Jesus, I'm gonna be sick!* Seems like I remember starting to fall forward and the dim candlelight going out.

I wake up I don't know how much later and bolt upright in the bed. "Where the hell's my gun! Goddammit, where's my gun?" I yell as I aggressively shake this strange woman next to me.

"Don't hit me! Don't hit me GI. You pass out. I get you to bed and take off your gun and boots." She points, "There. There in the chair!"

"My God, what time is it? I gotta get outta here! Jesus, my head hurts!"

I pull on my boots, sling my pistol belt over my shoulder and race down the hall yelling for Oscar.

"Hey for Chrissakes, keep it down out there!" Oscar finally shouts from his bedroom.

With a loud crash I burst through the door, rush in, grab hold of a foot and start pulling him out of bed. His ladyfriend bed partner unfortunately begins an ear-piercing scream. Jesus Christ! Her lung power was opera-star level, and doesn't help my pounding headache one bit. Her second shriek was even louder, and, aw, fuck—wouldn't you know it—now here comes Mama-San storming up the stairs cursing.

Oscar groans and struggles with me trying to make me let go of his foot as Mama-San rushes into the room fists waving and still cursing nonstop. Thank God, Oscar's playmate has stopped screaming. My ears were still ringing.

"Goddamn, Lee!" Oscar mumbles. "Lighten up. This is the first time we've been able to get away in months—go back to bed. And 'sides that, I didn't come here and I ain't leaving!"

I pause for a second and consider what he said. "Dammit, Oscar, that don't make sense! You're still drunk. Get your pants on and listen to me! We've got an hour before daylight, and one of three things is gonna happen sure's shit. If we don't get stabbed while trying to sneak back into camp, the guys on Berm Guard and this Red Alert have orders to shoot anything that moves, and if neither of those happens the Colonel is gonna court-martial our asses for certain!" Finally, I think I got through to him.

"Hey Lee," Oscar says as he slowly, reluctantly gets out of bed, staggers, and almost falls. He looks at me hard and mumbles, "I'm not as think as you drunk I am." Pissed off he stumbles around a good bit, but eventually collects and puts his clothes on. Soon, we're flying out of the house with me holding onto and pulling him while Mama-San stands in the door waving a fist shouting, *"Don't come back! You numbah ten GI. Don't come back!"*

Off we sprint down the back alleys of Tan An making our way toward the Army base. All the cool, suave bravery of last night is gone. I don't any longer, not even one bit, feel like the rugged, invincible John Wayne, Clint Eastwood, or whomever I thought I was the previous evening. We're now convinced that every shadow hides a crouching VC holding a cannon. Armed only with our .45s—a weapon I'm convinced is so ineffective it must be good only for a last-minute suicide—we push steadily forward to the unknown, but almost certainly disastrous fate that awaits us.

We squeeze into a smelly alley cubbyhole of a building's back entryway and pause to catch our breath.

Oscar whispers, "Nice knockers!"

Confused, I look for a knocker on the ragged, pitiful excuse for a door in front of us. None there. "What?" I ask, thinking I misunderstood him.

"My gal back there. She might not win the Miss Universe contest, but she sure had some nice knockers!"

"Jesus Christ, Oscar! Here we are in one helluva predicament and you're thinking, nice knockers?"

"Can't help it—it's a powerful image for one to get out of one's mind. But you're right, Lee. Guess what?"

"What? At this moment in time, Oscar, I have no earthly idea of what might be on your mind."

"I'm gonna turn over a new leaf. You know, something like this can change a guy's perspective. If we get out of this mess I'm never again gonna tempt the Fuck-Up Fairy."

I pause a minute trying to rationalize things and say, "Oscar, sometimes you can really amaze me. What do you think the fuc. . . Hey! Wait a minute! Did'ja hear that?"

"I heard something," Oscar whispers. "What do you make of it?"

"If I didn't know better I'd say it sounds like tracks coming down the street."

I glance at my watch. "Sure. Bet your ass it is! It's gotta be B Company coming in off night patrol. Come on, we're gonna stop them."

We leave our dirty, stinking hiding place in the garbage and rat-infested alley and run into the street yelling, "American, American, don't shoot!"

The company of armed to the teeth troops and tracks comes to a halt. Like two happy and excited kids at a parade, we run to the third track in line.

"Hey, Captain. Mornin'! It's us, Lee and Oscar. Can you get us back into base camp?"

"What in the name of nine kinds of hell are you doing in the middle of Tan An during an all-out Red Alert before sunrise?" He then pauses a minute. "Never mind! Don't tell me. I don't wanna know. In fact I haven't seen you and you aren't even here. Get down inside. We gotta keep moving."

As we climb aboard Oscar says, "Hey, Lee, I know it ain't no big thing, but didn't I make the exact same statement a little while ago? I mean . . . like I know what I meant, but I'm not sure it's what I said."

"Hmm." Shaking my head I look at the goofy prick. "Nope. You said something like, 'I didn't come here and I ain't leaving.' But that's close enough. Still and all I like the Captain's version better."

Back comfortably within the compound I look at my watch. It's 0530; I have 30 minutes before I report to the radio room. I grab a cup of coffee and sip on it very tentatively. Due to last night's heavy boozing balls-up debacle, the gag factor is ultra high just now. I pause for a moment of reflection.

Well, at least I don't have to worry about having the clap, syph, crabs, or whatever else. My God, what a night! And Jesus, what a hangover!

CHAPTER 5

BANDIDO CHARLIES

Our new Battalion Headquarters Commander, Eric Antilla, is a great guy, as was his predecessor, Lieutenant Colonel Steele. I enjoy my fine working association with him in the Rear Areas, but it is short-lived.

C Company's Commander is wounded and I'm assigned to replace him. I'm back to the front line, but now as Commander of C Company. My new unit is known as the 'Bandido Charlies.' The Bandidos have a solid reputation built largely by Lieutenant Larry Garner who was recently killed in action. He was a legend—one helluva guy! As with my assignment to Recon, I inherit a big pair of shoes to fill. However I am now backed by six months' heavy-duty combat experience, and I have another big plus: Charlie Taylor, my Company Executive Officer, is also a combat-tested veteran and a great help.

The 5th/60th is assigned the mission of participating in an operation called "Open Road." We set up a Fire Support Base on Highway 4 halfway between My Tho and Cai Lay, some 40 miles south and west of Saigon. The NVA have moved into this area and are raising hell with trade and traffic on this major road.

The first of the 84th Artillery pulls in and places four 155-MM guns in a pitiful rice field that is dry—baked hard as concrete. We're now in the middle of the dry season. B and C companies of the 5th/60th, plus an element of the 15th Combat Engineers, string out three rows of razor-sharp concertina wire. We also dig bunkers around the perimeter.

B Company, with their armored personnel carriers, is assigned to secure the west half of the perimeter. My company will secure the eastern half. The center consists of the four artillery guns and a temporary Base Headquarters consisting of two command tracks positioned back-to-back with Army green canvas stretched between them. Thus Fire Support Base Jaeger is now in operation.

Our activities are fairly routine. We send out foot patrols through the surrounding wooded areas in search of the expected battalion-size NVA force known to be working in the area.

On February 24th I am on such a patrol. With the dry season all the otherwise muddy rice fields, including the enemy's, are baked hard. Both foot and track mobility are enhanced in one sense, but the unrelenting heat and glaring sun bouncing off the hard earth make our lives unbearable.

Thank God, with this Search and Destroy mission, like so many others, there was no enemy contact. There was, however, evidence of a recent large-force presence in trampled vegetation and quickly deserted campsites. It will just be a matter of time before contact. That's guaranteed. And as usual, it will be at their time and call.

"This is Bandido 6," I call in to Battalion Headquarters. "Tree line cleared with negative contact. Request permission to return to Fire Support Base to prepare for night operations."

"Roger, Bandido 6. Come on in. Out."

Tired, hot and dirty we mount the vehicles and my Command track won't start—dead battery.

Pissed off, I say, "Get another track over here to give us a jump start, driver. And when we get back to Jaeger make damn certain new batteries are installed! When I need my track and all its radios, I need everything to work. No failures and no excuses. This kind of situation can and has cost lives."

"Yes sir, not a problem. I understand."

Like a wagon train we roll through the opening in the wire and spread out on our half of the perimeter. Our tracks, with their great fire power–a .50 caliber on front, M-60 machine guns on each side–make our security complete as we pull up to the wire between the bunkers.

Rest of the day we spend kind of relaxing as best we can. So damn hot! No shade, no breeze, no escape from the discomfort. Some clean weapons, some play cards, some try to nap. Everything seems to be in slow motion with everyone trying to move as little as possible in this all but unbearable heat. Our meals are like hundreds of others under these circumstances—all on your own, and all out of

C Ration cans. On the plus side is the typical trade process.

"Hey, I'll swap you beans & franks and a canned fruitcake for your turkey loaf and canned cookies."

"Okay, but you gotta throw in the pack of Lucky Strikes. You don't smoke anyway."

The night's only relief is the absence of the merciless, blazing sun. Out here on this baked concrete rice field, the nighttime temperature drops very little. What small comfort one can find is offset by the rise in apprehension and tension. These kinds of nights belong to Charlie, a.k.a., Victor Charlie, or the VC.

I make night assignments. Each track and crew will rotate. Sitting watch, manning the .50 caliber machine gun and listening to the radio. Everyone else tries to rest. I strip down to just my shorts and pants. Deep sleep is impossible.

At 0100 the struggle for attempted shut-eye is shattered. All hell breaks loose. We are under a full-attack!

I jump into my Command track and while pulling one boot on I try to get on the radio and assess our situation. I look out the down ramp at the perimeter. Machine gun fire crisscrosses the entire perimeter in the night's darkness, lighting up the night like fireworks. Yet another "Oh shit–oh dear" situation—we're completely surrounded! Like Cudgel, these are not the local black pajama farmers.

A bullet comes ricocheting around inside the track. Me and all others hit the floor and I shout, "Close the fuckin' ramp!"

The driver, knowing he's in deep shit, looks at me sheepishly and says, "Sorry Lieutenant, I didn't get things fixed. It won't start."

"You gotta be shittin' me. If we can't close the ramp . . . everybody out! Get out, now!" Bullets begin to zing in and bounce around inside the track like buzzing bees.

I'm the last to leave and just as I clear the ramp a huge explosion throws me several feet away. My track has taken a direct hit from an RPG and is now reduced to smoldering rubble. Face down, nose and mouth to the ground and breathing dirt, I roll to one side and check to see if I'm still in one piece. I think, *Private, thank you for not fixing my track—otherwise we'd all be dead right now!*

With my head throbbing and my ears ringing like mad from the concussion, I pick myself up. Damn! Close one. However, through the fog in my mind my position is perfectly clear to me—all fucked up! I have no communications, all radios destroyed. What I do have is what I have on me: my pants, no shirt, one boot, steel pot helmet and a .45 pistol with nine rounds. Yet another, 'Trust your guts or lose your nuts' operation.

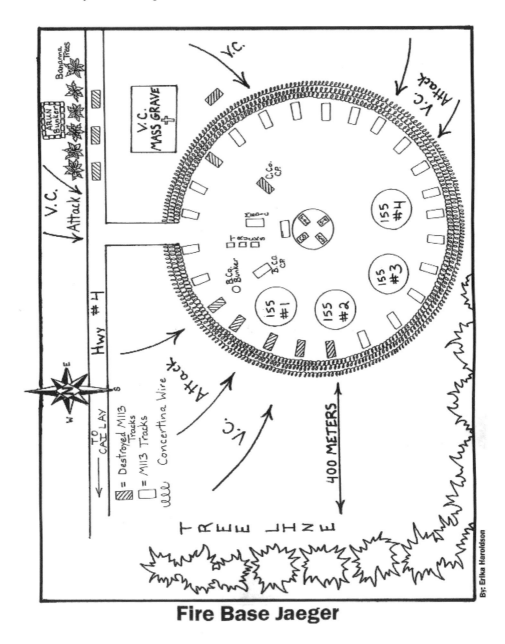

Fire Base Jaeger

Helluva way to go into battle!

First priority, as always, gotta check on my men, survey the perimeter, and get a SITREP to the Command tracks so we can adjust personnel and fire power accordingly.

Only way to do this is to beat feet from bunker to bunker. Off I go, bent over and at a hard run. One boot, pants and my .45.

By now the entire perimeter is ablaze. Smoke stings my nostrils, throat and eyes. I count eight burning hulks of steel meaning eight of our 20 tracks have already been hit. Small arms fire has not let up and the air sounds like a swarm of angry bumblebees from bullets whizzing by. When I reach the first bunker the report is no surprise.

"Man, Lieutenant Alley," one of my soldiers reports. "I'm glad to see you! Have two men wounded, and look over there, you can see the fuckin' VC coming through the wire."

"Yeah, I know. I've seen some already inside. Hold your ground. I'm going to the Command track to get some gunships and artillery called in. I'll be back. Stay strong!" Then I'm off to another bunker. Same response there. "I'll be back," and I'm off to the next and the next and the next. Same story at all stops. I've got to get to Battalion Headquarters! I dash to the center of the perimeter and duck into the canvas area stretched between the tracks.

It's full of wounded with more being dragged in. Screams, moans and more explosives. Damn! Nowhere to go and Medevac is impossible.

Then above the din someone yells, "Rocket! Rocket!" An RPG smashes into the tent aimed for the track beyond. No one moves. It's true! I can now positively testify that in those seconds when you sense death is imminent, the seconds pass extremely slow, like hours. Then after another three forevers we realize the rocket is just lodged here in the middle of us. Stuck in the tent. It didn't explode! Man, for the second time already tonight, and in short order. *Thank you my Lord!*

To my great relief the first person I encounter at the makeshift command position is an artillery liaison officer I have high respect and regard for, Alec Wade. He seems to be in command, caring for the wounded and using a radio. *This is good! We understand each other and I can work through Alec.*

"Alec, we're in a lot of trouble, partner. We have eight tracks gone. Bunkers are taking casualties and the VC are getting through the wire."

"What do we do, Lee?"

"Get on the radio and get some air support. Recon is overnight just down about six miles on Highway 4. Call them. They'll come if at all possible. I'm gonna make another round to check on things. I'll be back."

Still wearing one boot, my piss helmet and .45 in hand, I hit the trail again. Worse situation this time though. VC are in our artillery, in fact they're pretty thick inside the entire perimeter, and it's harder for me to move. Small arms fire still intense. The smell of scorched flesh, burning diesel fuel and brush gags me.

At each bunker, with the men's hopes temporarily raised for the moment by my showing up, I hear the same comments, *"Lieutenant Alley, are we ever glad to see you!"*

Unfortunately my response is always the same, "Hang-tough, guys. I'm just making rounds. We're trying to get some help in here."

All elements are under heavy attack and all in pretty much the same dicey situation. I later learn that B Company Commander Captain Schuerin has been killed in an attempt to reach a track. The B Company RTO, William Metzler, and two other SP-4s, a guy nicknamed, 'Arab' by Captain Siegfried, and Ernest Fisher are the only three mobile, and they're struggling to hold down that area of the perimeter.

I've known Metzler from my first days in B Company. He's a solid guy and a strong asset to any outfit. He later tells me:

"I see you making a mad dash across the compound toward our area. I think, *Great! About damn time, what a relief! He's here to take over command.* Just seeing you made me so happy I could shit! I didn't know you were just on another of your emergency circuitous check and survey missions and on your way back to Charlie Company. We'd been calling for reinforcements constantly since all this started. I see you and think, *'Thank God! We finally have some help!'*

"You visit us bareheaded, no shirt and shoeless during a short lull in the action. You took a quick look around and said, 'You guys seem to have this area under control. Keep up the good work,' then you haul ass out of sight.

"I was pretty sure you hadn't stopped by on purely a social

visit—tea and crumpets, serviettes, a small vase of fresh daisies resting atop our sizzling, red-hot machine gun turret—*but damn!*

"Arab and I are stunned. Here we've been yelling for help thinking we are hanging on by the skin of our teeth and you tell us we have everything under control!

"Arab looks at me quizzically and asks, 'Who the hell was that?'

"'That's Lieutenant Lee Alley. He's the C Company's commander!'

"'Jesus Christ, that was our help?'

"We looked at each other and laughed our asses off."

Back at Command with my unadorned feet smarting like a son-of-a-bitch, I tell Alec, "Hey, man, we're in deep shit! I'm running out of ideas and we're running out of men. We have to make a decision now."

"Lee, when I pre-registered all my possible artillery strikes I included the coordinates of this Fire Support Base. I say we call an Air Burst in on top of us to break the attack."

We look at one another long and hard. "Alec, you know that what you're saying could cause a lot of our own casualties?"

"Hey, guy, you've run the perimeter twice. You know our situation better than anyone. What are our other choices?"

I don't hesitate with my reply, "Call it in, Alec, but give me 10 minutes to make the rounds one more time and tell everyone to get down tight under something and plug their ears." I'm off again. Somewhere along the line I'd run out of my only boot. Both feet are now bare, cut, bruised and extremely sore. Been a long time since I've walked *anywhere* barefooted. We don't do a lot of that in Wyoming—rattlers, cactus and stones—and nothing like running this obstacle course almost three times around nonstop.

As ordered, within 10 minutes the heaviest of artillery rounds in the U.S. Army arsenal explode over Fire Support Base Jaeger. It turns the dark night into day. It's suddenly as brilliant as the brightest sunlight. Thundering above-ground detonations make the earth tremble and sprout bursts of fire and flame, which instantly scorch and burn the surrounding areas of dried rice, weed and bush. Those burning odors mix with that of the ordnance's explosives, incendiary, acetone, and other chemicals and spread low over the base and outlying areas. Even with heads covered, burrowed dirt-deep and fingers stuffed in ears, there are ear-piercing shrill whistling noises—screeches of exploding shrapnel that scream devastatingly through the air, shredding wood, rubber, plastic, tents, canvas, and anything other than solid metal into thin strapping pieces. The explosions totally mute all other sounds or noises.

I'm hoping and praying our guys have taken adequate cover in bunkers, under tracks, wherever or whatever. But, I also sadly realize there will be wounded from this friendly, but last-chance fire support effort.

Then just as fast—my God—it's so quiet! Is everyone dead, or has it worked?

The silence is broken by the clanking sound of tracks rolling in. They come with .50 caliber, M-60 machine guns and other weaponry blazing with firepower.

Two units have busted through. My old recon platoon coming from the east, and the 4th platoon of my Bandito Charlie coming from their overnight location to the west. I'm so proud of these men. I knew they would come. Only later would I learn of the great cost each rescue unit paid for their gallant charge to Jaeger. That is another story.

SUBJECT: Combat After Action Report for Firebase Jaeger, (location XS355495,) South of RVN Highway # 4 between cities of My Tho and Cai Lay, forty miles South and West of Saigon and ten miles North and West of Dong Tam.

1.   On the evening of February 24th, 1968, Firebase Jaeger was manned by approximately 210 men. They were:

A.   Bravo Company 5th/60th.

B.   Charlie Company 5th/6th, minus 1 Platoon.

C.   Headquarters Group 5th/60th.

D.   1 Platoon of Alpha Company 3nd/39th Infantry.

E.   B Battery 1st/84th Artillery (4 – 155 mm Guns).

F.   Elements of Bravo Company 15th Combat Engineers.

2.   In the early morning hours of February 25th these elements were attacked by units of the North Vietnamese: 261st, 263rd, 265th and 514th Battalions.

3.   The 5th/60th had been commanded the previous six months by Lieutenant Colonel William Steele. Lt. Col. Steele had just been reassigned to Division Headquarters. On the night of the Jaeger battle, the Battalion was under the command of the Battalion XO, Major Rocco Negris.

A.   Charlie Company was commanded by 1STLT Lee Alley.

B.   Bravo Company was commanded by Captain Daniel Schuerin.

C.   The 1st/84th Artillery was commanded by Captain Peterson.

D.   The 15th Engineers unit was commanded by Lt. Larry Corey.

CHAPTER 6

JAEGER—THE DAY AFTER

To most guys, the day after a battle is always the worst. Adrenaline is gone. Cold reality sets in. You're no longer on automatic, and there's a noticeable numbing of mind and body. Again, everything is in slow motion.

Through red, itching and swollen eyes I scan the fire support base we were guarding. I look at the SITREP in my hand. Twenty US troops killed in action. Seventy plus wounded. One hundred fifty VC KIA, and one captured. Weapons taken would amount to another several pages.

I sit on the back of a newly acquired Command track. Last night's battle, every bit of it agonizingly, slowly goes through my mind. The Medevac 'copters are all gone, the over 70 wounded are promptly transported to Emergency Rooms throughout the Mekong Delta. God bless our helicopter pilots and our medical personnel!

Many of my comrades are dead and difficult to recognize because of disfigurement, gunshot, explosion, or rigor mortis; with burning tears I stop, stare, and say a prayer for each of them. My fellow countrymen. Everyone a hero.

Another group of soldiers collects the Viet Cong corpses. The burning sun has begun to bloat the bodies. They are placed in rows of 10 to 15. Looks like about 10 rows. Our Intelligence Officers search each body collecting information, such as types of uniform, weapons, maps, papers, and anything that might indicate VC size of units and troop movements. Any scrap of information might save one of our men at another time.

Off in the distance comes the sound of a bulldozer. A pit approximately 30 by 20 by eight feet deep is promptly dug. I know there are some present, and I'm one of those, who feel a sadness for the death of any fellow human being. We watch as 150 bodies are moved into the mass grave. The pit is soon covered back over with dirt, the ground made smooth, and everyone leaves. All done. Quick as that it's over with. But still there are times now when I recall that burial. I remember the sight of all those dead bodies. And I see them not as enemies, but perhaps as husbands, fathers, sons, brothers, cousins, neighbors and friends to someone. Perhaps a someone who may have loved them, who misses them, and will forever wonder what happened to them.

"Lieutenant Alley. Hey, Lieutenant Alley!" A voice I recognize; I look up and see Sergeant Easter. He's a great soldier who stayed in Recon after I left. His tracks led the counterassault here last night which helped break the attack.

"Hey, Lieutenant Alley, last night remind you of anything?"

Our eyes lock and no other words are spoken—but we both understand—he was with me 60 days ago at Cudgel. Different battles, but the same feelings—exhaustion, numbness, and the same kind of bloodbath mission. Now, again, we must rebuild our units and try to prepare mentally for the next challenge.

There's no way then I could have known that it would come so fast, hit me harder, and this time nearly break me.

March 1, still at Fire Support Base Jaeger.

Nearly a week now since the Battalion elected to keep us here at the same Fire Support Base. This because it is obviously a hotbed of activity. The unit is operating at about 60-percent strength. Every man counts. Every man is valuable. Anyone with field time is placed in some form of a leadership role. Newbie replacements are scared to death. Everyone has a nervous knot in his gut.

Then it comes—the call that will trigger a lifetime of regret for me. "Bandido 6," my radio squawks to life. "Send a couple of tracks west toward Cha Lay. We have a possible VC sighting. Check it out!"

I pause and think, *Who shall I send?* My choice leaps out at me. Lieutenant Dick Bahr is my most experienced platoon leader and is a good friend also; of course, he's a great soldier. I call him in and brief him on the assignment.

Lieutenant Bahr's tracks are only minutes from the compound when a tremendous explosion is heard and felt. The deadly detonation and force is such that the sunbaked earth shakes and bounces us around some half a mile away. The smoke and dust cloud can easily be seen. All available tracks and men react immediately.

My Command track is the first to arrive and the horror I see sends my mind reeling and instantly makes me sick. Lieutenant Bahr's track is not here. In its place is a large crater some six feet deep and just as wide. The armored personnel carrier M113 has just been reduced to small pieces of metal.

"Bandido 6, Bandido 6!" the radio cracks. "How many men?"

Choked up I can barely respond, "I don't know! So far we don't see anything larger than a leg. We'll have to go through the pieces. I can't talk now. Don't call me back!"

My good friend, Lieutenant Tommy Franks, a part of the Reaction force, tries to comfort me. Tommy pats me on my back and stands silently, supportively beside me. He also could not believe he was looking at the remains of Dick Bahr's track.

Some men use rain ponchos as makeshift stretchers, and we all begin the horrific and gruesome task of collecting body parts. A leg, an arm, a torso, a head, then two, then three, then four—six men now each in shattered pieces in the ponchos. Six fine courageous men, and closest friends—now not even recognizable!

"Lieutenant Alley, we found wire. It was command detonated and leads to that hootch over there near the tree line."

"Take six men," I order, "and see what you can find."

Minutes later the call comes, "We have a prisoner, a twenty or twenty-two-year old hiding in the hootch."

"Bring him to me!"

As the squad approaches with the bound VC, I began to shake. I can't focus. My mind suddenly is not my own. All I can see is the carnage, Dick Bahr's and the others' arms, legs, heads. All I can smell is dirt, mud, gunpowder, blood, and the odor of death of *my men*. Once more I get a strange roaring inside my head. Rage and a vengeance seeking insanity overcome me.

"Gotta kill him!" my choked voice slurs as I draw my razor sharp survival knife.

The Vietnamese drops to his knees and begins to plead for his life. No one else speaks or moves.

"You son-of-a-bitch! You command detonated—*you* punched the bomb button that killed my men! You goddamned lousy bastard, slimy, stinking son-of-a-bitch! You're gonna die a slow miserable death. And that'll be too good for you. Your ears then your eyes first." I grab his left ear and slice through the cartilage. I hear a scream break through the fog I seem to be swimming in.

"No, Di wee! No! You cannot do this! You are too good a man. I owe you my life and I now beg you to spare this one. If you slaughter him it will trouble you forever. I know this. Please, Di wee, do not degrade yourself like this in front of us."

I turn and look into the eyes of Sergeant Trang, my faithful interpreter who has followed me from Recon. He's always by my side. His astute interpretations and suggestions have always been solid. Is this occasion different?

I look down at my bloody hands. They begin to shake uncontrollably and the knife falls to the ground. Tears well in my eyes and nausea and bile rise in my throat. *My God! Who do I think I am? Judge, Jury and Executioner? What have I become?*

"Doc, fix him up and get this rotten son-of-a-bitch piece of shit out of my sight!"

I call to my driver, "Sergeant, I want all the bodies in my track!" *They're my men. Goddammit it, they're my men! I'm the one who sent them. I'll bring them back!* "Let's get out of here. Let's go. Now. Move it!"

I walk the short distance back and mount my track.

At my desk in my dimly lit tent, with mosquitoes still pestering the hell out of me, I look down at the papers. It's my job to write the letters back home to the loved ones. Damn! I can actually see my men's faces in front of me. Mostly always smiling, good hearted, joking, vibrant and full of life. They were—everyone of them—super special. Like each of us, they had their quirks and idiosyncrasies, but good buddies and finer guys never walked this earth.

Lots of the good and bad times we had together come flooding back and overwhelm me. Slumped over, I begin to cry. Hard. Can't help it. Tears blur my vision.

What do I put on this paper to his family? How can any of this make sense and be made right? Twenty-six of them. And now twenty-six letters to write home. Letters that will forever ruin lives and break the hearts of those waiting; the hoping, praying parents, wives, children and other loved ones.

God, please help me as I try . . .

Lt. Charlie Taylor, the XO, quietly entered my tent and without saying a word surmised my situation. He patted me on the shoulder lightly, pulled up a chair and asked quietly.

"Can I help you, Lee?"

CHAPTER 7

THE LAST BAG-DRAG

Still on active, hot, dirty, sweating, Recon Search & Destroy duty—still getting shot at by VC and still killing VC through the long hot months of May and June. Finally it's hard to believe, but it's time to pack up and move to the rear area for final out-processing.

When you get short (very little time left In-Country), emotions run high. Seems like the last week is the longest of the entire tour. The days seem interminable and the nights beyond long. Can't sleep. Think constantly about home. Count my blessings and thank my lucky stars I've made it to this point. *God, please don't let a stray mortar or sniper round get me now.* Damn. Hurry on clock!

Finally my last day at the unit arrives. The Battalion has a small get together send-off kinda thing for me. They present me with an Officer's Sword with the 5th/60th engraved into the blade. There's lots of hugs and backslaps all around.

"Man, you are one lucky Mother's son—wish it was me leaving," seems to be the most common remark.

"Yep, I'm ready to hit the road and get the hell out of here. Been the longest year of my life."

"Well, Lieutenant Alley," someone says to me, "the Supply Convoy is getting ready to leave for Long Binh, your clearing station. Don't miss your ride. Good luck, sir, and God bless and God keep you."

"Thanks, the same to you and no sweat about missing my ride. I'm out of here." I turn around waiting for the Jeep to pull up. As the convoy is about to go out of the compound gate heading north through Tan An, then Saigon, I turn around for a last look at the 5th/60th Base Camp Binh Phuoc. My home for the last rugged and probably most momentous 12 months of my life.

Small tears form in the corners of my eyes. I don't really know if they are tears of joy because I made it, or tears of the guilt and sorrow I find myself feeling for leaving my men and the greatest, once-in-a-lifetime friends ever. Strange as it seems to me, I know I'll miss this place, and for damn sure I'll miss my comrades. Throughout the two-and a-half hours the convoy takes, I don't speak. Don't have anything I want to say to anyone. Lost in thought I guess.

My two days in the rear area are going to be full. A lot of lines; lot of paperwork. A thorough check of all items I'm taking home. I carry a Chi-Com Chinese rifle, one of the few weapon souvenirs allowed to be removed. It is checked, double and triple checked then tagged 'Okay' to make the trip. I also have my 5th/60th sword. I look more like I'm coming in to combat rather than going out—but tonight will mark my last bag-drag in Vietnam.

Around 1400 of this, my final day, I finish all of my processing and am good-to-go—locked and loaded for a night flight out. Well, I have five or six hours to kill. What the hell, they have an Officer's Club here, and a couple of drinks, *actually with ice,* can't hurt!

The Officer's Club at 1400 is nearly deserted. I like that. I sit with my back to the wall in self-isolation. Don't want to talk. Just want to drink and think. About 1700 the place begins to fill up. *Some of these guys have fuckin' banker's hours, eight-to-five, and it's now going on happy hour for these warriors.* It suddenly becomes hell for me. I'm building up a big pissed-off attitude. Demon firewater strikes again?

I sit and listen to what I perceive as bogus tales of bravery and secret missions. As the drinks wear on, their trumped-up stories become dumber and dumber, louder and louder. I've had enough and can't listen to any more.

There's a sudden crash of furniture as I kick my table and chairs. It gets everyone's attention. I rise and stand wobbly. At this point I'm not sure if I'm John Wayne, or Clint Eastwood, but I know damn well I'm tough. The words coming out of my mouth are slurred, but good and loud. "You rear end pansy-assed warriors are the sorriest bunch of fuckers I've ever met. If you want to be able to tell some *real* war stories, take a trip to Binh Phuoc and meet some of 5th/60th guys. They are truly, bona-fide soldiers. And if any of you believe or say different you're invited to step outside with me."

Wiser and more sobered minds prevail. Most just simply turn

back around to the bar and ignore me. Someone says, "Don't miss your flight, asshole!"

Rather unceremoniously, I thought, I'm shown to the door. With duffel bag in tow I stumble out into the night heading towards Base Operations and the flight line. There's a long queue of people waiting to board the big jet. There's Army, Air Force, Navy, Marine; sergeants, lieutenants, captains, all ranks and each of them, finally, headed back home. Most just stand around and fidget in line. Few talk. When I'm about halfway to the plane's entrance I turn and bolt for the eight-foot chain link fence surrounding the airstrip. I grab the fence with both hands and forcefully toss my cookies. Damn! I hold onto the fence with all my strength and throw up with gusto, repeatedly.

My mind is a blur. Vision too. I turn around and look toward the plane. Oh fuck. Where's the line? Oh my God, everyone is on board the plane but me! I let go of the fence and stagger/run to the plane, climb aboard, and claim the last seat just as the ramp closes. Damn, that was close. Departing planes out of here don't wait for anyone.

We leave in 'Blackout and Crash Conditions.' No lights on in or outside the huge aircraft. Buckle-up, head between knees. The jet engines roar, the plane vibrates noticeably and shudders, the brakes release, and we hurtle down the runway. In seconds we're off like a rocket and immediately go into a steep, seemingly straight-up climb to quickly get out of any enemy weapon's range. *Come on, Lord. Come on. Please, be with me just one more time. Don't let them get me now after all of this . . .*

After some dark, bumpy and anxious minutes the lights finally flicker then come on. "We made it. We're at altitude. We're off," the pilot calmly announces over the intercom. Shortly the plane levels and a pretty, round-eyed girl comes down the aisle with a beautiful smile and says, "I'm taking orders." Everyone on board cheers!

Chapter 8

It's Great to be Back Home?

After my last couple of weeks in 'Nam, when the time seemed to drag by at an agonizingly slower than slow pace, finally it's airplane wheels-up time and back to the good ole USA and my release from the Army in July. Then suddenly I'm a student on campus at the University of Wyoming in September—no real decompression or readjustment phase down; forget even five minutes transition time from war to peace back home.

I'm extensively and superbly trained to kill, with that training put into real-life situations and actual practice, sometimes on a day-to-day basis for over a year. Now, seemingly overnight I'm out into another world. One completely different and strange from the past 12 months. Twelve *full* months of living 24 hours a day with the experiences and images of killing people. Never before imagined I would, or could, kill someone. Me? Actually killing people. And also, far too often, seeing my friends and comrades shot, their faces, arms and legs blown off, grenades and bombs disintegrating their bodies. I've shot enemies from a distance and at other times, like when our fire support bases were overrun, been involved in hand-to-hand combat where one or the other of us fighting would surely die. It don't get any closer than that. Easily, too easily, I can still see a knife in my hand. I'll never forget the sight or the smell of his blood all over me. Then presto quick-like back home. I'm given a piece of paper and walk out of that military door into a totally new and different life. One that I find somewhat disturbing.

Our government is exceedingly generous at sending our most valuable resources—our youth—around the world in defense of democracy in these troubled times. I applaud this and salute those who go. Yet, as a nation, we fail miserably when it comes to the care of our veterans when they sometimes do and too many times, don't return home—at least in the same condition they left.

Our young soldiers, sailors, marines, and airmen are not machines that can be turned on and off as you do a light switch. Hey! They have feelings, emotions, fears and nightmare experiences they are burdened with as a result of answering their country's call to duty. Many return with horrible wounds and heartbreaking deformities. Some are blinded and have fingers, arms, legs missing; they are paralyzed, impotent, some have brain damage from half their head being shot away, and there are still others who show no scars, but mentally carry troubled baggage which overwhelms them. What can be the thinking behind a government that sends its youth to fight in far-away God-forsaken deserts of the world? To swamps, rice paddies, reed fields, rugged, rocky mountain terrain like Afghanistan, Kosovo, or cities, mosques, villages and houses, hootches, or hut-to-hut, of late, and then coldly separates them?

Early autumn near Laramie, Wyoming, 1968.

I'm registered for the fall semester at the University of Wyoming, Laramie. Everything seems to be happening so fast. I guess the transition of returning home from a year of damn near daily fighting for life and limb in Vietnam has me kind of confused. Maybe a feeling like going through a sudden time-warp—abruptly transported from one entirely different dimension into another. Initially, it's great to be back with family. No pressures here at the old homestead. Fall's in the air. A pleasant relaxed feeling of loving, caring and comfort . . . But there are subtle changes, something—I don't know what—but I have this strange, uneasy and worrisome feeling.

Among other things I amaze my family now by getting up well before dawn and anyone else—even Dad. He says, "I suspect it's a nervous energy kind of thing. Before long you'll probably be back wanting to sleep till noon again."

This morning I quietly leave the house well before sunrise. Last night Mom prepared me a sack lunch that I take along with me. I carry a canteen of water and am joined by our old family dog, Poncho, as I head up into the Snowy Range, Thunder Basin high country above Laramie. Guess I just want some time alone. Nothing really bothering me that I can put my finger on, but feel like I want some remoteness. And I've always loved the autumnal masterpiece of beauty way up in the Sierra Madres—my absolute favorite place and time of the year.

At the lower levels by the wandering creeks and streams, large cottonwood trees are beginning to turn color. Sheep that summered in the high meadows have returned to lower pastures. It's quiet and peaceful as we begin our hike into the elevated terrain. Poncho meanders alongside me and looks up at me now and then, kind of odd-like. Probably wondering what in the hell are we doing way out here at this time of day and season? I pat him on the head and momentarily think of our Vietnam Recon mascot. I know Dammit is in good hands and gets lots of attention.

Not unusual for our area, the higher elevations have already had some heavy frost and light snow. Some of the purple peaks are mantled lightly in white, which make the darker, rich green fir and pines at timberline stand out. The aspen, in patches, with their brilliant white bark and striking brilliant gold, orange, and red leaves, are magnificent. In the valleys they quake and seem to actually glow when touched, like now, by a light breeze and the rising sun. Further on flowers such as the yellow mustard plant, red Indian paintbrush, goldenrod, and purple chickweed mix with the aspen, lodgepole pine, spruce, fir and the ponderosa which carpet entire mountainsides. They present absolutely beautiful fall landscapes—a palette of colors. The cusp of our Wyoming autumn is near and everything seems poised for change.

Unlike fall in other parts of our country, autumns here are not long and lazy. The first beckoning sign of the coming winter can and does often unexpectedly swoop down from the high Rockies at any time from August on. Today the breeze is a mix of warm then cool winds and filled with odors of pine, wildflowers and the pristine snowmelt of the stream I walk beside. Tomorrow, or the next day, we could have a blizzard.

I find a shady spot and sit, pausing early for my lunch, which I share with Poncho. The wind whispers through the pine overhead. *Love that sound.* I look up through breaks in the branches and watch a hawk ride a thermal through the morning's deep blue sky. It will soon be filled with skeins of geese flying south. This area of conifer and aspen will become a habitat for elk and herds of deer. It's one similar to the areas where my father used to come with his rifle to harvest game for the coming long winter months. We always had elk and venison steaks, roasts, hamburger and dried jerky. I wish now that I'd spent more time, like hunting, fishing and other things, with Dad before he became ill.

With early afternoon shadows beginning to lengthen, I recall Mom said for me not to be late returning. Have supper with all the family for a change. I turn around and head back. I've walked farther than I thought, but it has been a good outing and I feel better for it.

As I near home I smell delightful kitchen odors wafting about, carried by a gentle, cool breeze. My Mom's a great cook. I pick up the smells of her terrific Wyoming Pioneer soup filled with onions, potatoes and other vegetables, and her melt-in-your mouth warm homemade bread, with slabs of butter. I also imagine her pumpkin pies and bread-puddin' with raisins and that great, sweet gooey stuff on top. Big flaky homemade biscuits, chokecherry preserves and the large steaming blue enamel coffeepot ever present and perking on the stove. For darn sure, no C-Rations tonight. My mouth salivates.

But I have an odd feeling and it's a departure for me because I've never been an introvert, or anything resembling a recluse, but tonight I feel a definite anxiety about being with even my immediate family. Maybe just nervous about being around others? *But, why now this change?*

Choi-Oi! What the hell, I say to myself. *It's been a terrific day! Cleared out some mental cobwebs. Breathed some good, sylvan high-country mountain air and, for a change, had lots of good thoughts. But still, if I today feel awkward being around my own family members, I dadgum sure as shit can't help but wonder what, come Monday, will college and a totally new world of strangers be like?*

Much to my disappointment it doesn't take long to find out. I bottom-line the experience with the concise summary that I guess I'm a 'confused' (for the lack of a more definitive term) 22 year-old veteran suddenly back home and in a changed world at the University of Wyoming. I find the turmoil of campus life troubling, a very uncomfortable place for me to be.

I see numerous Students for a Democratic Society who have booths set up in the Student Union halls and yell "Baby Killers!" Vietnam Veterans Against the War are dressed in fatigues most likely purchased from some Army Surplus store. I note their uniforms bear patches of the Third Air Force, which is headquartered and located only in Europe—not SEA—makes me wonder if they were ever in Vietnam, or the military. They also wear silly looking headbands and shout ridiculous slogans. They make spectacles of themselves and try to attract new members, anyone who'll listen. They're fanatical.

Damn! I try to avoid the Student Union. I can't believe what I am seeing and hearing. *Is this our America? Our world has changed— my God, what has happened to us? What has happened to me?*

Because of my love for the University of Wyoming in Laramie, and its prestigious football team, the Cowboys, which I've bragged about for so long, all of the wonderful memories I cherished and clung to while in Vietnam, they, sadly, no longer exist. I just don't seem to fit in with campus life. I agree to be interviewed by the WU's Branding Iron (BI) Student Paper:

BI: *How do you think the peace groups in America have affected the war in Vietnam?*

Alley: Generally, the peace groups have been successful in at least bringing to the surface some of the problems which come with this type of war. But I don't think the peace groups realize how their demonstrations affect the individual who is doing the fighting. There is nothing more disheartening to a fighting soldier who has just seen his buddy killed than to discover that his own peers back home are calling him a fool. Recently the Veterans for Peace Group, of which I am not a member, were organized on this campus. Their purpose is good. Anyone who says he is against peace should take another look at life. But from my point of view, this organization is working in the wrong direction. By setting up a table in the lobby of the Union Hall manned by individuals with long, shaggy hair, headbands, and Vietnamese flags on their clothes, that group lost my support. I think it would be safe to say that this influenced many other UW veterans to think as I do about the group. They are getting recognition, but to me it is negative. If they want recognition, why do they identify with something the average American conservative is tired of seeing and hearing?

BI: *Do you like the American attitude toward dead soldiers, maimed soldiers and returning soldiers?*

Alley: *Death to me is a very tragic thing. But the average American has very little sympathy for Vietnam war casualties. With the exception of personal contact with another soldier or friend, death in Vietnam is easy to overlook. My best friend had his head blown off by an anti-tank rocket. He had no family and was lucky to get a simple white cross in Arlington National Cemetery. He died fighting for his country. When an athlete dies, an entire university opens their arms and their pocketbooks to keep his memory alive. At times I think our entire value system is distorted. As an officer, I toured many of the Army hospitals in Vietnam visiting wounded men. For those who think they have it rough— well, they should visit some of these hospitals. The beds are filled with thousands of our young men who will never lead a normal life.*

Not surprisingly, I was never asked to become the poster boy for the Students for a Democratic Society, the Vietnam Veterans Against the War, or the Veterans for Peace group.

I'm a serious college student by day. But I find the nights difficult to cope with. I spend most evenings in a local bar with my favorite drinking buddy, my brother Ralph. Ralph is also a 'Nam veteran. Sometimes he gives me a sort of serious-like look then smiles and says, "I don't think you're normal. Maybe you ought to be committed." That probably has to do with my changes of attitude, thought processes, and sometimes-weird actions when I get into the sauce.

Even being back home I still, for a while, have some quirks. Can't sleep in my bed. Too soft, or something. I sleep on the floor. When I was younger and we knew our sheep were safe, I always liked the nighttime yelping of coyote, a high quavering cry and a series of short high-pitched yips, but now they make me bolt upright out of a dead sleep, startled and instantly wet with sweat. When I go to the bathroom I really prefer to go outside, but no one knows that. Have some other, what Ralph calls, "out of control" oddities, but he tolerates them as well as my mood swings. He's a great companion and brother.

It's yet another night at the good ole Buckhorn Bar. As always I don't go to the bar for the camaraderie and socializing. I just plain flat-ass go to get drunk. I believe it helps me to cover up things I want to forget. Coming back from the john I look around and ask, "Where's Ralph?"

"He called somebody out," a patron said. "He's outside and I'm thinking there's going to be a fight."

I burst out through the bar's door and find Ralph standing chest to chest in the middle of the street. He's facing someone I don't know. I walk up beside the two and ask, "What's going on?"

"This son-of-a-bitch is talking about what went on in Vietnam. He's bad-mouthing all the lieutenants and said 'they shoulda been fragged and killed themselves because they were such terrible leaders.' That means he's talking about you, Lee, and I'm not going to put up with it."

The stranger turned to me and said, "I fragged a lot of lieutenants in Vietnam, and as far as I'm concerned, everyone of the fuckers shoulda been killed. They were all a bunch of egotistical unqualified bastards who shouldn't have been put in command. I was a private. Me and those like me were doing it all. If *you* were one of those lieutenants, asshole, *you should be dead.*"

Suddenly rage boiled up within me, immediate and volcanic,

and I became someone else. There was a roaring inside my head. I swung as hard as I could and caught the loudmouth on the left side of his jaw. He dropped like a rock.

"Jesus Christ, Lee, I think you've killed him!" Ralph shouted.

By now a crowd had gathered. Someone said, "Get him up and see if we can bring him around."

With an angry voice I shout, "Don't touch him. Don't anyone touch that son-of-a-bitch! If he really fragged, or even thought of fragging one of his own country's comrades, he deserves to be killed himself, and certainly far, far worse than what I gave him. Leave that worthless bastard piece of shit in the gutter to hopefully die there!"

Ralph shouts in amazement, "Lee, by Christ, you could have killed him! What's the hell's the matter with you?"

"Back off. Goddammit. Back off! You don't understand. Nobody understands. *Yeah, goddammit, I am a 'Nam lieutenant! I did send patrols out, and some got caught in ambushes. I'm the one who sent a track out that hit a mine and everyone on board, my closest buddies, were killed. Blown to bits. The biggest piece we could find of any of my six men was a leg. I'm the one who blames myself, the one who failed in too many missions. Goddamn, don't you know, can't you understand that even just one injury was too much. I'm the one forced to live with those decisions, memories, and nightmares day in and day out. I don't need this dipshit worthless fuck or anyone to remind me of Vietnam, the war, the deaths and slaughter.* "Don't anyone touch him. Let the son-of-a-bitch lay there."

Ralph grabs me by the shoulders and pulls me aside. "My God, Lee. Come on. C'mon now, Lee, let's go. We're gonna have to get some help."

My mind is a jumble. I look again at the stranger lying in the street in a puddle of his own blood. Still enraged, I want to kick him and stomp his head into mush, but Ralph guides me as we stumble off into the cool Wyoming night. We wander around aimlessly for some time just walking and avoiding other people.

Neither of us says a word. The good old Wyoming wind picks up, and its cool gusts are sobering to me. The rage and loud roar in my head slowly fades and I calm down. *What the hell has led me to this? I've always respected human life, others' feelings, their weaknesses and sensitivities. That's the way we were taught and grew up.*

What the fuck now causes this sudden build-up and explosion of rage, frustration and anger in me?

If the bad memories and awesome nightmares would just leave me alone!

Goddammit! Am I going nuts, or what?

CHAPTER 9

REFLECTIONS
IT STILL COMES BACK

July 1985, Wheatland, Wyoming

Life is good. I am blessed with my wonderful wife, Ellen, and two great children, Kresta and Bo. The waters are warm at the Little Reservoir where we are spending the day with some of our best friends, the Hortons. Their children and ours are nearly the same age. In a sapphire blue Wyoming sky the play of a midday sun and summer's puffy clouds make patches of shadows on the water and gently sloping shoreline. It's been a great day. We've been boating, had a nice picnic lunch, and are now just kicking back in our lawn chairs enjoying the special peaceful and serene afternoon. A perfect setting. I lean back in my chair, keeping a close eye on my daughter, Kresta and son, Bo, who is very young at this time. Bo begins to waddle toward the water and suddenly I panic. I try to jump up from my chair, get tangled in it, stumble and fall. My heart is in my throat. "Stop!" I scream, "don't let him go into the water!" The water level there is only ankle deep and other children, younger than Bo, are enjoying themselves, just squatting, splashing and playing in the water. There is absolutely no danger.

But all of a sudden it isn't a peaceful July 1985 sunny afternoon, and I'm not at Wheatland, Wyoming's Little Reservoir. It is, in that instant, November 12th, 1967. It's another gloomy, gunmetal gray day. The clouds press low to earth, and there's a clogging heat mellowed to liquid breezes that seem to waft through the tops of the palm trees in the Mekong Delta of Vietnam. It's almost like breathing water.

My Recon platoon is on alert. B Company has gone into a zone to sweep a tree line and river area looking for some suspected Viet

Cong. They come into contact with a squad-sized VC force. Five are spotted. B Company gets three of them, two escape.

I'm sitting on my cot in my tent cleaning my weapons, sweating, swatting mosquitoes, and wondering what the coming day might present. Suddenly the landline rings. Colonel Steele, my Battalion Commander, says in his crisp voice, "Lieutenant Alley, B company has made enemy contact. They got three of the five they sighted. Two got away. I want you and your boys to find the remaining two. I have every confidence in you and your men, Lee. Company B will secure the area until you arrive. Report back ASAP. Good Luck."

Once again I shout to my men the familiar words, "We're rolling. Get your gear and head out to the helipad." There's no longer any question about what the new day might bring. Within minutes we're all aboard and promptly airborne. Seems like only a few minutes pass before we land.

We are met by the Commander of Company B, Captain Steve Siegfried, who briefs me on the situation. He is one of the most outstanding leaders I've had the pleasure of knowing and working with. He is affectionately referred to as 'Captain Sieg' by all who know him well.

Serrated silhouettes of the trees reflect morning shadows on the surface of the river, which runs through the tree line.

It's a muddy river and as we stand near its edge there's an odor of desiccation, dead fronds, wet earth and slow rot. I quickly check things out and scan the area for any possible hiding places of the two remaining VC. *Can't be in the trees—they've been searched and strafed—so they've gotta be in the water. But where? Sons-a-bitches could pop up anywhere, any time.*

I turn to Double L. "We have to get 'em—they're underwater and gotta come up some time—let's go." Without hesitation my men follow my orders and we begin single file, into the river guided by our point man, Double L Willson. Point group enters first followed by the command group made up of myself, Private Westphal, my RTO, my hippie medic, Doc Coutant, and my interpreter, Sergeant Trang. Within a matter of yards the water is waist deep and stinks.

We press on with our search through the murky waters cautiously and in a practiced manner. Step and pause, step and pause. You can't see two inches into the water it's so dirty. Nerves are strung tight and our eyes constantly search in all directions. We continue with our extremely slow, methodical search. We're quiet as possible, no noise, no talking. Long afterwards, for some reason—and I'll never know why—I pause for just a second. I look down and see the back of the head of a VC suddenly pop up for a second as he gulps air—inches—maybe a foot from where I've stopped. He hasn't seen us and resubmerges just as fast. I freeze immediately and turn to the sergeant behind me. "Hold up! I gotta stand still. Can't move," I whisper to him.

"What's going on Lieutenant?"

"Fire right here beside me. One of them's touching me. Shoot! Shoot now!"

His M-16 bursts to life and the high-powered rifle bullets strafe the water right next to me and around where I stand. Suddenly I can actually feel the Viet Cong's hand jerk and spasm, clutching my leg, then releasing. Instantly the muddy water turns crimson. The sergeant's shots have found their mark. Presently two bodies float to the surface. All this water and all this space and I stop damn near on top of them. *Jesus!* Once more, *I knew* I could *feel* them.

Turned out it was a good kill. The two have maps and intelligence on them and a large amount of piasters. Musta been on a payroll mission with all this money.

"Steele here," the voice on the radio answered. I am reporting to my commander.

"Lieutenant Alley, sir. We got 'em."

"Great job Recon. Congratulations! Knew you would. By the way, the Province chief wants to hang these two with the other three in the Village Square. A reminder to those in and around his community that this is what happens if you do not cooperate with the Americans."

The helicopters returned to pick us up. We loaded the dead. Another routine, mission complete.

It's early afternoon back at base. We shower, clean up, dry out and contemplate what the coming night might have in store for Recon.

My wife, Ellen, brings me back. "Why can't Bo play in the water with the others?"

75

I'm kind of in a befuddled state of shock. Confused big-time. My mind momentarily is a jumble. Seconds ago when my beautiful, precious son waddled into the shallow waters, *I once again felt that Viet Cong grab my leg. That's all I could think of.* That day we were lucky. Those VC hiding in the water could have detonated grenades that would have blown us all to pieces. That has happened too many times. I become frigid, get nauseated, and uncontrollably outraged all over again with the memories of picking up the body pieces— arms, fingers, limbs, even horrifically blown off heads of my friends and comrades. These two VC could have popped up out of the water, surprised us by tossing grenades, or sprayed us with a killing spread of machine gun fire. May not have got everyone, but certainly they would have killed some of us.

Why, in God's name, can't I separate myself from what happened in 'Nam so many years ago?

Of course Bo should be able to play with the other children in the water. *Why must my family suffer from these screwed up anxieties I have pent up inside of me? Why can't I shake this? I have to find a way to live with myself—some way to control this.*

PHOTO SECTION

Lee Alley on patrol,
Mekong Delta, 1967

Lee Alley, motor pool,
at Binh Phuoc, 1967

Lee Alley
Saigon, 1967

Lee, Vietnam, '67-'68

Mail Call-Sgt Trang,
Lt. Alley, Lt. Sweet

Lee and Hoi Chan, Vietnam,
Fire Base Jaeger, 1968

Tan An Marketplace in
daylight, not as I saw it
after escaping from
the brothel

Captured VC Weapons,
Fire Base Jaeger, '68

Lt. Alec Wade, my forward
observer, Fire Base Jaeger, '68
RPG didn't explode in tent

Fire Base Jaeger, 2/68
My command track after
the RPG rocket attack

M60 Machine Gun
in helicopter

Flying Crane bringing
105 Howitzer into
Fire Base Cudgel

The Song Van Co River
from a helicopter

Pfc. Gerald L. Milbrodt, KIA 16 FEB 1968

William Milbrodt, who wrote "The Letter,"
the father of Gerald L Milbrodt

The U.S. Military Assistance Commander, Vietnam, General Creighton W. Abrams, presenting one of the nation's highest military awards, the Distinguished Service Cross, to Lt. Lee Alley. Gen. Abrams would later become a Chief of Staff of the US Army.

Lee Alley and family today . . . son Bo, wife Ellen, daughter Kresta, and Lee

2005–Retired General Tommy Franks and Lee reunite 37 years after serving together as lieutenants in Vietnam, 1968

PART TWO

BACK FROM WAR:
FINDING HOPE &
UNDERSTANDING IN
LIFE AFTER COMBAT

CHAPTER 10

GENESIS OF THE
5TH/60TH INFANTRY ASSOCIATION

After leaving Vietnam in 1968, I had no contact with the men I served with until the year 2000. There had always been a noticeable void in my life that I couldn't put my finger on. This re-association has most definitely filled that void.

I take no credit in building the 5th/60th Infantry Association. The following chapters are from those great, dedicated guys who took those many needed extra steps.

It all springboards from here—from them—*God bless 'em!*

— Lee

CHAPTER 11

COME JOIN YOUR FAMILY AGAIN

My name is Curtis Hatterman. I survived Vietnam, but I don't know how. I know I worked my guardian angel to death during that time. I proudly served in Bandido Charlie Company, 5th Battalion, 60th Infantry Regiment, and 9th Infantry Division. I was released from active duty the day after I reached the States having served my year in Vietnam. In fact, Uncle Sam still owes me one day of vacation, which I don't plan on collecting. From California I purchased a first-class airline ticket for my final trip home. I figured that it would be less crowded in first-class and I would have fewer problems with the war protesters.

Life was hard for me when I first got home. I missed the excitement of battle. I got married six months later after running into my soul mate. I was happy, yet I felt like something was always missing. A few times at night, after the wife was in bed, I would go outside and sit on the back steps of our apartment house and just break down and cry. I think they call it withdrawal from adrenaline addiction or something like that. I didn't realize it at the time but I was also missing my buddies I had lived with daily for an entire year in Vietnam.

I had bad memories from Vietnam. The whys and what ifs would fill my mind, as I would recount things that had happened back then. The memories. Those damn memories just wouldn't go away! No matter how long it had been, I could remember things like it had happened yesterday.

When the very first personal computers (PCs) came out, I purchased one and learned how to write computer programs. I found that while I had my mind occupied with writing a program, I was forgetting about Vietnam. I must have either liked writing computer programs or I had a lot of memories to block because I've written a lot of programs in my lifetime.

When the Internet became available in my area I got hooked up right away. The very first thing I did was look for my buddies from Vietnam. At that time the Internet was still brand new and there were only a couple of military Web sites to search. After a while I began to wonder if anyone I served with was even alive after 28 years, as I couldn't seem to locate anyone. After searching for about a year, I decided to create my own Web page so my buddies could find me instead of searching for them.

My first Web site I wrote was for my Bandido Charlie Company. I purchased a book and learned how to write the code used for Web pages. I wrote it at about the same time that I attended a mini-reunion with three other guys from my platoon. That mini-reunion showed me just how important it is for us to get together again. It took me three days to get the grin wiped off my face after it.

Several months later, I got an e-mail from a guy who called himself "Shorty." He had been a Forward Observer in our Charlie Company. His e-mails were always filled with excitement about our company, and he asked if I needed an historian for the site. So, Alan Kisling and I began filling the site with information to attract others.

After about six months or so I received another e-mail one day from a retired Lieutenant Colonel named Earl Massey who had served in our 5th Battalion in Vietnam. He wanted Alan and me to help create a Web site for our 5th Battalion. And I believe it wasn't very long, maybe a month or so, when we all decided that we should have a membership on the site and create an association. We elected Earl to be the president of the new association simply because he seemed to know what direction we should go with it, and it was his fault for getting us into all the work involved with forming a new association in the first place.

As the membership grew we decided that it would be good to have a reunion and get together so we could meet each other. By this time we had elected some guy I had never met or heard of before as an officer. The new guy's name was Lee Alley. Alan Kisling was our historian, and our secretary who had served time as an RTO in Bravo Company was William 'Metz' Metzler.

Our first reunion was held in beautiful Denver, Colorado. During my drive to Denver from Enid, Oklahoma, I had plenty of time to think while fighting the prairie winds of Kansas in my pickup, and I realized that I had made the very same trip almost 30 years earlier to the very day. When I had returned from Vietnam the last part of April, I wanted to visit my sister and brother-in-law who lived in Denver because I wanted to see snow again after returning from a year in hot Vietnam.

Metz had mailed us 9th Division hatpins to wear to help us in finding each other when we arrived at the hotel in Denver. I checked into my room and went to the lobby to see if I could find anyone amongst the crowd. As I recall, I was sitting in the lobby when I heard someone call out Lee Alley's name and I looked up and saw the 9th Division pins on several individuals. After a lot of good hugs, the guys went to work on our very first reunion that was scheduled for the next day.

During that reunion I got to see others get their very first Vietnam hugs. Smiles and handshakes were everywhere. We were becoming a *family* again. All of us Vietnam veterans were beginning our healing process because inside is where all the bad scars from the war are. To heal for the future, one has to face the past. And the only way to do that is with someone who knows what you've been through, shares the same guilt that you have, has been where you've been, suffered the pains that you've suffered, and knows and understands why you are the way you are. This is why we have our "family" reunions. This is why I work so hard at the job I dearly love, as your webmaster.

Sometimes the e-mails I receive are rather tough to read without getting teary-eyed. I get stories about guys who looked for their friends from Vietnam for years and finally found them on our site. These e-mails are what keep us going. Every one of the officers of the 5th Battalion Association does his job out of love for our Vietnam brothers.

For anyone who reads this and has not joined our 5th Battalion Association, I say this to you: *Come, join your family again. We're all waiting for you. You won't regret it!*

May God bless Earl Massey and Lee Alley.

Your Brother,

— Curt

Footnote: Curtis Hatterman passed away Wednesday evening, the 14th of December, 2005. He was not only the webmaster for the 5th/60th Infantry site http://5thbattalion.tripod.com but also one of the three founding fathers of the association. Without his effort as association founder and his maintaining of the award-winning Web site, we would not be enjoying the success the reunions have given us. Heartfelt thanks to you, Brother Curt! We miss you.

Chapter 12

Our Little Group Grew Ever So Slowly, But Now—Wow!

My name is Alan D. Kisling. I am a Vietnam veteran and would like to explain my thoughts, my feelings, and what pushed me along with two other 'Nam vets to form the 5th Battalion, 60th Infantry, 9th ID Association.

The Association was formed in October 1999, by Earl Massey, Curtis Hatterman, and myself. It is a loose-knit group of former vets who had been part of the 5th/60th from the beginning of the original formation of the 9th ID in Fort Riley, Kansas in mid-1966 to the folding of the colors in Dion, South Vietnam in Oct. of 1970. (The 9th ID was subsequently moved to Fort Lewis, Washington.)

In early October 1967, at 18 years of age, I volunteered and was sent to Vietnam. There I was attached to A Company, 5th Battalion (Mech,) 60th Inf., Binh Phuoc, Republic of South Vietnam (the Mekong Delta). Eventually I was attached to Bandido Charlie, C Company, 5th Battalion (Mech)/ 60th Inf. until my return to the states in October of 1968.

My attachment to the unit was as part of an Arty Forward Observer Team, which consisted of a radio operator, a Sergeant and a Lieutenant. I started out as the radio operator and quickly moved up. At times when the officer pool was depleted I took the lieutenant slot. I spent my entire year in the field with the grunts of the 5th/60th. I had such a respect and admiration for these very young men who, like myself, were performing their jobs to the best of their ability, under the most extreme combat conditions. I survived both small and large unit engagements with these men. I never ceased to be amazed at how they cared for each other.

Upon completion of my tour of duty 1967-68, I came home to the States briefly, then returned to Vietnam for an additional year and a half. Never in my follow-on tours did I find a unit with men who impressed me as much as did the men of the 5th/60th.

My final return home at 21 years of age was uneventful. I attempted to step back into society. Just sort of pick up where I had left off. I married, we had children, and life just went on.

I would often hear of Viet vets in trouble with the law, alcohol abuse, and drug abuse. For me that was their problem! Not mine! The truth was I was one of them with the alcohol abuse, and for a few years, drug abuse. Once or twice pushing the line of what society thought was proper. I believed our marriage was normal, compared to the standard in society. In retrospect it was a poor relationship due in part to my inability to let someone get close to me. I was one of them. I was a Vietnam vet who moved back into society and never left it behind.

If someone asked me about Vietnam in the years following 1970, I had to be drunk to talk about it. Then I would tell them the most gruesome story I could just to get them to drop it. I never thought about Vietnam. (I told myself.) The truth was it was the first thing I thought about when I awoke in the morning and the last thing I thought about before sleep. It never left me alone.

In early 1999 my job required that I become mildly proficient in the use of a computer. This led me to the Internet and the world of e-mail. One day for fun I typed in Bandido Charlie. To my total shock, up popped the Web site created by Curtis Hatterman. Through a flurry of e-mails I discovered other Web sites pertinent to Vietnam vets. I began to do as many other vets were doing. Looking for my buddies from 'Nam. Curtis and I became fast friends exchanging memories and memorabilia. It felt exhilarating to think I had found someone who would, could, listen and understand my feelings.

Somewhere in mid-1999 Earl Massey joined our round robin of e-mails. Once again we became fast friends and through our e-mails the three of us decided to form some type of an association. In its infancy we struggled with everything from bylaws, to association officers, to any number of other questions about reunions, dues, etc. Eventually Earl became President, I became VP/Historian, and Curt the obvious Webmaster. Eventually (thank God) William Metzler, with his abundant skills as an organizer, became Secretary/Treasurer.

Our little group grew ever so slowly. We spent many hours searching the net for guys from our unit to join with us in the Association. It was a lot of work, but a work of love.

I threw myself into my historian role. I spent my time and money for whatever task was required. I retrieved information from sources such as the National Archives, the War College, or any place I could find material concerning the 5th/60th stay in Vietnam and Cambodia. As more contacts were made the task became easier. The Association was growing but not without its share of road bumps. Soon there were individual company reps and Association members, all those things that gave us depth. When Earl decided to retire as president we were stumped as to who should replace him. No one wanted the job. We were at a turning point. The next president had to take us through our first reunion. He had to be a true leader and a dynamic personality.

So who shows up on our e-mail list, the only man in retrospect, who could lead us through the next stages? When I asked him if he was interested in being our president, like a true leader of men, he said, "If that's what it takes to have our first reunion, I am your president." (Lee Alley never missed a beat.) With Lee as our president the Association has never faltered. We have had three very successful reunions. We continue to grow, as I had never thought possible.

As the Association has grown my role has diminished by choice and by circumstance. The act of helping to create the Association has been a great tool for me to remove the past from my soul. By helping others to perform my tasks as historian, and reuniting with old and new friends through the Association reunions, I have been able to finally remove the ugly monster from my closet, look at it, and discard this excess baggage. Vietnam has to me become a distant and uninteresting memory. My life now moves on, treasuring the important things in life such as family, friends, and the short time I get to be with them.

Chapter 13

Hey, We Can Laugh—Off to Denver

Lee Alley

When the 5th/60th Infantry Association officers—Earl Massey, President; Curtis Hatterman, Webmaster; William Metzler, Secretary/Treasurer; and Alan Kisling, Historian—took me into the fold, the groundwork for the organization was already well established. An award-winning Web site was up and running. A set of basic bylaws was intact, and company rosters were being compiled. As the new president, I made it my mission to plan a reunion. It was time to put faces onto the hundreds of phone calls and e-mails that had been exchanged. A location and date was selected—Denver, June 15-17, 2001. We were locked and loaded.

At this point, everything had been done long distance. As the reunion date neared, last-minute anxieties began to build. Two of the officers, Metz and Alan, decided to fly into Denver two days early to drive up to my house in Wyoming for final preparations. I was elated. I have always been much more comfortable in dealing with matters face-to-face. Perfect way to ensure all is in good order for this first reunion.

Then very real apprehension set in. For 30-plus years I had avoided Vietnam and everything associated with it. In a cold sweat I began to have a flashback–not of the battles in Vietnam, but of the images I had of the professional veteran from my college days and their antiwar rallies. What if these guys show up dressed in jungle fatigues, with patches of every unit in the Army sewn on their jackets, braided hair to down below their asses, and wearing red, white and blue headbands? What in the world would we talk about for two whole days?

I paced, I wrung my hands, I swallowed antacid tablets, and

thought about hitting a jug of whiskey, too. But no—I needed a clear head—I might have to escape. Then the doorbell rang. Oh shit! Too late. Can't run now. Well, here we go! Standing at the front door were two normal-looking guys in civvies. They do look a hell of a lot older than I do, but I can live with that.

I swung the door wide and greeted my brothers with big, open bear hugs.

"Welcome to my home. Welcome to Wyoming." I said as a flood of warm, happy tears and emotions overwhelmed me.

The tension of our initial small talk immediately melted away– these are two great guys. Our common experiences in Vietnam, all three of us having been in the 5th/60th at Binh Phuoc Base Camp, coupled with our burning desire to make this reunion a success, instantly bound us together. We began to share stories we hadn't spoken of for over three decades. It was so easy. Just seemed right.

Their stories and reflections captured me, but it was rather puzzling at the same time because although we were in many of the same battles, their memories varied so greatly from mine. It reminded me of a football game. If every player was interviewed after the game, I'm sure the story told by the center who gets smashed in the mouth with every snap of the ball would be far different from the story told by a wide receiver who caught two passes and was never touched. Same game—differing points of view. It was great to revisit our experiences in a new light, through each other's eyes. I had relived my battles so many times when no one else's existed. What an eye opener.

"Hey, Lee," Metz asked, "remember when the whole Battalion was pinned down, and we were all in those damn canals full of leeches?"

"Do I ever." I responded. "Had to be one of the longest nights of my life. I finally gave up and just let the leeches take over."

"Not me. I declared all out war. Let me tell you how it went. I remember it like it was just yesterday . . . "

Metz continued, "When the Greyhound helicopters dropped me and the rest of Bravo Company into our landing zone on 11/16/1967, they came under immediate enemy fire. One of the birds was shot down and our unit took several casualties. We could see that the nearest woodline was thick with enemy soldiers. The field of reeds we jumped into looked like any other from the air, but when we landed, we discovered that the water was up to our waists and the reeds were well over our heads, giving us a visibility of only a few feet. At this point we couldn't see the enemy, but the reeds that were cut down by rifle fire showed us that the enemy knew exactly where we were.

"Between the woodline and us there appeared to be an earthen dike. As we approached it we could see that it was actually a canal. We entered the canal and the water rose up to my chest. Some of the shorter guys were struggling to stay above water. This was one of the nastiest landing zones we had ever encountered. The air was thick with mosquitoes, and by the time we reached the canal, I could see several leeches on my arms and on the arms of my nearest buddies.

"As one of the company radiomen, it was my job to stay close to the captain. He needed to be able to speak to the colonel, who was directing the operation from above in his observation helicopter, or to speak to any of the lieutenants in charge of the various platoons. As I stood next to the captain, I could feel myself slowly sinking into the muck. When the captain was finally finished speaking, I moved off a bit to present less of a target to the enemy riflemen. With each laborious step I took, I could feel a strange tugging on my penis. What in the hell is this? I unbuttoned my fly and reached in to have my worst fear confirmed. The grandfather of all leeches had attached itself to the tip of my doodle.

"It was at this precise instant that I ceased being an effective infantryman. Bullets, hand grenades, and rockets be damned, I now had one problem and one problem only. Everything else paled in comparison. This sucker, and I mean that literally, had to go. As an average red-blooded American, 20-year-old male, a good deal of my waking, and for that matter, sleeping thoughts revolved around my penis. This current situation was completely unacceptable.

"There were several recommended methods for removing leeches. One's initial reaction is simply to grab hold of the disgusting thing and yank it off. However these nasty buggers have very sharp little sawing teeth, and if yanked off, they have a bad habit of leaving some of these little teeth behind in the wound, which then quickly becomes infected. This fact, oft repeated by my medic buddies, caused me to have a flash vision involving needles and scalpels and tender places. I discounted Option # 1.

"The other two methods have less drastic repercussions. You can either burn the creatures off with a lit cigarette or pour salt over them. The leeches dislike each process equally well. As a nonsmoker, I moved quickly to Option # 3.

"Soldiers in Vietnam wore the very same style of helmet their dads wore in World War II. While the helmet itself is uniformly olive drab in color, in Vietnam the GIs covered the helmet with camouflage cloth secured by a thick rubber band. This band was used by the grunt soldiers to hold and carry any number of things that they hoped to keep relatively dry. Most of the guys I knew, and myself included, carried several packets of salt in this area to use as "leech therapy." The problem with this method is that the affected area must be on dry land.

"I had the unfortunate choice of allowing this leech to continue dining on this most personal of places or to expose myself, in more ways than one, to the enemy, and then try to remove it at peril to my life and limb. The decision was quickly made. I hauled myself up onto the dike and lay there flat on my back. My presence did not go unnoticed by the NVA soldiers as the ground around me quickly came alive with bullets. I frantically went about the business of salting my pecker as quickly as I could. Fortunately my aim was true and Leechzilla let go of his death grip. I threw it toward the enemy soldiers in the vain hope that it would cause them the same problem. I slid gratefully back into the ooze which, amazingly enough, now felt comforting, and I went back again to being a soldier. I have sometimes wondered what this harebrained operation must have looked like to the colonel aloft in the helicopter?

"I have often remembered this day as my life moved along down through the years, using it as kind of a yardstick against which to compare other trying days. Compared to this, most other days have been just ducky."

With the arrival of my veteran pals, my wife, Ellen, who has always been a most understanding spouse, obliging and accommodating hostess, excused herself and went to a movie so the three of us could have the house to ourselves for any and all uninhibited conversations and reflections. When she returned, Alan and I were on the floor laughing so hard we couldn't stand. Metz, with Herculean, aggressive thrusts, had been demonstrating how to attack an unseen leech with a salt shaker.

Ellen, with her beautiful smile, graciously said, "I don't even want to guess. . . Good night—gentlemen—I'm going to bed."

Once we finally regained our senses, an internal awakening light went on. *I'll be damned– I can actually laugh about Vietnam.* There had been some good and fun times. We do have a bond cemented not only by the horrors of that war, but also by the crazy antics of 19, 20, and 21 year olds . . . just being boys!

Hey, I think we're okay. Let's have that reunion—and we're off to Denver.

CHAPTER 14

THE DENVER REUNION

Approximately 0530 hours, June 15, 2001, Denver, Colorado

I've always listened to my inner feelings. I'm not sure what that'd be called. Perhaps in less stressful situations, serendipity, or just plain luck. On other occasions maybe something akin to Extrasensory Perception (ESP)—a sixth sense, or an unusual, and innate receptive awareness—I simply call it my gut-feeling.

Without fail during my military service, those feelings alerted me when danger was near. They told me when to be cautious or *extremely* cautious. When to reach for my stiletto-like survivor knife, and to use it to strike silently. The weapon has utilitarian purposes but its deadly design makes it a perfect killing piece. Or instead, with a total abandonment of stealth, use either my large bore .45 caliber pistol, my M-16, or grenades. They've signaled to me when to mount an all-out attack, or when to run, and try to escape. What I do know is that during combat those feelings saved my life and the lives of many of my men countless times over. Yeah, maybe odd, but nevertheless also a sort of *comforting* feeling.

For more than 32 years after the war when things were supposedly calm, at least to outward appearances yet still troubling to me, the same feelings have sometimes quietly, but unrelentlessly instructed, "Don't talk about it, just keep your friggin' mouth shut! On other occasions they've *shouted* warnings, *"Run! Run now goddammit! Just escape!"* And so I did.

My impromptu getaways were easy—no one even knew. Using the excuse to check cattle I would saddle a stout gelding and lope for hours. The beauty of the Laramie plains combined with the magnificent strength of the horse beneath me always brought me back around. It was as if my horses knew I needed some space, to just slip away for awhile. They never let me down. Again, maybe odd, however, still a comforting kind of feeling.

But not this day. I am out-and-out absolutely trapped. I can't run. My guts churn, my palms are sweaty. I breathe deeply seeking control of my emotions. The urge to run once more is strong and unrelenting, troubling me in no small amount just beneath the surface. I struggle trying to hold my ground. *No, nope, and Hell no—no comforting kind of feelings now.*

My area of entrapment is a hotel room in Denver, Colorado, where I tread silently across the carpet trying not to disturb my sleeping wife, Ellen. Sleep for me for many nights now has been a hard bargain. At the window I watch the beginning of a brilliant red and yellow sunrise slowly appear in the east to awaken the vast expanse of the Great Plains. I leave and quietly close the bedroom door. In the still-darkened outer room I open the drapes, turn to the west and see the first pink rays of light strike the jagged tops of the snowy Rocky Mountains. I prepare a pot and sip a cup of hot, black coffee—and for the ten-thousandth time in the past few days—once again ponder *this day. Damn!* Sweaty palms become sweatier.

In just a few short hours I will be downstairs addressing the opening session of the 5th Battalion, 60th Infantry of the 9th Infantry Division's *First Reunion.*

What will I encounter? Professional veterans still in jungle fatigues? I hope not. Having looked at all the pre-registration cards, several men from my command have signed up and will be here. Some will be disfigured from their war wounds. Do they blame me? What are their feelings from that long-ago, but still yet today, troubling war? I was the one who gave them orders. Me! I can't even begin to imagine the possible range of consequences or answers to that question. No wonder I can't sleep.

Before I've always had an escape—but not today, and not here—not now. What has led me to this? I have positively convinced myself there are veterans out there who have never come to terms with their war experiences. I know that for a concrete, ironclad solid fact. *Hell, I'm one of 'em!* And yet I say I'm putting this reunion on *for them?* What about me? Christ, have I just been trying to fool myself—in fact—actually lying about *who needs the help?*

The new golden sun continues its slow climb and has riveted my gaze. Indeed, I stand as if captured looking out the large hotel window, hypnotized by the power of this beautiful breaking day.

Well, there's no landline phone ringing like crazy this time, but I'm just as excited and antsy as hell as if it were once again another one of those long ago's 'Recon Call to Roll.' There's no urgent rush to grab weapons and race to the tracks or helipad. Now, instead, it's just finally time to begin dealing with the past decades of pent-up emotions. *It's time to begin to find hope and understanding in my life in earnest.* So, guys, let's roll once again. We go downstairs.

A copy of my Talking Notes from the June 15th Denver Reunion.

• Good morning and a hearty Western welcome to beautiful Denver, Colorado, and the first of many to follow reunions of the great men of the 5th/60th 9th Infantry Division and their relatives.

• First I would like to give you a breakdown of what we have planned for the next two and one-half days:

Tomorrow – Saturday June 16th
• Saturday morning we will begin with a General Session then break down into smaller numbers. Group discussions will be held on many of the larger battles the 5th/60th were in.
  Also rooms are provided for Company-size mailings.
• Saturday evening will be our banquet with several guest speakers.

Sunday- June 17th
• Sunday may be one of our more difficult days as our comrade, and the now Reverend Ron McCants, will conduct a Memorial Service in which the names of our fallen brothers and sisters of the 5th/60th will be read.

Today, Friday, June 15th
• Now, let's talk about today. Before we go any further we need to get to know each other again. We served together thirty years ago and it's time for us to get reacquainted. We won't leave the room until everyone has had a chance to speak.

For a sample reunion agenda, go to page 235.

The tension within the room quickly melted away as one by one the more than 50 veterans stood and shared their experiences. Some simply stood and said, "Hello, I'm John, a lawyer from Chicago. Went to Vietnam from 1967-68, glad to be home, thank you." But we also had a lot like: "Hi, I'm Bob. I lost both legs to a mine. I should have died. I was saved only by the excellent care of my medic. Never thought I'd see him again, or be able to thank him for saving me. That's him setting over there at the third table. Thank you, Doc!" The tears flow.

Yeah. Tears do flow. Many find happy occasions for real belly laughs. There are uncountable pats on shoulders, obviously sincere and emotional bear hugs abound. The reunions work for me!

CHAPTER 15

A STRANGE KEY TO UNLOCK THE DOOR

May 2002, Wheatland, Wyoming

Many questions still haunt me. How do I—how does *anyone* returning from a war zone—make sense of the why, when, and how we have changed? How has this strong metamorphosis of mind, thought, and emotions been formed? In many cases, I wonder, how has it so consumed and overtaken us?

Today, years since World War II, Korea, Vietnam, the Gulf War, and other conflicts in between where we, wearing a uniform of our country, have picked up our weapons, killed, been wounded, deformed, paralyzed, and witnessed too many of our comrades' and closest friends' deaths in far off countries—so many questions remain, unanswered. The right-up-front and in-our-faces primary question is: **How can we find hope and understanding in our lives after combat?**

Keys needed to unlock forbidding and frightening doors sometimes come in surprising forms that we may not recognize. For me my key came as a telephone call. I tried to explain it in a speech I made as President of our 5th/60th Association at our second reunion in Charleston, South Carolina. The transcription of that speech follows. My prayer is it might help someone . . .

Video Tape Transcript
Second Reunion—Charleston, SC

Good evening.

It's absolutely great to be here. It is such an honor for me to stand before you. However, one of the biggest mistakes I made when I set this reunion up is I allowed myself to go last in the lineup of speakers. I should have pulled rank. When a guy has to follow

General Siegfried, Tex and Metz, I liken that to the frustrated ant that was climbing up the elephant's back leg with rape on his mind. I feel rather inadequate for the job. Nevertheless I guess I'll give it a go.

A couple of years back when we were putting this thing together and tossing a lot of thoughts, concerns, and problems around, a very good friend of mine, Metz, said, "Hey Lee, let me tell you something. There's nobody shooting at you now. You don't have leeches hanging off your butt, life has got to be good, pal!" Now when times get tough I always remember Metz's philosophical and optimistic statement, *Life is good!*

I can guarantee you it is good to be here with each of you. As I look out into the audience I'm confident there's one thing we all have in common. We served our country when we were called on. General Sieg touched upon this earlier in his talk. With sixty-some veterans here I'm certain if we went around the room as we did this morning with our Grippin' and Grinnin', there would be sixty different fascinating stories. And there's no one story more important than another.

Another thing I'm sure we had in common is at some point during our tour in 'Nam I suspect we all got a little bit homesick. Just plain bound to happen. Let me share with you one of those stories that would maybe not otherwise be told.

There was this supply sergeant . . . we were headed into Tan An. "Lieutenant Alley," he said, "I heard there's some women in Tan An that work in those—you know—those kinds of houses?"

Still today I'm puzzled as to why he thought I, in particular, would know about those kinds of houses. But I told him, "Yeah, as a matter of fact there are, Sarge."

In town we pulled over and went into a house.

The sergeant promptly pulled $300.00 out of his pocket, handed it to the Mama-San and said, "I want the ugliest woman you have and a bologna sandwich."

"Danh Tù, Sergeant!" she responded, "for so much money you can have our most beautiful woman and a seven-course meal."

"Hey," he said, "I ain't horny, I'm homesick!"

The man did seem to have a problem.

But at any rate I don't want to use my time here this evening to talk about my tour of duty. I just want to talk about how proud I am of you, my fellow veterans of the 5th/60th. For one year of my life I met the most incredible people ever! I met people who did things that were absolutely above and beyond, and they did that on a daily basis. I trusted my life to them—to you—and would again in a heartbeat without one thought or reservation. You've been tested under fire, and proved up.

But know what? Something happened to me once I got back home. I lost you. We lost contact and I couldn't find you! See, what had happened is Hollywood, and the antiwar movement created a Vietnam veteran I didn't recognize.

We were labeled baby killers. They said we raped, plundered, stole, robbed, beat and tortured—we did only everything that was bad, shameful and horrible. Those of us who did make it back home were not greeted with open arms but stared at as if we would snap any minute. "You're a drug addict, you killed babies," they said. What happened is *we let them label us* and lie about things they said we did as soldiers. We didn't counter and said nothing in response but remained quiet and with fading hopes tried to quietly once again settle back into the life and America we used to know.

The really crazy thing about this entire situation is, I guess after awhile, I bought into that idea. I allowed them to drag me from what was pure and rightfully proud fact into pure, unadulterated gross fiction. And, in fact, it got to a point with me where I couldn't tell the difference anymore. Tremendously confused, I began to doubt my own memory. This was such a terrible war and time; I began to wonder how could you, my comrades, or me have done anything over there that was heroic?

If you went to see a film about Vietnam, or read a book, you couldn't find yourself in there. Anywhere! You couldn't find a Lieutenant Garner in there. You wouldn't find Lieutenant Beechenor, or Captain Sieg in one of the books. Instead, there were people in the 'Nam stories that I did not want to be associated with. So, the easiest thing I could do was withdraw. And I did. I had convinced myself to get rid of everything I had that reminded me of Vietnam. I took it all, wrapped it up, and placed it away deep in a closet—I thought I didn't want to see it again. Unfortunately the biggest fight I ever had with my family was over that incident.

I want you to understand something. I come from a very large family, seven of us children. My parents were blue-collar workers. They were outstanding parents. They worked hard all their lives and did the very best they could for each of us.

One day when I was attending the university, my mother and father, searching for something or another, got into that closet and came across my medals. They dug them out, took them downtown, and had them placed in a beautiful framed display.

When I came home and found the medals hanging on the wall, I went berserk. You see, at this point I was actually embarrassed by the medals. I had allowed myself to be caught up in this false stereotype of the returning drunk and weird Vietnam veteran. And I robbed my parents of the pride they had for their hero son who was blessed enough to return home from the horrible war where 58,245 of our fine young Americans were not so fortunate, and their precious lives were lost.

I actually seriously hurt and heartbreakingly robbed my parents of their parental pride. Did any of you do anything like that? I hope not. It hasn't been easy to live with.

I tried to erase all the memory of my Vietnam experience. Buried. Forgotten. Gone. But the funny thing is I've since learned from many veterans that you guys, for me and them, *you are and always were there.* You never really left us! I'm now confident that special people and each and every special kinda time like we endured over there never really leave us. Never. But back then I just didn't know where you were or how to get you back into my life.

One day I came home and there was a message on my answering machine about a reunion in Kansas City, Missouri. I was invited to attend and speak on the battle at Fire Support Base Cudgel. I'd never attended a reunion in my life. I'd never been in a VFW Hall. Had no desire to. I had never even been in an American Legion Hall and I didn't want to go to this thing.

I returned the call and said, "No, thank you." Well, then, for some unexplainable reason, my reluctance changed and something happened—and I went to the reunion. There I was blessed to meet up again with one of the most incredible individuals I have ever known, Jim Deister. Jim was at Cudgel. He was shot through the head and placed with our others killed in action that day. Onboard the helicopter someone noticed Jim began to move and wriggle. The medics saved his life. Today he has no hearing. He wears hearing aid packs and has a speech impediment. But none of that slowed Jim down. He came back from death. He carried on and pushed himself to do incredible things like earning his Master's Degree in counseling and has helped and still today continues to help countless others.

"Jim," I asked him dumbfounded, "how in the world have you done all of this?"

"I did it, Lee, because I needed to."

His profound, sincere eight words touched my heart—and changed my life.

I prepared to return home from the reunion. I found I wasn't comfortable with a person or two I met there. Other than Jim I knew very few of the attendees. As I was saying my goodbye to Jim he said, "Lee, that outfit you commanded in 'Nam has a Web site. When you get home do me a favor. Please take a minute and look it up."

I did and was absolutely blown away by the things I saw on my monitor. They literally leapt out and grabbed me; they gave me chillbumps and caused a lump to form in my throat.

This reminded me of a disconcerting situation a long time ago when I was a young boy. I stood very near and was frightened by this big, wide lake out in front of me. I wanted to go swimming but this lake was so big. Probably cold, and for sure it was deep—well over my head. Nervous and indecisive, I just wasn't sure about plunging in. So, that evening I decided to put my toe in and sent out an e-mail.

The next day when I got home I had 23 responses! That amazed and told me there are *positively others out there*, like me, wanting and needing contact! Some of the e-mails were very emotional, some were entertaining. I was happy and excited about every one of them. Well, I now had my toe in the water. Some of these people I started to call, just to feel myself out a little, maybe I thought, I'll put another toe in the water.

Later I was thoroughly enjoying a telephone conversation I was having with a fellow veteran that lasted quite a while. Unfortunately I hated to, but had to cut it short to attend a meeting. I was president of the Platte County Fair Board. No big deal. But there I was sitting in the board meeting and I could not get my mind off that conversation with my comrade. I couldn't concentrate on the meeting that I was supposed to be conducting. It was a struggle for me to pay attention. Some were arguing about the problem with cleaning Tom's horseshit out of the parking lot, and others were hung up on what to do about getting Mary's horse's shit out of some neighbor's yard. Well, we finally got things cleared up and I dismissed the crowd and called an executive meeting where I promptly resigned from the board.

Several said, "Hey, wait a minute! What are you talking about—you can't just quit, up and walk out."

I said, "Sorry, but it's time for me to get the horseshit out of my life. I have some things I *need* to do."

I left the meeting and took a solitary drive up Palmer Canyon Road leading to the backside of Laramie Peak and had a big time self-analysis and heart-to-heart talk with myself. I felt a strong need to re-evaluate my past. I decided to redirect things and plunge both feet into the water of that lake. With doing so I became active in the 5th Battalion, 60th Infantry Association and eventually became its president.

We decided to have a reunion in Denver. The greatest thing about that get together for me was to look around and see the many familiar faces of my fellow veterans and the warm, pleasant realization that the gathering was actually taking place! What a thrill.

My feet are in the water my friends, and I'm getting in deeper. So, now I'm walking up to my waist. I have begun to make calls and made other wonderful, if emotional contacts. I've located my point man, Donny Teague. I found my RTO, Don Westphal, I found my medic, Doc Coutant. None were in those movies, but I found my guys anyway! I couldn't find them in those phony movies, I couldn't find them in those phony books.

I found Vito and I found Tex. There've been other fantastic gains. I found Lieutenants Sharp, Sweet, and Schlee. Initially we were kind of like the Four Amigos over there. All young lieutenants and scared spitless. Every chance we got we'd get together, hit the sauce, and share some concerns, problems, past good times, and thoughts of going home. They weren't in any of those phony books or movies either.

Then I found Ernie, then Curtis, Toby and Tim. I made more calls and found Colonel Steele. He was a very respected father image to me over there. I made another call and found General Sieg. My hero.

He's not in those phony dang books or movies. Where did I find him? He's teaching at a leadership academy. That's where I should have thought and known to look.

Where else would he be?

It truly is so fantastic to be here with you. I was able to once again make contact with my friend, Captain Russell. And do you see what happened guys? It finally dawned on me. I began to realize I was looking for you in the wrong places. I was looking where Hollywood tried to influence us all to look for Vietnam veterans. "Look for the down and outs. That's where you'll find them."

Not so! Just absolutely plain not so. I have found you and continue to find you as the good husbands and fathers—the doctors, clergy, lawyers, teachers, farmers and all the other fine, reputable and honorable people you have always been and continue to be. You haven't changed. Thank God, and bless your hearts, *you haven't changed.*

See, what has happened is really simple. The Vietnam vets have quietly become the backbone of America. *You guys are the backbone of America.* I just didn't know where to look for you. But right now, I'm up to my neck in this Association, and I gotta tell you it feels good. I look at you and am so proud. I wonder how in the world could we ever have let our pride and dignity be taken from us? Maybe *now* is the time for us to get some crap out of our lives. Perhaps like our fantastic comrade, Jim Deister, *maybe it's something we just need to do!'*

What has it taken to get you here this weekend? I'm certain it was a stretch.

How many of you have shared things this weekend with your comrades? Concerns, fears or problems with your special 'Nam buddies that you've kept hidden and locked up tight for years? Maybe some troubling things you, like me, just could not bring yourself to discuss with others?

I know very well how difficult it is to conjure up some of the memories of our times in Vietnam. Especially the perilous ones, the ones that scared the crap out of us, and would have scared anyone nearly to death. Hunkered down in a bunker, canal, rice paddy, reed field or wherever with explosions, mortar, grenades and rifle fire all around us and knowing for certain we wouldn't—couldn't possibly ever—see another day. And then there're the heartbreaking memories of carrying our seriously wounded, and sometimes tearfully, the lifeless bodies of our closest friends. It's damn hard! I know it's hard to open up old wounds!

But, know what? We *did,* by the grace of God, make it through those times. And although I'm not a doctor I know that sometimes before a wound can properly heal, the old wounds have to be opened up again, as a necessary part of the healing process.

If you have taken some time here, opened up and shared things that have troubled you—*good on you my friends*! If you haven't already, get to it! As these reunions continue I see more clearly the need to voice the past. Don't let this opportunity escape. Please believe me it's positive and therapeutic, and I know you'll feel better for having done so. It's darn sure worked for me, and many, many others I've talked to.

I honestly believe that now is the time to open those locked doors of the past. Let reunions like this, e-mails, phone calls, a letter or a post card, whatever, be a key for you to open the doors.

After thirty plus years we need to record the actual and factual SITREPS and get away from the fiction! Don't let this Association die. Don't let the contact between us *ever* slip away again.

And, there are many more of our comrades out there who feel lonely, troubled and confused. They have maybe glanced and looked tentatively, but for whatever reasons haven't stuck a toe in the water.

They need to test the water, and all of us need to help them. Make calls. Make that contact happen. Let them know there's lots of help as near as a phone call away.

So, my friends in summation, thank you for attending, for letting us one and all become close as a family once more. Thanks for sharing the memories of some fascinating once-in-a-lifetime times and the many soul-touching experiences we've made it through together. Some of those were most certainly deeply painful, many dangerous, some heartbreaking, some fun, and I'm sure most all of them could never, ever again be duplicated.

I know I'll never forget them. And I'll never forget you.

My parting words then to you my friends are these: Hold your heads high. Walk tall and be proud. Feel like the true heroes you are. *For you are the bravest of the brave.* Rest assured *you are my heroes*, and *you are also America's heroes.*

I am honored, proud and humbled to be here with you.

Thank you and may God bless and keep you until we meet again!

PART THREE

REFLECTIONS OF
FAMILY MEMBERS AND VETERANS

CHAPTER 16

OUR RELATIVES SPEAK

One of the great offshoots of the reunions that I never anticipated was the attendance of caring family members. Often *Finding Hope & Understanding In Life After Combat* is not exclusively restricted to veterans. Their loved ones— wives, children, brothers, sisters, mothers and fathers—they, too, have also often been affected.

The following are reflections of four relatives of veterans: Bo Alley, Misty Woodall Costner, Linda Tiffany and Kim Cooper Findling, and the Vietnam veteran father, James M. Cronan, Sr., UH1C Helicopter pilot in Vietnam, who writes about his son, James Michael Cronan, Jr. (Jimbo).

They and thousands like them have experienced struggles for hope and an understanding, for guidance that might allow them to help their loved family veteran in some way, or perhaps sadly, to learn the truth of final moments and circumstance surrounding his or her heartfelt loss. God bless our families.

— Lee

Chapter 17

Forgotten Honor

My name is Bo Alley. I am the proud son of Lee Alley. The following are some of my reflections on being the son of a hero of the Vietnam War. I also comment on some of my thoughts and experiences growing up in the shadow of my father, and of the eye-opening occasion of attending a Vietnam Military Reunion with my father in Denver, Colorado in 2001.

I often wonder what it takes for someone to go into war, and with that same thought, I also wonder what the war takes away from them when they come out. Growing up I knew that my father had fought in the Vietnam War; I also knew that he was still fighting to get out. He never talked about it, and I never asked, but sometimes I could tell that the ghosts were not far away. Whether it was his body tensing at the sound of a loud noise, or his uncanny ability to sense when someone was behind him, he was always ready for an enemy that was no longer there. The jungle swamps and rice paddies were a world away, but his mind would transport him back into them in an instant.

One day we were out on a deer hunt. During the hunt there was a time in the early morning we both paused to rest and just kind of survey the area for game. Evidently for some reason this seemed to be a melancholy time for Dad. Later on I wondered if maybe it was because we were out in thick woods searching, and he was once more carrying a rifle. Perhaps that stirred some past memories.

At first when we stopped he just seemed to be lost in deep thought. Then as we rested he began slowly, and in an unusual manner, to share some of those thoughts with me. He spoke quietly and took me with him back in time to Vietnam—not too far, just enough to get a passing glimpse—I was 16 years old, and not ready for what I was going to hear.

It was a story about blood, guts, and cries for help. It was brutal. It was real. This was just one of his many memories; he had seen so much, he had fought so hard. He still fights; his memory has proven to be a tougher foe than the enemy. For a minute I felt his pain. But then it was gone. Not so for my father. His pain would not go away.

I began to wonder how he could keep so much inside. But who could he turn to? Like me, others might feel his pain for a minute, but that was all they could do. What relief would come from others who could not fully understand? His feelings and emotions from the war were trapped. He needed help . . . and finally it came!

Our phone rang one afternoon and the voice on the other end asked, "Is this Lee Alley? Lieutenant Lee Alley?" It was an ex-soldier, one who had been looking for my father, among other Vietnam veterans. As they spoke the extended conversation seemed to spark some hope, optimism, and a more upbeat outlook for my father.

The caller explained that my father was not alone, there were many men just like him, men whom he had once known in Vietnam. They were now facing their pasts.

They had been together in the war and this contact, this conversation, was proving it was time for them to be together again.

A few years later there was a meeting. A reunion of Vietnam veterans gathered in Denver, Colorado, where I happened to live. My father asked if I would be interested in attending. I was honored at the invitation and leapt at the opportunity to go.

The day of the reunion arrived and with sweaty palms and a turning stomach, I entered the banquet room. It was not what I expected.

Hollywood had portrayed a distinctly different, but vivid picture of the Vietnam veteran, *and it was nothing like this!* These men were not longhaired off-the-wall activists; they were good men, all of them, just like my father.

I tried to sneak to my seat, but was quickly spotted, well sort of; apparently I looked very much like my father did back then.

"Lt. Alley! Look at you. You haven't aged a day!" I heard several shout.

Sneaking to my seat would not be an option. I met Doc, Tex, Metz, Shorty, Charlie, his son Sam, the list goes on—all remarkable people. I heard so many stories, and learned of so many sacrifices.

Emotion was building and soon it shot wildly around the room, no one could escape it. There was joy from reunion, pain from harsh and hurtful memories. There was laughter from past follies. There were many reverent moments and tears for fallen brothers. So much was being let out that had been trapped for so long; it was beautiful. In time everyone found a seat and men made their way to the podium to tell their stories. Stories about when they were boys, 18, 19 and 20 years-old. My God they were young! It really hit home. I was 22 at the time of the reunion; I would have been a veteran in their ranks, and yet those stories, they were not stories about boys, they were stories about men. My mind could not fathom the innocence lost.

That night I learned a little about the war and a lot about life. These men were bona-fide heroes, who had returned home from the war only to find that they no longer fit in with the rest of America.

They tried to hide their experiences and mask their pain because that's what we told them to do. We told them to forget, to go on with life. That's not what these men needed. They needed to be honored. And honor cannot be given if that which is to be honored is forgotten.

I cannot say the reunion gave my father back everything the war had taken, but I can say it allowed those of us who love him to better understand him.

The reunion also made me realize that I had been wrong. Before going I felt that I couldn't help my father because I didn't under-stand his problems, but I now had a new perspective. Thankfully I could help.

I just had to listen.

May God bless all of our veterans!

CHAPTER 18

I DON'T BELIEVE IN COINCIDENCE ANYMORE

My name is Misty Woodall Costner, daughter of Charles M. Woodall, Jr., KIA Jan 25, 1969. My father was with the 5th/60th from November '68 until that time.

I just want to give my thanks for Metz's generous time and effort with the Web page. I can honestly say the Web page has changed my life. I had been searching for years to find men who served with my father. My mother and I had basically no information about what happened to Dad other than he was leading point.

I had worked with a veteran I met through *Sons and Daughters in Touch* and he found the 5th/60th Web page for me. After that I began e-mailing everyone, and Metz was kind enough to pass along my letter to others. Almost immediately I began to get responses. There was even a picture of my father on the site.

On July 25, I got an e-mail that I had been praying for. I received a note from my father's company commander. He had gotten together with two of his squad leaders for a weekend, and they had done almost nothing except talk about my dad. It was an amazing and terribly emotional experience for me.

For 30 years I thought no one would remember my father. I learned he had and *still has many friends.* I learned he was a very brave man and that he insisted on leading point the day he died. I also found out his comrades risked their lives to save my father. I cannot explain how much this information has meant to my mother and me. We always felt so alone in our grieving for my dad. We discovered there was someone who had thought about him just about every day. Thank God, all of this happened because of the web page.

Since that time I have corresponded with my father's company commander, and on Veterans Day, my mother and I met him in Washington, D.C. It was amazing and wonderful. We were waiting for him at a party in a very large room of about 400 people, and he walked right up to me because, he said, I look so much like my dad. It was such a happy time for us.

After that I continued to search for the medic who was with my father when he died. I didn't have a name or any information. Someone said the medic died from injuries he sustained trying to rescue my father. I didn't have much hope of finding him.

Then one day out of the blue I received an e-mail from the medic. He had found the web page and my name on the membership directory. He told me exactly what happened when my father was killed, and he also told me many good stories, too. He remembered Dad laughing and cracking jokes at Diablo Fire Base. This is the first time we have heard any happy news at all coming from Vietnam.

This has truly been a wonderful miracle for us, and I certainly don't believe in coincidence anymore.

You can be certain that I will be at the next reunion, hopefully along with some of my father's buddies. I just wanted to share this information and let you know how much Metz's hard work on the web has meant to us. I'm sure it means a great deal to all the guys from the unit as well. If there's one thing I've learned from Vietnam veterans, it's that they care about their fellow soldiers.

We thank you all for your caring, for your wonderful help in getting so many people in touch, and may God bless and keep you.

CHAPTER 19

A VIRTUAL WALL OF REMEMBRANCES MIRACLES & REUNIONS

Linda Tiffany

The loss of a loved one stays imprinted on the heart, and though the years may fade, the memory and yearning do not. Veterans Day 2003 caused me to turn to the Vietnam broadcast on PBS in my living room in Salt Lake City. Little did I know that my niece, Kirsten, watched the same program in her home in Oregon. In an effort to know more about her Uncle David (my brother) and his tour of duty in Vietnam, she searched the Internet and found the most beautiful Web site, The Virtual Wall, with a page in his memory and honor. I will never forget the day my sister Laurel, Kirsten's mother, began to forward e-mails from men who knew and loved David. Kirsten's inquiry brought a gold mine of information to us and was the catalyst in an amazing series of events that has not ceased.

As I read the e-mails sent to Kirsten, I pondered the words written by these men. I thought it remarkable that after 34 years from the time David was killed in battle, May 28, 1969, we now had contact with former soldiers who remembered and loved our brother. I found such joy in reading the David L. Tiffany page on the Virtual Wall! I pondered deeply with feelings of awe, and I knew I would at some point respond to this event, though I was not sure how. I did not have a clue about the chain of communication yet to happen that would unfold unknown stories and events. Ahead was an unfamiliar journey, and I would in many ways retrace David's footsteps. I did know that I would, in turn, go down a path of my own. My heart was in charge and I followed its lead.

Because David was killed with five other men in an ambush, one of my first desires was to locate family members of the other men who died that day with him, so they would be able to share in a similar experience to mine, if they chose. One of my first phone calls was to Henry Dixon, Patrick Dixon's brother. He was easy to track down. Patrick was the Reconnaissance Platoon Leader, for the Special Forces unit that David joined a month prior to his death. Patrick's sister, Linda, returned my call and we quickly found that we had much in common with our losses. The connection was one that was created because we both knew the horror and tragedy caused from the death of a brother. I found comfort in our conversation. I later met Henry via the telephone and found he had done a great deal of research, and he was able to answer many of my questions. We've become close friends. With persistence, I was able to locate Marvin Briss' sister-in-law, who is the keeper of the family records. To this day, however I've not been able to locate a single family member of Dick Whitney, or Earl Godman. The sixth man killed was the Vietnamese Tiger Scout, and I have no name or information as to who he was.

Barney Tharp, the former Platoon Sergeant who instigated the David L. Tiffany ("Doc" Tiffany) Virtual Wall web page, and I communicated several times a week. He would answer questions for me and was eager to assist in my quest. Barney was so helpful and concerned that I receive answers. He began sending photos continually and we became fast e-mail friends. I will be forever grateful to Barney for taking the time to post the web page: http://www.virtualwall.org/dt/TiffanyDL01a.htm (Eventually I added information to this page and the site named me, as a family member, as point of contact.)

His love of and commitment to "Doc" was evident. I felt privileged to communicate with Captain Anderson who also honored David by posting a memorial message. I just knew in my heart that David would have been very attached to him as his Company Commander. E-mails led to many phone conversations. I talked with many of the "brothers" as the soldiers called themselves.

I eventually pulled out David's scrapbooks – the ones which were sent home with his personal effects after his death. They had been stored away for years. After my parents' death, I became the keeper of his memoirs. Our mother had compiled a beautiful book filled with photos and David's letters. Oh, how I longed to hear my brother's voice again, and so I searched in vain for the "reel to reel" tapes that he had sent the family from Dong Tam and Rach Kien.

I spent hours and hours searching the Web for any information I could find that would let me know more about David and his tour of duty. One snowy weekend I posted messages on as many Web sites as I could find—even ones that were even remotely related to my search. *The 5th Battalion, 60th Infantry Association* http://5thBattalion.tripod.com was a very helpful site. Many of the veterans highly recommended it, and they encouraged me to consider coming to their reunion in Dallas, Texas, June of 2004. I must admit I was greatly intrigued; however, I thought I might feel out of place.

About a month into our family's discoveries, I knew I needed to compile David's story once again, updating it with the new information we were discovering. Ever since the early years after his departure, I had this inner desire to share his story and perhaps write about him someday. I wanted to do this for our extended family. Now in the age of advanced technology, I decided to compile a DVD with "Doc" Tiffany's memoirs and thought perhaps I would share it with the former soldiers who served in the Army with him. I asked Barney Tharp if he would consider showing the DVD at the upcoming 5th/60th reunion to those who might be interested. He said he would be honored, but he wished I would consider attending. The more conversations and e-mail communications I had, I soon realized that indeed I wanted to meet the men who served with my brother.

As I compiled information, this DVD grew into a much bigger project than I realized. The photos and conversations kept coming– more research resulted. The process of creating a DVD was immense. My sisters were completely in agreement with me and supportive of the project, and we all financially shared the expenses. I sought technical assistance and then decided to learn the process and do as much of compilation as I could.

Every day became an adventure, wondering if I would discover something new. Phone calls and e-mails, and photos and memorabilia in the mail became routine now, most men who responded knew David, and some did not, but everyone had something to share. The former soldiers often connected with their buddies, and they'd call or write, too, many telling experiences, sending photos, and making recommendations of ways to continue in the search. As we communicated, I felt the pain of these men, and the concern of many of their wives. One evening to my great surprise, I received an e-mail from a man named Doug Bates. He had found one of my posted inquires on the 5th/60th Web site and responded. I was awestruck, once again, as I read these words:

> *Dear Linda,*
>
> *This is a letter that I never dreamed in my life that I would write... here is what I know about David. He was the bravest man I ever knew and totally dedicated to his profession as a field medic... David's best friend was a guy named Skinner... I have some excellent color slides of your brother and would be happy to have photos made and send them along to you...*
>
> *I recently published a book about my tour in Vietnam and I used a fictional account of the May 28th mission in the book, "Circles Around the Sun." Linda, your brother was an incredible young man and I count it one of my life's highest honors to have known and served with David Tiffany. I would like very much to speak with you and await any contact you choose to initiate.*
>
> *Blessings,*
> *J. Douglas Bates,*
> *"Doc" Bates*

Doug held keys to many critical elements of David's tour, the nitty-gritty everyday stuff. It certainly made sense that David would have best friends while there. I instantly wanted to find this "Skinner" and I couldn't wait to read about my brother in Doug's book. Doug's memory was amazing. His book is fiction based on facts and was very descriptive and gave me a sense of life as a soldier in the Mekong Delta. His knack for detail is profound. Because Doug was also a field medic, he had many similar experiences to David. He was also stationed at Ft. Sam Houston, and Presidio (San Francisco), where David had been prior to Vietnam, so I was glued to his recollections. I counted our connection nothing short of a miracle, just as the discovery of the Virtual Wall site.

My search for Skinner began immediately. With the aid of the Internet, I hunted. I called. I researched. I found about 126 Skinners and started the countdown. No luck. More calls, more research and time was passing. Still no luck at all. One day I talked to Doug again, and told him of my disappointment. He immediately said, "Linda, try Kettlesen, then. Kettlesen and Skinner were close friends and they grew up near each other. Kettlesen isn't a very common name, and so he may be easier to find."

It seemed like I was hitting a dead end and I wanted so much to find this Skinner and talk to him. So I turned my research to Kettlesen. To my amazement I found only three, and one of them lived right in the same city I now call home. How remarkable, I thought, could it be possible that this former medic might live nearby? I called, and a woman answered. I explained that I was looking for the Kettlesen who was formerly an Army Medic who had served with my brother in Vietnam. I told her my brother was killed and that I was researching his former associates to gather more information. She gave me no clue really, except that indeed her husband had served in the war and that she would relay my message to him, but couldn't promise that he would respond. When I hung up the phone I had such mixed feelings, as I was elated that just maybe I had found the right one. Still things seemed sketchy. Most everyone had responded so quickly in my search, and I wanted to hear back right away. I tried to be patient, though I thought of many different scenarios as to how this would turn out.

My initial call was made on a Friday morning. I waited patiently, no return call. Saturday came and went, and no return call, then Sunday came and I decided that if I had not heard anything by late Sunday afternoon I would call again, as many families gather then, and life is a little more relaxed. I thought perhaps this woman had forgotten to share my call, and that maybe with any luck Kettlesen himself would answer the phone. Well, he did not answer and Mrs. Kettlesen was brief when she said, "I gave my husband your message and he said that he would contact you, and that's all I can tell you." I was so disheartened when I hung up the phone and knew that now I needed to hope and pray that he would call and that he was the right one, because the other two Kettlesens did not check out.

Well, this second conversation was on a Sunday, and the following Monday night I was compiling information on the computer when I received a call from Pakistan. It was Kettlesen, the Kettlesen that did indeed know my brother, and knew Skinner. We visited for a bit and he shared a few stories with me. He said that he was still involved in medical operations and had a medical supply company in Pakistan. I could hardly believe that the man I was searching for lived just a few miles away from me yet was calling me from across the world!

As for this Skinner, Kettlesen told me exactly the name of the town that he lived in and thought he was still there, even though he hadn't been in contact with him for a few years. He said just call all the Skinners there and someone would be able to find him. I knew now I may be very close to ending my search. Of course, I didn't know if "Doc" Skinner would even want to talk to me, but I was unwavering in my search to find out.

As soon as I said goodbye to Kettlesen, I searched for more Skinners. Voila! I found a few that matched the location and began calling. A woman answered the first number I dialed. As I began introducing myself, I said, "This is Linda Tiffany and I'm looking for the Skinner who knew my brother in Vietnam. I don't know if I have the right number or not, but I'm hoping you can guide me to the right man." The friendly woman said, "You've dialed the right number all right, and I know who you are."

I said, "You do?" I was very taken back. I thought, now who has already called her and told her I'd be calling, but didn't let me know? I was so puzzled. Little did I know no one had called her and that she truly did know who I was.

"You're Dave Tiffany's sister, aren't you? I know all about Dave. In fact, we named our daughter Tiffany after him."

I was completely astounded. I couldn't even imagine such a discovery. I was totally overjoyed. "You did?" I responded in amazement, with my heart pounding in my chest and tears filling my eyes as I held the phone. I knew at that moment I was in the middle of a miraculous discovery, a discovery far greater than I could have ever imagined.

She then introduced herself and said her husband had gone to bed already and that it would be pointless to try to wake him, but she was sure he would call me first thing tomorrow. Then she told me the story of how Tiffany was named. She said that before their second daughter was born, she had suggested that they name her Tiffany, but Skinner had expressed his concern, feeling that it would be too difficult to do that. She said however, after the baby was born, she handed her to her father and said, "You name her." He said, "Her name's Tiffany." I cannot begin to express the immediate bond I felt with this family. The memory of this conversation and the words expressed are imprinted on my heart forever. To think that someone loved and cared for my brother enough to name a child after him was truly awesome. Our family has often deeply felt the loss of David, as well as the emptiness knowing he would not have his own children like the rest of us. I then imagined what it would be like if David had come home safely, married, and had a daughter.

The next morning, not long after I arrived at work, I had the long-awaited phone conversation with the real Doc Skinner! As we became acquainted he shared some of his recollections of the time he spent with David in Rach Kien. It was immediately apparent that he and my brother (both medics) were very close friends. He told me about his family and I could hardly wait to meet all of them. We immediately shared stories and photos and continue to share to this day. This has been one of my life's greatest unexpected joys.

My progress creating the DVD project was steady, keeping me up late many nights, but I found such happiness in the process. My youngest son Britt, age 23, was visiting me from California, and of course I shared all the events of getting to know so many wonderful veterans. I told Britt they were having a reunion in Dallas in June and that I wanted to share the DVD with them there. Though I had been invited by many to attend, I had a little apprehension about going. When I played a preview of the DVD for him, tears filled his eyes and he said, "Mom, you have to go. You need to meet these men and these men need to see this. I'm going to buy a plane ticket for you for your birthday." I was thrilled at his gift of love, patriotism, and his reassurance. I contacted a few of the men I had communicated with and told them I was coming. Word was spread from brother to brother by e-mail that there would be a "sister" joining them. I talked to the Skinners and asked them to consider coming so I would be able to meet them. I called Henry Dixon, Lt. Dixon's brother, to see if he was going to attend. We both thought it was very compelling. Barney and Doug were very excited that I had accepted the invitation.

My family gave me the encouragement to venture the flight to Dallas. As I finished dressing the morning of June 18, 2003, I carefully put on the American flag pin that had been my Christmas gift to my mother the year David was killed back in 1969. She left it to me after her death in 1995. This simple piece of jewelry was extremely symbolic. Yes, I was nervous as I flew across the skies that morning and then landed and boarded the shuttle bus to the hotel. The man sitting by me on the bus said, "It's obvious you're patriotic with the flag pin you're wearing." I smiled and my heart was warmed, and then he said, "I'm patriotic too, and I'm on my way to a reunion with my Vietnam brothers." We instantly felt a connection as I told him I was attending, too.

I checked into the Marriott Hotel, feeling as though David was close by. It was midday now, and very muggy in Dallas. As I left the front desk and turned the corner to the elevator I heard a voice that was newly familiar to me. I instantly knew the man was Doc Bates. When I approached him I held my hand out and said, " You must be Doug Bates, I'm . . . "

"Don't say a word," he said. "I know who you are. You've got David's eyes." We both had tears as we embraced. A few minutes later in the lobby, I met Barney Tharp, and the awesome A Company brothers. It was already a very emotional reunion, and I was still in the lobby. In the faces of each one of these brave men, I could see glimpses of the vitality of their youthful photos, the ones who were treasured in David's scrapbooks, the ones that I had carefully created into a DVD. In the hearts, though, of these men I sensed a deep intensity from burdensome months of war and individual losses. Without question, a reverence prevailed amid all the introductions and activities.

Where were the Skinners? It had been three months since our connection and I could hardly wait to meet them. I knew I would get to hear more stories about David, and I wanted to hear all about their two daughters, especially Tiffany. It wasn't long until we met in person and I loved getting to know them. I wanted to hear every detail. Skinner said his daughter Tiffany has the same quick smile that David was so famous for. Everyone who knew David always commented about his smile. Our conversations were very dear to me and very comforting. We laughed, shed a few tears, and enjoyed this time together. I was glued to every word that Skinner spoke as he revealed things that were so typical about David. I could easily picture in my mind the things he talked about.

With these, my wonderful newly found brothers, I was escorted into the large meeting room, where I heard many men briefly share their stories. I quickly learned that each and every man had a story wrapped intently around his heart. It was a sacred experience to hear their words as they communicated. The microphone was soon passed to a man that I knew must be Henry Dixon. I related to all of his words as he spoke. I felt his deep love for his brave fallen younger brother. His words were gripping. As he spoke he looked across the room and acknowledged me, even though we had not met in person yet. When he was finished he passed the microphone to me. Though I was startled, I briefly expressed why I was there and how I came to know about the 5th/60th Reunion. Of course I told of the miracle of discovering Barney and Captain Anderson and their postings on the Virtual Wall site. I shared the miracle of Doug Bates' response to my web site requests, and the miracle of the Skinners and their beautiful daughter, Tiffany. I was there because of so many compassionate veterans who cared. After I spoke, the microphone was in Skinner's hands. The bonds of fellowship in that room were incredible.

Later, when it was picture time, I was honored as Captain Anderson asked me to stand with the A Company men and represent my brother and theirs, Doc Tiffany, in the group photos. This was such a privilege. Lee Alley and his wife asked me to speak at the women's luncheon the following day and share my story with them—yet another honor. Following my words at the luncheon, each of the women who desired had the opportunity to share a bit of their own stories—stories of being married to men who had suffered much and given much of their lives emotionally to the raging war years. They shared what it was like for them and their families. It was a beautiful experience to hear words spoken with deep emotion and healing. This was an experience I still treasure.

Saturday evening was a beautiful banquet and program. The tables were gorgeous with large shimmering patriotic centerpieces. There was an awesome spirit of fellowship and goodwill, as speeches were given. I was so impressed to hear beautiful prayers and talks that centered on men who had turned their lives to God in an effort to heal the atrocities of war. This touched me deeply. Henry and I were given a standing ovation as we were asked to come from the back of the ballroom and receive recognition in honor of our brothers, Patrick and David. My heart was bursting from the unified outpouring of love and compassion that filled this event as we received tokens of remembrance. I was utterly speechless as I choked back tears.

This reunion was an unmatched experience in my life, so unexpected yet so rewarding. I now have a new circle of friends which has bonded me even closer to my younger brother, David. All these years—35 years—David has had friends and Army associates who have remembered him and have stayed connected to him through their bittersweet memoirs and their own stories of war. I am so blessed to have entered into this band of brothers for a time.

On Veterans Day last year, I sent a patriotic e-mail remembrance to many of these newfound brothers. Their replies were very touching, especially the one who shared how for the first time in 35 years, he was finally able to have a moment of peace in his heart on that day. This was from knowing of my search and desire to be united with David's comrades, knowing that newly found friends have loved and accepted me, just as they did my brother. On Veterans Day and Memorial Day this year, I know I can expect similar connections and reassurance that life has not been given in vain; conversely life has been found. There is much more now than memories of David and a legacy left to our family. Indeed, there is a legacy of lasting true brotherhood, fellowship and love.

May its rippling effect endure for generations to come.

CHAPTER 20

WITNESSING

Kim Cooper Findling

I was born in October of 1970, 15 months after my father returned from Vietnam. When I was young, I knew that Dad had been in the war, but Vietnam was not a topic of conversation. Dad never talked about it; now, I realize neither did anyone ask him about it. Perhaps people believed they were protecting Dad by not asking him to recount what was a horrid and painful time; probably, they were protecting themselves, too. Dad's silence was assumed to confirm the collective decision to avoid the subject. Therefore, paradoxically, the Vietnam War loomed even more significantly over our lives than it might have simply by the mysterious silence that surrounded it.

In spring of 2004, Dad asked me if I would like to accompany him to a reunion of his Vietnam battalion. He'd only recently discovered the 5th/60th Association, but it was already clear that the long conversations he'd been having with the group's members were both invigorating and healing for him. Frankly, I wasn't at all sure that I wanted to attend the reunion. I didn't particularly care about war stories; in fact, I kind of dreaded hearing them. Further, a trip to a conference center in the middle of Texas in June didn't sound like much of a vacation. But I did recognize the opportunity for what it was—a rare chance to understand what had, up until now, been a shadowy time in my father's life. The trip would also allow me to share something with Dad that was incredibly important to him. Of course I would go.

Because I am a writer, Dad hoped that I would document some aspect of the reunion in writing. I wanted to do this for him, but found the task, after we'd returned home, to be difficult. The reunion had indeed been challenging for me; the stories of the war were often unpleasant, and hearing them and being immersed in a vet's world, even temporarily, had been a struggle for me. I wasn't sure that revealing my honest experience of the reunion was what Dad—let alone his vet friends who he also hoped would read whatever I wrote—wanted to hear. Nor did I want to write a casual piece just to get something on the page; that would have felt false to me.

In the end, I did exactly what the men of the 5th/60th had done in Dallas; I relayed the truth as I had experienced it. And also like them, I have found myself grateful to those who have listened.

Witnessing

For some, it was the first time they'd spoken of their war experiences. The real stuff, anyway—a friend's blood splattering across your face, traipsing through a jungle village and killing people before they killed you, the sights and sounds of torture and death that can't be erased from the mind even 35 years later. Through the long morning, into the lunch break, past the afternoon's scheduled end, 110 Vietnam veterans stood and spoke. I fidgeted. I waited for an opportunity to escape—the pool, maybe, and my paperback.

In some ways, each story was similar. Dust, heat, the constant chop-chop of Huey helicopters, the thwack-thwack of gunfire. Creeping through the jungle on instruction to engage the enemy—which simply meant hiking around until someone shot at you. Blind, terrifying nighttime battles. Searching for meaning in the melee and finding little. Hot dirty hours merging into eternal blurry days. The sheer folly of hoping you'd be the one to survive 365 days in hell when men fell around you in a spray of fresh carnage every day. Throwing yourself into the only oblivion available—beer, cigarettes, prostitutes and the most morbid, self-defying humor you could muster. The sheer, oppressive aloneness of coming home from an unpopular war to people who didn't understand your experience and never even really tried. "We disappeared into our lives," said one vet, and because he was not just another in this sea of middle-aged men, but my father, I realized that it was my life that he disappeared into as well.

I worried that my presence would interfere. These men—men with huge bellies, men with no legs, men with every one of their fifty-odd-years etched on their faces like scratches on a cell wall—would edit themselves for my sake. There were other women in the

room, a few wives, but no other daughters. Would I remind them of
their own daughters back home: the girls they were protecting most
when they swallowed yet another private horror story? Eyes followed me when I left the room at the break—penetrating, somber. I
tried to make myself invisible.

The soldiers' stories diverged at tour's end. Some went home to
rural America and became mechanics or factory workers, made a
family, got by. A smaller number went to college and became teachers or bankers. A handful stayed in and made the Army a career. But
it wasn't so much what they did for work that was notable—it was
what they did for a life, after the promotions earned and children
raised and marriages saved or broken. How much of the war did
they carry? Some had never really left Vietnam. If they stood, they
stood rigid and anxious. If they spoke, they ranted, choked, spit
crude, bawdy jokes. Their stories were of divorce, alcohol, thrown
jobs, bar fights. Their bodies were very big or very small, as if they
were trying to expand outside of or vanish within their own emotional space.

Others had survived; some, even, had thrived. They had found
the thread of their lives waiting back home and followed it somewhere good. There was no reliable war trauma-to-current trauma
equation. The man most physically injured was perhaps the healthi-
est emotionally—at least on the surface—and the guy who never
saw combat might still be waking with night terrors.

My uneasiness was not just because the vets wouldn't be able to
speak freely in my presence. Their stories were not easy for me to
hear. A bomb exploding—your leg—but it's too far away to be your
leg. Pubescent Vietnamese whores visited. Buddies blown into
pieces, then collected by your hands from rice paddy sludge. Enemy
bodies, heads removed, piled, rotting. The atrocities weren't even
the worst—it was the constant fear and uncertainty, the unbearable
strain and loneliness; a supreme misery marinated in an unrelenting
suspicion that it was all for no reason at all. Some men wept, some
blustered and bragged, some simply quivered in a familiar fight
against an enemy that at some point had morphed from a VC soldier
with an AK-47 into three decades worth of an invisible emotional
tidal wave. I watched, I listened, I hoped for an end. I stayed for the
duration, even though the day, for me, was an unlikely mixture of

trauma and tedium. I didn't want to be there. I didn't think I needed to be.

I was wrong. After the last man spoke, I stood from my conference chair and, head down and moving quickly, began to dart through the thicket toward the door. I tried to make myself small, to leave and let these men say what they needed to say, to escape the ache of hearing it. But as I passed through the room, eyes locked on me, and then arms reached for me. "Thank you for coming," a man with an impossibly droopy face said. "Thank you for being here." Then, another, with a deep Southern drawl—simply, "Ma'am, thank you so much." Startled, I managed replies, and began to see something new in the steady and contemplative gazes I'd received all day.

In my discomfort, I'd forgotten what it can mean to simply bear witness. Having your story heard—not only by those who were with you but by those who weren't, and who otherwise would never understand, and therefore never understand you—validates it. I had said nothing and done nothing but simply be present. Somehow, that had been enough.

Kim Cooper Findling's father Bob Cooper was in Vietnam July 1968 to July 1969. He was a 1LT with 3rd Platoon Company C, 1st Battalion, 16th Infantry, 1st Infantry Division and with 3rd Platoon Company C, 5th Battalion, 60th Infantry, 9th Infantry Division. Later, he served as Civil Affairs Officer (S-5) for the 5th/60th.

CHAPTER 21

JIMBO FOUGHT HIS BATTLES ALONE

James M. Cronan, Sr.

Well, I guess this is about my son, James Michael Cronan, Jr., or as he came to be known, Jimbo.

He arrived all boy, redheaded and Irish-blooded, freckles and all. I loved him so much it hurt. He was my first-born and my namesake. He was my morning and night. To give you an idea of the stuff he was made of: at about age five I got him a Shetland pony. One day as we were fixin' to saddle the horse I was taking particular note of how he looked in his cowboy hat, chaps and boots.

I was enjoying the look of him and the horse together. All of a sudden the horse just ups and bit the fool out of Jimbo. Guess like most fathers I was waiting to gauge my response to his. You know if they cry you hold and comfort them, and if they laugh, you laugh. Well, before you could spit, Jimbo, standing face-to-face with the pony, calmly took hold of the horse's halter and delivered a straight-on punch to the nose, left-handed. He didn't say a word, but I could tell by the tears in his eyes he was hurting.

I didn't know a horse's eyes could get that big or a Shetland Pony could kick that high and fast. The cool part was Jimbo never let go—and the horse never bit him again.

Yeah, he was tough as a boot, but he was also all smiles and tenderhearted as they come. Jimbo was the sweetest little boy a daddy ever had.

But here's the twist. If you think he grows up to be the veteran in this story you are wrong. Most heartbreakingly, I'm the veteran and my precious Jimbo is the casualty.

On my first tour to Vietnam I was lucky enough to qualify for the gun platoon-flying UH1C helicopter gunships. My call sign was T-Bird 3.

I was proud of being a helicopter pilot, and I was damned proud of being a gun pilot. Unfortunately, due to high combat losses, I went from training as a wingman to flying as the company's senior fire team leader in less than one month.

I was green as grass and dumb as a stump. On my first few missions everything I touched turned to shit. However, after a while with lots of help from everybody times two, I began to learn my job and things got a lot smoother.

I learned that the word 'brave' didn't mean what I thought it did. It meant shaking so hard you almost couldn't fly the aircraft, but did it anyway, simply because the crew was counting on you. It meant doing your job because you would rather have been shot than let anyone know how scared shitless you actually were.

Fortunately, in all this doom and gloom there was one saving grace. Between coordinating the mission, flying the gunship, leading the fire team, covering the lift ships and shooting the bad guys, I was one busy son-of-a-bitch. (Sorry, Mom!)

When I got home one of my brothers asked me what I did when my day's missions were complete. Told him I'd grab a shower and head for the 'O' Club to get some scotch and shake off the day. Then he asked what time I went to bed. I answered, "Just as soon as I threw up."

At any rate I would write letters home and send tapes telling of my exploits and how we were kicking ass for America. Just like our dads did during WWII and Korea. I guess our dream was that if we could just live through this shit we would also be soldiers returning from war. You know, the heroes and the guys everyone liked and was proud of.

Surprise, surprise! We had absolutely no idea we were all "baby-killers, rapists and dope head smokers." Hell! Nobody told us that while we were in 'Nam doing none of this and being shot at and killed on a daily basis. Confident we were honorably serving our country.

But you know what they did do—they told and tried to brainwash my Jimbo that Vietnam soldiers were doing the above horrible things every day!

The news media drug us through the mud on TV at five every day, and at school the next day the children would say bad things about Jim's daddy and tell him how his father was going to come home dead and in a box. After endless taunts by his schoolmates, my Jimbo began to change. He became quiet and sullen. At age six my son became a fighter. As he got older he became an army of one—for me.

We both fought a war. I got to fight mine with guys I looked after and that looked after me. Jimbo fought his all alone. We had men who were taken prisoners of war while my precious six-year-old became a prisoner of unwarranted pain, ridicule and slander.

Turns out he spent his life angry and alone. The only time he seemed at peace was when he was going really fast. After owning two Corvettes and two Camaros, both Z1's, he finally found his true love—a Harley-Davidson Fat Boy. He would take his Harley out on the highway and for awhile in his mind be like his father. He was a T- Bird 3, flying his gunship, young, daring, bulletproof and invincible. You see, I was his hero.

Can you believe it? What a great personal thrill. *I* was my son's hero.

Jimbo was my best friend in the whole wide world. I lost him last year, 2004.

Now, this day and with this, I confess to you: I don't have much left to offer, to give, or even to say—except maybe this. Please, I beg of you in the name of, and help from our Lord God Almighty, don't treat our veterans coming home from the Middle East like our fellow countrymen and women did us back then, we, the veterans of Vietnam. The pain that can be caused—the pain our fellow American loved ones, friends and neighbors have caused in the past—can go much deeper and be more horribly hurtful, even life-devastating than one can imagine.

Please! I and all of us who've worn the uniform of our blessed country beg of you, *please,* give our returning veterans all the love, care and support you can. They have pledged and offered *all* they had for *you.* Some, by far too many have, in fact, indeed given their all. Let it not be in vain.

CHAPTER 22

THE LETTER

When I asked Hector Villarreal to be one of the speakers at the third reunion in Dallas, Texas, I had no idea how his speech would so compassionately touch such a vast number of attendees—veterans and family members alike; those seeking closure.

Thank you, Captain V for your selfless and wonderful lifetime of caring for and supporting our veterans—all of our brothers and sisters.

You are indeed one rare individual, and we all love you!

— Lee

A true story by Lieutenant Colonel Hector Villarreal, US Army, Retired, Vietnam Veteran

It was on a Sunday evening in the early spring of 2004 when I returned from our church's evening services, that I noticed I had a message on our answering machine. When I listened, the message said: "My name is Louis Balas. I am looking for Captain Hector Villarreal who was with the 5th/60th Infantry in Vietnam in 1967-68. If you are that person, please call me at the following number."

The voice was deep, clear, and to the point. I noticed somewhat of a Texas accent so I figured this caller lived not too far from me, as I live in San Antonio. My mind went flashing back to Vietnam with the 5th Battalion 60th Infantry and names that I had long forgotten but was now desperately trying to recall. My questions were: Who is this man? Why is he calling me? I have been retired since 1983, so why is someone looking for me now? My heart pounded a little bit faster as I anxiously and excitedly picked up the phone and made the call that took me back 35 plus years in time.

I said, "Hello, this is Captain Villarreal who was in Vietnam in 1967-68. Who is this?"

"Tex," Louis Balas said. "Captain V, I'm the soldier you had a conversation with concerning my name one sunny afternoon at Binh Phuoc. Do you remember that conversation? You told me that my name Balas meant 'bullets' in Spanish."

This commenced a conversation which rekindled a relationship that had begun more than 35 years ago, with most of those years in between having no communication at all. In fact, because of the way we had been treated when we returned, I tried to put Vietnam behind me, permanently. For those who had survived, I really did not know where my soldiers had gone to, or if they had retired, or left the service, or if they had recovered from their injuries caused by ambushes, command-detonated mines, incoming mortars and artillery, emotional stress, and a thousand other reasons.

As we spoke I remembered that for 25 years or so my awards and decorations that I received in Vietnam had been rolled up in towels and put away because I was not sure how I felt about all that. The memories these awards brought caused a mixture of pride, pain, and sadness as I recalled the horrors of what we as a group and as individuals had gone through.

Tex and I carried on with one of the most exciting and self-satisfying conversations I had ever had. As we talked and shared memories, it was like we were back in Vietnam at our Fire Base next to the village of Binh Phuoc. In fact, as we spoke, I could almost smell anew the different odors that reminded me of that part of the world and specifically our Fire Base. Tex then told me he was happy to find me, and that there were other soldiers looking for me via the battalion's web site, specifically Harvey Shapiro, my Company Clerk. He also wanted to tell me that there was a reunion of the 5th/60th Infantry coming up in June and he wanted me to attend. I accepted the invitation and reassured Tex that we would keep in touch. He said the reunions helped many soldiers deal with their war problems.

I will never forget that at the end of our conversation, Tex said to me, "Welcome home, Captain V."

A few days later, I received a call from Lt. Alley, Lee Alley. He was a hero, one of many in our battalion, and was the first soldier I had the honor of writing up for the Congressional Medal of Honor. He had distinguished himself selflessly over and over again one night in a combat situation where a much larger North Vietnamese unit had attacked our battalion, but because of our fantastic men and the leadership of those like Lt. Alley and others, our unit prevailed and won the battle. Lt. Alley asked me if I remembered him.

"Remember you?" I said. " I still have a copy of the form we wrote recommending you for the Congressional Medal of Honor. Throughout the years, I have spoken to many people about what you did. I will never forget you, Lt. Alley. It is my honor to be speaking with you now."

Lt. Alley said he remembered me saying in a joking sort of way that I was the only Mexican-American Captain in the U.S. Army. After we laughed and reminisced a little more, he then invited me to the reunion and asked if I would be one of the guest speakers. I agreed and asked, "What do you want me to speak about?"

And he said, "You can say whatever comes to your heart." I told Lt. Alley that besides his document, I also had a special letter that I had kept all of these years and wondered if I could read the letter, speak on it, and what it meant to me. I told Lt. Alley that every time I read that letter it brought tears to my eyes and gave me courage and strength to deal with the hardships in life.

He said, "Do it Captain V!"

The reunion was held mid-June 2004 at a Dallas/Fort Worth airport hotel. It was convenient for everyone to arrive and depart without having to rent an automobile, the facilities were very nice, and the hotel staff was very accommodating. All seemed to look at us with different eyes. Somehow we attracted a special kind of attention. I brought pictures I had taken while in Vietnam, the final draft document of Lt. Alley's Congressional Medal of Honor recommendation, a copy of orders of which I am very proud—the fact that, as a Captain, I had signed for the 5th/60th Infantry Battalion, for about one week. The rank of a Battalion Commander is a Lieutenant Colonel. I also took along 'The Letter' that changed my life and that I was going to read and speak from.

Throughout the years I had read and reread the letter and each time, it touched me deeply. Each time I read it, I gave serious thought to calling the author of the letter, but I was concerned that I could open up old wounds or that I could be violating his request to keep this information secret. I never called but it did not leave my mind. I came to know that it was not God's timing.

On the special evening of the reunion we enjoyed our dinner and then had some remarks from the leadership of the Association. General Steele, our Battalion Commander, spoke from his heart and honored all of the vets attending as heroes. He made us laugh and made us remember those days way back then by relaying two stories of people going above and beyond the call of duty. One was about Captain Tom Russell and the other was about Lt. Lee Alley. Both stories touched everyone's hearts and, in some cases, brought forth new information as to what had actually happened during those specific combat situations. In closing, he saluted everyone present and honored all. We all stood proudly as we were acknowledged, and some for the first time were acknowledged by a General Officer for doing our part as soldiers in Vietnam, in a war that was not popular.

Lt. Koeneman, the Master of Ceremonies, and now a Lieutenant Colonel in the U.S. Army Reserves, then stood up and introduced me as the next speaker for the evening. The tone I wanted to set was a different one from the previous speeches, which had been light-hearted and humorous, where possible. The tone I wanted to set was a serious but compassionate one that dealt with the reality of life and death and moving on with life. I wanted to make the point that if a father could let go of his son because of death, then we, too, could also possibly let go of those things that might be holding back our recovery from the horrors of war. I knew that this specific letter had changed my life, and I wanted to encourage the audience that this letter could also possibly change their lives. I thought that maybe some of our heroes might want to share their experiences with veterans and or units returning from the Middle East. Help them out with closure.

When I got to the podium and thanked the master of ceremonies, I commented, "Don't worry, Tim, my wife cannot pronounce my name correctly either." And I then continued, "It is such a humbling experience for me to be up here. I want to speak to you from a different perspective than my distinguished and cherished comrade speakers before me. However, as with them, my words and feelings come from my heart."

As I got started with my real message I was floundering somewhat as you will see because I still was not exactly sure how I was going to bring meaning to the phrase in the letter, which changed my life— 'I have to believe it was God's will'—without offending anyone.

"What I want to do is, and I am not one to speak from notes, so this will be a little tough for me. What I want to talk about at this my first ever reunion are things I truly believe and feel in my heart—perhaps you—my dear friends and comrades also share similar feelings. Maybe these are some of the same kinds of things that motivated each of us to come here.

"I proudly say that you, each and every one of you, and me—we can honestly say we are all heroes. God bless you. For everything that you are and all that you've done, God bless you. We came here to reflect, to laugh, to cry, and that's OK. In fact, it's great. It's funny, it's wonderful, and although we may not be able to do this elsewhere, it's OK because we could do all of this here and it is good, and doing this is healthy.

"Since arriving I have seen men hug each other, talk, reminisce, laugh, and cry and that's good, too. Because it lets out old steam which possibly has been bottled up for these past 35 years or so, and that's good too!

"When I was the Company Commander of Headquarters and Headquarters Company, I received a letter from a father of one of our members. Now we here consider ourselves brothers in combat, but we also had fathers, mothers, sisters, wives and children that were at home. They, too, were part of our extended brotherhood. This is a letter from a father—the real McCoy—a loving father and son relationship from first breath at childbirth on. I've learned from this letter. I cry every time I read it and have saved it for personal reasons. This letter changed my life because it led me to a different path, a more serene and honest way of thinking and loving, a more peaceful outlook on life. With your permission, I would like to read this letter now and interject as I go. (For the reader, I have added some additional information to my interjections that, because of scheduled and allotted speech-time at the reunion I didn't say then, even though I felt them. The **dark print** denotes the words of Mr. Wm. Milbrodt, those following are mine.)

Wm. Milbrodt
W –Rice St
Sleepy Eye, MN

Captain Hector Villarreal

Dear Sir:
  I am writing in regards to our son Gerald who was killed while serving with your Company.
This statement alone took a lot of guts to write. As I now continue to read this letter I want you, in the screen of your mind, if you will, to please close your eyes as you listen to this and visualize the following: As a Vietnam veteran you can possibly help some of the commanders and service personnel who are coming back to your state or local community from the war in Iraq and/or Afghanistan and future wars which may come our way. Or you could see yourself helping others in your community cope with their frustrations that people have—fathers, sons, daughters, or loved ones in different war zones fighting the enemy. Or maybe you could step up to the plate and help provide guidance, experience, and encouragement to these folks

in your local or state communities. Mr. Milbrodt's letter continues.

The address I gave you is where I am employed, the reason I am giving you this address, is to make sure my wife will never see the letter I hope to get from you.

There was tenderness and love in these words for his family and it showed. He wanted to keep any grief away from his wife, but he wanted to have closure. He wanted to know. He wanted to know what happened. He was prepared for my answers and was letting me know in no uncertain terms in a very sensitive way. He was quietly, bravely crying for help from me.

First of all I want to tell you that I served with the Infantry in France, Belgium and Germany during World War ll.

He was telling me that he was a fellow combat-in-arms brother. He was telling me that he had lived through the horrors of combat, of war. He was leveling the playing field so that I would know we were equal in combat experience. He was complementing us in Vietnam, and could have easily added this name to the countries he had fought in, because war is war.

I know what combat is, as I was badly wounded on the 18th day of March 1945, spent nine months in a hospital before being discharged, at the same time I was wounded, three men in my squad were killed.

Most of you were not even born yet. He was sharing very personal information. He was being vulnerable. He was allowing me, and now as I share with you, he wanted me to know where he stood, that he had the courage, that he wanted to know more, and wanted me to know that he could handle this information he was requesting, as brutal as it may be. He was also leveling with me and letting me know what it was to lose combat brothers in action. I could feel his pain, his suffering. He was one of us.

The reason I am telling you this is because I am going to ask you some personal questions, which I hope you will answer, and give me the exact details of what happened as it won't bother me any. I know I will feel better if I can know exactly what happened.

Now when I read this for the first time, I said, "Oh my good-ness. By regulation I'm not supposed to even answer this letter!

What do I do?" I spent several sleepless nights before I made my decision. In my heart I knew he needed to know. I felt his plea in my heart. I reasoned that the Army leadership would understand and support my decision.

I identified Jerry when he was brought home. Several people told me not to. It was a hard decision to make, but I did, and I'm glad I did. And I know for sure it was our Jerry. It doesn't bother me now, so whatever you tell me won't either, so <u>please</u> tell me everything.

I could see the word please underscored as I read it. I could sense his heart, his mind, and his determination to know. How do you not answer this man and live with yourself? As a father, I, too, would have needed to know what happened to my son in order to have closure and peace of mind.

What time in the evening of the 16th was Jerry killed? The reason I ask is because we have a canary, and the morning of the 16th, this canary acted very unusual, and I think the time in Vietnam is 12 hours ahead of our time. Were there any other men killed or wounded when Jerry was killed? Was he in a vehicle or on foot when he met death? What part of his body was hit? I could see nothing on his face or head. Here is one question I hope you will answer me to the best of your knowledge. Was he killed instantly? If not, how long did he live after he was hit? This answer will not bother me any and nobody except me will ever know. I promise you.

One thing I cannot understand is that on the 20th of February we were notified that Jerry was missing in action since the 16th day of February, then we wondered for another week and were notified on the 27th day of February that Jerry died on the 16th of February. Then we get a letter that death came quickly, I cannot understand it.

In today's environment in Iraq and Afghanistan, we hear in the news, men and women getting killed there and loved ones here have to wait; imagine how frustrating this must be. You can help. Get involved and help these families, these soldiers, airmen, marines, sailors, civilians, and all others involved in their respective wars.

Share what you have learned and help them begin to find closure, to learn to move on, to learn to let peace into their hearts, if at all possible.

The last letter we got from Jerry, he had told us that a number of Viet Cong had defected to his Company. I wonder if those ex-Viet Cong could have led Jerry into a trap?

Well, so much for that. We had three letters from Jerry since he was in Vietnam, and each time he told us that he was in a good outfit. He was very proud of his unit, and I know that the 9th Division has always been a good outfit. Jerry's funeral was on the 9th of March. The people here in Sleepy Eye say it was the largest funeral ever held in Sleepy Eye.

Now, our brothers who died right next to us in combat, in some cases, we personally took them back to battalion and from there they went on to the States, but we did not see their funerals. Their fathers, mothers, brothers, sisters, their wives, their children, their friends and neighbors did. We were part of the beginning and they witnessed the end—the funeral, the tears, the pain, yet the quietness of it all, the reflection of a life that was, and the changes this would have on those remaining, the color guard, the folding of the flag, and taps playing as our brother-in-arms was laid to rest.

Today, people like those mentioned above need closure too and, in many cases, we can help if we only make the effort to assist, and the earlier the better.

Jerry had many friends. I don't believe there was a single person who didn't like Jerry. He had many friends. He was a wonderful boy and we were very proud of him. He was Salutatorian of his graduating class. He was a natural artist, we have some of his paintings and so do some other people. He had told me that he wanted to take that up as a profession. He would have been very good at it. But it's all over now and we miss him so much, but our only comfort now is to believe that it was God's will. We know that the parents of the other boys over there feel the same way we do.

The line 'but it's all over now and we miss him so much' was a very tough line for me. But Mr. Milbrodt was not quitting; he was getting ready to move forward, to move forward with his pain and grief, but to move forward with the reality that with life comes death. He was also moving forward with his memories of his son. What I am saying to you here is for you not to quit on yourself. We understand what happened to us then, but if we are going to help others today and tomorrow, we, too, must move forward with our lives and help others do likewise.

I did not fully understand the impact of his most touching line: . . . **but our only comfort now is to believe it was God's will.** *I will talk more about this in just a minute.*

I will close now, just hoping and praying that you will answer my questions. Nobody but me will ever know, I promise you.

Gerald Milbrodt's Father
William Milbrodt

P.S. Was Jerry in good spirits when he was over there? Or was he depressed?

I wrote Mr. Milbrodt at the address he requested and I answered his questions to the best of my ability based on questioning the few remaining soldiers who had been involved in that battle.

In closing I said: "Gerald's spirits were always high. He was proud to be in our unit, and we were proud to have him as one of our men. I would have been proud to have him as my son. I most sincerely hope this letter can bring you the tranquility you might need.

Sincerely,

Capt. Hector Villarreal"

I have always revered the Bible, but I had never read it. I did not know what exactly Mr. Milbrodt meant when he said, "it was God's will." As time went on, I started studying the Bible and began to understand what he meant by his statement. I started a trek that continues today. I want to share one thing, but I want you to know I am not preaching. I'm merely sharing my own experience with you. An experience that changed my life and has brought me continued peace.

I found in the Bible a man who had written in the New Testament, a man who was under house arrest with no air conditioning, no heating, no carpeting, no latrines. A man who knew he could be beheaded at any time and yet he wrote the following:

> *Rejoice in the Lord always. I say again, Rejoice. Be anxious for nothing, but in everything by prayer, and suppli-cation, and thanksgiving, make your requests made known to God. And the peace of God, which surpasses all under-standing, will protect your minds and hearts through his Son.*

At first, I had a hard time understanding this but as I did, it helped change my life. This letter changed my life. Being in Vietnam with you guys and having the responsibility to read and respond to letters like this one changed my life. I pray, just as I heard General Steele earlier this week say that he prays, too.

Whatever it is that is going on in your life, I believe the best book is the Good News Book. Go to it, read it, find it. He will guide you, and again, I am not preaching, I am just sharing with you my experience. I have to tell you what I found and am very much now at peace.

As I close, much to my surprise, my wife wanted me to share something with you indirectly. She wrote me a card. I found it hid-den in my suitcase. I didn't know she'd put it there. May I please share with you what she said?

> 'Dear Hon,' not like in Attila the Hun, mind you. I think she meant Honey. 'I am so glad that you will be able to renew old friendships from long ago. I can only imagine that the remembrances will bring mixed blessings. Please know you will be in my prayers. I know also that God will use you to share the tremendous changes He has brought to your life since Vietnam. May your friends be open to what you have to say. I am very proud of you. I love you, Bonnie.'

My brothers, my comrades, my dear friends. Thank you very much for listening to me and for allowing me the pleasure to be in your company once again. I salute you."

Footnote: My reunion presentation about The Letter had a very touching and emotional impact on me. I had tears in my eyes pretty much throughout the presentation. Immediately after the meeting adjourned I was approached by many at the gathering. When we met I noticed they, too, had tears in their eyes.

One of those was a Mrs. Nixon who didn't just have tears, she was crying.

"My husband," she said while gripping my hand, "Larry Nixon, was part of the patrol the night Gerald was killed. We thank you from the bottom of our hearts for sharing The Letter with us!"

The following comments are those of the sister and brother of Gerald Milbrodt (KIA, 16 February 1968) concerning how The Letter from their father to me about the death of his son, Gerald, years ago, has moved their lives.

My name is Linda Milbrodt Lang. My first thoughts as I am told of my father's letter was: *Do I want to go back thirty-seven years to the time of my brother Jerry's death in Vietnam?*

It was so difficult to even think of such a gentle, kind soul going to war. Did I want to relive the grief I saw on the faces of my parents and my younger brother, Joe?

I'm grateful to Larry Haglund for posting a tribute to Jerry on the web site. It was through that tribute, Mark Slama contacted me.

Mark explained his outlook on his time in Vietnam, and afterwards, changed since he heard Captain V read Dad's letter at their last reunion. Mark and his wife, Rita, have become our close friends. The Letter has given my brother and me a multitude of wonderful things to be thankful for.

I'm thankful for the uplifting and meaningful phone calls from Captain V. My father would be proud to know The Letter has had such a positive influence on Captain V's life as well as so many others'.

I'm thankful for Jim Miller and Larry Nixon's phone calls. They gave us information concerning the night of Jerry's death. They answered hard and sensitive questions that have lain heavy on our hearts for thirty-seven years. They weren't easy calls for either of them to make. Finally, through them, I have found peace of mind knowing Jerry did not suffer at the time of his death.

I'm thankful for the increased and closer relationship between my brother Joe, and myself. The distance in time and the separating miles between us had perhaps weakened our relationship. Due to the letter, we are now communicating routinely. The Letter has brought many people together.

I imagine our parents and Jerry smiling down on us from the heavens.

In closing, I would like to say to all the Vietnam veterans who may have known or served with my brother: I have never felt that my brother's death was in any way due to anything you may have done or didn't do. I send my heartfelt gratitude to you for your brotherhood-in-arms, caring, and help. I thank my Lord for each of you and for all you have done—*and I am thankful you came home!*

I truly believe it is as my father would say, "It was God's will." Peace be with you!

Linda Milbrodt Lang

My name is Joe Milbrodt.

I was not surprised to learn my father wrote 'The Letter,' but I was surprised by the way he worded it. Dad only had an eighth grade education.

I didn't just see a father trying to gain information about his son; I also saw a soldier trying to get information from another soldier.

My father, to the best of my knowledge, didn't tell anyone about the letter he wrote to Captain Villarreal. He also didn't tell anyone about the letter he received from the Captain, which showed respect from one soldier to another.

I'm glad my father's letter has eased some of the anguish that all of you who served in Vietnam had to deal with. I hope it can help anyone who reads this book.

My father's letter has helped me get in contact with some people who have firsthand knowledge and have told us my brother Jerry didn't suffer at the time of his death. I also feel that I may have lost a brother, but because of my Dad's letter, I have gained several new brothers.

I would like everyone who has served in a war, any war, to know I have nothing but respect for you. I have special feelings and respect for those who served in Vietnam, I guess because we lost our brother, Jerry, in that war.

To the people I have talked with on the phone who were with my brother on the night he lost his life, I feel as if I've known you for a long time. I consider you a friend. I'll even go so far as saying I now look at you and feel towards you as family.

I'm very proud of my father for having the courage to write that letter. I would like to thank Captain Villarreal for having the courage to respond to my father's letter.

I also would like to thank all of those who served in my brother's unit for having the courage to be involved in combat and for serving our country so valiantly. I pray you are not troubled by any possible after-effects you may have encountered while keeping our nation and us safe.

You are all heroes! God bless you!

Joe Milbrodt

Closing comments of Captain V

True and factual comments in the form of reflections and statements from our fellow comrades, their loved ones, doctors from the medical profession and members of the clergy follow in the next few chapters. They are the very touching and emotional testimonies of men and women who were directly or indirectly impacted by war.

So, even after 35 plus years, I believe God has seen to it that there can be a degree of closure for our troubled comrades. Our desire is that those who read this book will find there is hope in reunions, in coming together via e-mails, phone calls, visits, notes and letters with your comrades-in-arms, your loved ones, and openly discussing the unresolved issues that needed closure.

As this chapter ends, The Letter is still changing lives. It also teaches us that all wars have a common denominator and that is human life, human emotion, pain, love, laughter, and reflections. If you are troubled, our sincere hope is this book and maybe The Letter will help you in some way to change your life for the better. We hope they will give you the strength to move on toward closure in whatever your specific situation may be that has been caused by the horror of war.

You have a good shot at overcoming your problems if you get together, as our battalion has done, and openly share your hearts and minds with your brothers and sisters-in-arms, your families and friends. It is not a guarantee, but it is surely worthwhile if you just take the first step. Be open; let the truth come out. Deal with it honestly, without reservation.

This, of course, while knowing you cannot change the past. But please believe me—you can sure change and get ready for tomorrow with a new perspective in life, and possibly a new beginning for your family and loved ones. You can do it! *You can do it!*

Sometimes it may take for you to say, "I am sorry" or "I forgive you" or "Please forgive me." Sometimes you may find you must say these words, but cannot say them now mouth-to-ear, or heart-to-heart as you want, because those to whom you want to say them have long been gone. However, because you say them, you may find the peace you are looking for. Let those words work sincerely in your own mind, and in your heart, and then peacefully, let it go.

Remember, if the man under house arrest by the name of Paul could find peace and hope in his situation, if the men and women you read about in the chapters following could do it, or even the many who are presently doing it, you can do it too, my brothers and sisters-in-arms.

May I suggest you get started today? God bless you and speed you through these steps.

Captain V

CHAPTER 23

WELCOME HOME, MY BROTHERS!

My name is Larry Nixon. I arrived in Vietnam on February 2, 1968. I was assigned to the 9th Infantry Division, 5th Battalion, 60th Infantry Recon Platoon.

Two weeks later, the day of February 16th, 1968, will linger in my mind 'till the day I am finally laid to rest.

Recon Platoon was pulling security for a small artillery battery just outside the village of Cai Lay. It was my shift of guard sitting on top of the track. Everything was quiet. There was a little fog. But off in the distance you could see red ribbons coming down from the sky. Cobra gunships were at work. That meant some American unit was in contact with Charlie.

Suddenly word came that Recon was moving out to assist a unit engaged in a firefight. I remember a knot was forming in my stomach as we rode on top of the tracks headed down the road.

When we reached the other unit, we were told contact with the enemy had been broken. We were directed to get down off the tracks and sweep the right side of the road.

As we moved off the road and down the dike, Gerald Milbrodt was in front, then me, followed by Cullen Quin, Tim Agard, a guy named Pierce, and several others. Once Gerald got to the first dike that paralleled the road, he turned and started walking beside the dike. I was about 10 to 15 yards to his left. Quin was about the same distance to my left, and so on down the line with the rest of the troops. Flares were popping overhead as we moved on line through the paddy. We had gone maybe fifty yards when Milbrodt suddenly screamed "Ambush!"

I looked to see a VC standing next to Milbrodt firing an AK-47 into him. I turned and fired at the VC, and saw him go down as another VC immediately popped up next to him. We shot each other.

I fell and discovered I couldn't move my legs; bullets whizzing front and back were churning the ground around me. I tried crawling toward Gerald by pulling myself on my elbows while firing at the muzzle flashes. I wanted to help him, but every time I moved and fired, bullets came streaking back around me like a swarm of hornets. I started inching my way back toward the tracks and came across Quin lying with his M-16 toward the dike. He was dead. Shot in the face.

I remember pulling myself along on my elbows and firing at the VC. Each time I fired I would roll, and where I had just been, the ground would be sprayed with bullets. I don't know how long I was in the paddy trying to get back to the tracks. I finally made it to a position close enough to call for help. James (Chip) Miller and James Simmons ran out, grabbed my arms, and pulled me back behind the tracks.

I returned to Recon after spending two weeks in Long Binh and then another four weeks in the convalescent hospital at Camh Rahn Bay. I never talked about that night. A lot of the guys were gone that had been there. Miller and Simmons were gone. I never got a chance to thank them. Not that they would have wanted it. I never asked where they were because I was afraid to ask—afraid of what the answer might be. Guess I just assumed the worst.

I took all the memories of Vietnam and crammed them into like a small trunk. I locked it and put it in the back of my mind—never going to let it out!

They laid and festered there for all those years; the nightmares, night sweats, thinking about the things that happened over there, blaming myself for not being able to help Milbrodt, Quin, and Agard. All the memories lay in that internal trunk, and the poison-filled thing grew like a boil. It grew bigger and bigger and finally the trunk lid couldn't contain it any longer, and all the memories erupted and came flooding to the surface.

The only person I had talked to about Vietnam once I got back home was my father, who had been in the Pacific during World War II, and Louis (Tex) Balas. My dad died a couple years after my return and Tex and I lost contact. The years passed and I knew I was missing something. Certain sights, sounds, smells and countless small things reminded me of Vietnam. I wondered what might have happened to all the guys I knew in 'Nam? Their names stuck with me: Louis (Tex) Balas, Willie (Tiny) Taylor, Willie Martin, Chip Miller and James Simmons. I wondered if they were still alive.

More years pass. One day I go in my office and find a note: 'Sergeant Nixon, call this number.' I looked in the phone book and the prefix was from Texas. Who would be calling me from Texas? Then it hit me. Louis Balas. Tex! As soon as I heard his voice the years instantly faded. Memories came rushing back and we talked and talked. Pressure was being released with that phone call and I didn't even know it.

I started looking on the Internet and found the 9th Infantry site, the 5th/60th site and old thoughts returned strong and then stronger, as if they had never been gone. I started e mailing people on the Web site, but no one from the Recon Platoon that I remembered was there.

Next there was talk of a reunion in Denver and I thought, *Man, that would be great.* I went by myself because I didn't know what it would be like. Louis Balas and his wife were there, and I met Lee Alley who was the Lieutenant of Recon before I got to 'Nam. *It was great.* Those people had been there; they all knew what it had been like. I no longer felt alone. It was really strange because I didn't know hardly any of these people, but at the same time it was as if we all knew each other because we were war brothers. We had all been exposed to the horrors of war; we knew things other people didn't. We had experienced life and death as only brothers-in-arms could do. We were not strangers; we could talk of our experiences without shame and know and understand what one another said because we had been there. The pressure was released from my trunk and then it closed again—for a while.

The next reunion was in Charleston, SC. My wife Mary Alice went with me to that one because I knew other wives would be there for her to talk and visit with. More men from the Battalion came and brought their wives. And more healing took place.

Then came the Dallas reunion. This was the one I was really looking forward to. The two guys who pulled me out of the rice paddy the night I got shot would be there, James Miller and James Simmons. I had earlier been able to learn their phone numbers, called each of them, and thanked them for what they did for me that night. Neither wanted my thanks because I think they knew I would have done the same for them. My wife was as thrilled as I was to see them. As comrades we, Miller and Simmons, and many other of the reunion attendees hadn't seen one another in over 30 years, yet it seemed like only yesterday we were together in 'Nam. More healing was taking place.

Saturday night was the banquet with guest speakers. Lt. Alley was the first, then Captain Tom Russell. My wife and I were seated near the back of the room with some other people. The next to speak was Captain Hector Villarreal who had been the Company Commander of HHC. He began by reading a letter from a father of someone in our Company who had been killed.

Suddenly it hit me like a ton of bricks. What he was reading sent me back in time to February 16th, 1968. I was once again in the rice paddy, wounded, unable to move my legs. The guys around me were dead. The letter was from Gerald Milbrodt's father. Gerald, my comrade who had yelled, "Ambush!"

He was the first to die that night. One of my buddies I tried to help, but couldn't.

All the pain, the memories, the shame I felt for not being able to save them, and the never ending question of "Why them and not me?" came rushing back.

Crying was something I had done very little of in all those years. Guess it's always been hard for me to cry. But amazingly, not that night. Tears came flooding. I arose from the table and went to the back of the room. My wife hurried to me and asked what was wrong. I explained to her that the letter is about the night I got shot. It's from my friend, Gerald Milbrodt's dad.

I felt extremely weak and emotionally rattled. I really wanted to leave the room, but forced myself to remain and listen to Captain V. After everything was over with, I was just standing around in the crowd. My wife came to me and wanted me to follow her. She led me to Captain Villarreal and explained our, and Gerald's, Vietnam association. Captain V gave me the original letter and said I could make a copy if I would like.

That night I promised myself I would get in touch with Gerald's father. Mr. Milbrodt, Sr. had since passed away, but later Captain V called to tell me he had located Gerald's brother and sister, Joe Milbrodt and Linda Lang. He gave me their phone numbers. I was hesitant to call them because I didn't know how they might react. I wondered if I could even talk to them about 'that night,' but I had given Captain V my word I would try.

I called Linda Lang's number and it rang several times. Each time it rang my heart beat faster, and a lump was growing in my throat. The answering machine kicked in and I said, "This is Larry Nixon. I was with your brother the night he was killed. If you'd like I'll be pleased to talk to you," and then gave her my phone number. I also tried to call her brother, Joe Milbrodt, and again had no success.

The next day when I got home Linda had called and said she'd been hoping I would call after she had talked with Captain V. I tried her number once more. No answer. I tried Joe's number again and this time he answered promptly.

I told him who I was and that I'd been trying to get in touch with them. I told Joe I hoped my calling would not bring back a lot of unwanted memories, but I felt it was something I needed to do. I asked about his father and was told Mr. Milbrodt Sr. had passed away some years before. I told him I wished I could have talked to him about 'that night' and maybe helped ease his pain. We talked for probably 30 minutes. I told him I didn't think Gerald suffered and probably died instantly. I told him I would continue trying to reach his sister.

When I later contacted Linda Lang, her voice, when she answered, sounded happy and washed away any fears I had of talking to her. We talked for a long while and I, again, felt my pent-up pressures easing away. It was really strange because it was almost as if I was talking to long lost friends.

The one regret is not being able to talk to Gerald's dad. I wish I could have told him of that night and that Gerald was probably one of the reasons I'm alive today. I wish I could have told him how the loss of those guys that night now feels like the loss of my own brothers. In a sense, we *were* like family, tossed together by a war that none of us really understood.

During this time I was looking for a car for my son and daughter-in-law to carry my new granddaughter around in. I ended up buying one from a young man who had just returned from Iraq. I told him I had been in Vietnam.

"Will it ever go away?" he asked with a serious and concerned expression.

"No," I responded, "but it can be made easier to live with." I then told him about our 5th/60th Association and what it meant to all of us who are a part of it. I'm sure, if you are like I was when I came home, you want to forget about Iraq and war. But take a few minutes and write down all the names and addresses of as many guys as you can. Don't lose contact with them because they are your help; they are your brothers who were with you, and they are the ones you can talk to when you need release from the pressures and bad memories that might build up inside you.

Don't make the mistakes that many of my comrades and I made. Don't roll your memories up in a ball and try to hide them away in the back of your mind, a footlocker, trunk or closet. *That doesn't work.* Keep in touch with your brothers and sisters-in-arms. Talk to one another. Give support to one another. *Please believe me—you will be far better off for the effort.*

I hope my ramblings might help others who have been in war, and are now coming home from Afghanistan, Iraq, or—any war. *Welcome home, brothers and sisters.*

CHAPTER 24

REUNIONS A.K.A. MIRACLES

The term Reunions is a catchall phrase I have used throughout the second portion of the book. I say catchall because there arc so many things going on, which in the mix of large reunions seems small, but taken by themselves are a very powerful aid in helping with one's quest.

The following are veterans' stories which include humor, mini-reunions (spinning off Squad and Platoon size) get togethers from contacts made at the Battalion gatherings, and the great comfort, and peace of mind in turning it all over to the Lord. All three are excellent ways of finding hope and understanding in life.

— Lee

CHAPTER 25

A MAN-MADE HELL CALLED WAR

My name is Louis Balas. I'm from San Angelo, Texas. The only ones who call me Tex are the men I served with during my tour of duty in Vietnam.

I arrived in Vietnam August 12, 1967, and was assigned to the Reconnaissance Squadron, 2nd Squadron of the 11th Armored Cavalry Regiment. I was with E troop, 2nd Platoon. I served seven months with the Cav., one of which was spent in base camp preparing to go on the Cambodian border. I spent five months in combat on the Cambodian border. At the end of January 1968, my unit was sent to the Long Binh-Bien Hoa area to fight in the Tet Offensive. After Tet we were sent back to the border. The 12th of February I received orders that I was being sent to HQ, and HQ, Company 5th/60th 9th Infantry Div.

I reported there on February 15, 1968, and was immediately informed I was assigned to the Recon Platoon. This came as a complete surprise. I had been told I would be going to a supply unit. There were two other men who came with me: Willie Martin and Gregory Andrejeski. We'd each been told we were to be assigned as supply clerks. Well, they clerked our asses right on over to Recon. Shoulda known it was a trick.

In the orderly room we met Capt. Villarreal, the Company Commander; Lt. David Evans, the Company XO; Clerk, O'Brien; and First Sergeant Payne. Then we went to the Armory and saw a guy named Hamby. We were issued our M16s, and went from there to Supply where SSgt. Spencer issued us new boots, a blanket, poncho liner, and two sets of new fatigues. That was as close to supply as we ever got.

We were escorted to Recon's area and told to find a bunk. We didn't know whose bunk was whose, but with the help of some short timers, Sgt. John Miller, Sgt. Lades and a guy named Partner, we found some vacant bunks. Those guys showed us around Recon's area—the mess hall—I only ate there twice in five months, and that was twice too often—worst food I ever put in my mouth. Was shown Recon's own club, a 24-hour Reaction Force tent so we wouldn't have to leave our area. Thank God, we had that, our own beer joint. Was showed the outhouse—like we couldn't smell it—which was right outside the club. The only shower was next to the outhouse (nice). That was our Recon's area.

I noticed the guard tower sat beside Recon. I remember thinking, *Damn good aiming point for a mortar attack.* And it was. I'd been in Recon about three months when Capt. Villarreal called me to the Orderly Room. He wanted to know if I was of Mexican descent. I told him no. He asked how I got the name Balas, and explained it means 'bullets' in Spanish. I told him mine is a Czech name. He said he was from San Antonio, Texas, and I told him we are neighbors 'cause I was from San Angelo. Never forgot that conversation.

The following day I was instructed to get on a deuce and a half and ride out to where Recon was camped. When I got there I asked someone what track I was supposed to get on and he said, "Just pick one out." I wound up on SSgt. Manallo's track. That night, my first night in the field, we had a bad firefight. Four of our men were killed: Milbrodt, Agard, York and Quin. Several others were wounded. One of them I would see once more. I never saw the others again. As it was my first night in the field, I didn't know any of those killed or wounded. Next day I was assigned to Sgt. Vito Guitilla's track and during the following week I met the rest of the guys in Recon.

On the evening of February 24, 1968, we were set up at our night position at an ARVN compound. Around 0100 we got a call that Fire Base Jaeger was under heavy ground attack. We responded and helped turn back the attack. That night there were a lot of casualties. Recon lost a man named Richard Scala (KIA), many of us were wounded. Several of those who were dusted-off—Medevacced out on helicopters—never returned to Recon. Two of the men placed aboard were "Round Rob," the driver of Sgt. Vito Guitilla's track, and a man named Tanner. He was the mechanic who was riding on Sgt. Vito Guitilla's track, the same one I was on when an RPG hit it.

I helped put both of them on a dust-off.

Too late, after the chopper left, I found another man lying in the road. I couldn't remember his name so I nicknamed him "Tiny." Later learned him to be William Taylor, from Robertsdale, Alabama. When we were hit he had been blown off the track and landed on his head in the road. Tiny weighed 235 pounds and is 6' 4" tall. I had to get him off the road or he'd be shot. I dragged him into a ditch beside the road. When I got him there he asked, "Are you gonna leave me?"

I wanted to punch him and say, "Hell yeah, man. Damn tootin'. I'm gonna bop on down around the corner to the store and get some coffee and donuts. Maybe pick up the February issue of *Playboy,* too." Instead, I patted him on the shoulder and said, "There's only two ways it's gonna come down, pal. We'll either die together, or we'll see the sun come up together." We watched the sun come up together and have remained close friends to this day. RPGs hit all but one of Recon's tracks that night.

At times there would be someone in the Company who wanted to get out of base camp for a night or two so would go out with us on Recon. I always wondered why on earth *anybody* would want to do that? SSgt. Dan Spencer, our supply sergeant, did.

He joined up with us on the night of February 24th. He rode with Platoon Sergeant Williams' track, which was also hit by an RPG. Great timing. That also happened to be the night of the blood-bath at Fire Base Jaeger. Come the next morning when we pulled back into base camp, I don't think I ever again saw him outside of the supply room. Neither I nor anyone else could blame Dan for that. Unfortunately he'd just picked the wrong night for a ride-along. We can laugh about it now, but it wasn't at all funny at the time.

On March 10th, 14 days after the Battle of Fire Base Jaeger, Sgt. Vito Guitilla's track, which I was again left gunner on—same position as at the Battle of Fire Base Jaeger—ran over a land mine. This time everyone was wounded. SP5 Andy Wescott and myself weren't hurt as bad as the others so we stayed on and helped with the fire-fight. Sgt. Guitilla, PFC Magnusson, PFC McCaskell, and SP4 Sanchez, were dusted-off and never returned to Recon.

I spent 11 months and 23 days in a combat mode. However, and thank God, during that time there *were some good times.* In

September 1967, 2nd Sqdn, 11th ACR was carrying out combat operations around Tam Ky. Second Platoon was short one track so my Platoon Leader, 1st Lt. Gerald Rudisill, sent me and PFC Robert M. McCarter (KIA11/17/67) to Chu Lai to pick up a new track.

When we got to Chu Lai, the track, an ACAV–Armored Cav Assault Vehicle or Armored Personnel Carrier–had been left on the beach where it had been unloaded from the ship. We had to hang around a few days to have the gunshields and weapons mounted before we could take it back to our platoon.

The second day we were there I walked to the mess hall, about 800 meters up from the beach to get some coffee. When I got back to the track, McCarter, who weighed in at 215 pounds, stood 6'2", and looked like a blond gorilla, was washing his feet and toes with Dial bath soap, water and sand. I'd never seen anybody scrub down like that with sand before.

"Holy shit, McCarter," I said, "what in the hell are you doing, boy?"

McCarter gave me a stern look. "Damn, Tex. What does a man look like where you come from?"

It took me a minute to realize he didn't like me calling him boy. Later on that night, we were sitting in the track talking about home and how we were raised. He told me his family was so poor the county let him and his family live in the upstairs of the funeral home. He was one of eight children in the family, and they all had to wear hand-me-downs from the county welfare.

I told him my family was so poor my momma couldn't buy us clothes and toys both. So when she bought me a pair of britches, she'd cut the pockets out on the inside.

McCarter turned, looked at me kinda funny and said, "Damn, Tex, how come she did that?"

"Well, that way I'd have a new pair of britches to wear, and if I needed something to play with, I could just stick my hands in my pockets."

McCarter stared at me for a minute then gave me a slight smile. "Tex, my buddy, you're a motherfucker, you know that?"

I guess McCarter could have pulled my head off if he'd wanted to. But we'd formed such a close friendship that whatever we said to one another was always okay.

The following night I needed to make a trip to the outdoor

latrine. McCarter asked me why I had to go to the latrine at midnight. Seems he always took care of his business like that in the daytime. He didn't like getting up and going at night. I told him that I was sorry but I just couldn't plan my trips like he could.

The latrine was a big one, about 12 foot long, six foot wide, and seven foot tall. It was a fancy four-holer, with screen wire and wire mesh, hail wire, over that. It was pretty much open air all around. Don't guess people on the outside, including me, appreciated that too much, but what you going to do?

The month of September in 'Nam was typhoon season. Earlier in the day we read on the Bulletin Board we would have a high tide before morning.

In the latrine, just as I sat down and squirmed into a comfortable position to take care of my business, I could tell by the increased sound of the ocean that the tide was coming in. I was just sitting there twiddling my thumbs waiting to do my duty. Kinda nice to hear the heavier surf. I had no idea the high tide was gonna arrive as a raging 12-foot wave wall of ocean.

A water force like huge gushers shot up out of all four holes. For a second I was reminded of Old Faithful in the Yellowstone. Helluva thing to think of at such a time.

Like an eruption I was literally catapulted up off the hole I was covering and thought, *Damn! I don't even have my water wings on!* The entire latrine was flipped over and immediately filled with water, sand, and all the contents from the now overturned and empty latrine barrels.

I had to kick, pull, and rip my way through the screen and wire mesh in order to get out. Respecting the unmentionable dousing I just had, I made certain to keep my eyes and mouth shut. Believe it or not, during this entire scenario the most worrisome thought I had was of the Army telling my momma her son drowned in a shithouse during the war. My God. There's no telling what she would think.

When I finally, stinking and stumbling, made my way back to the track I still had a lot of soggy toilet paper, magazine shreds, and God only knows what *other stuff* covering me.

McCarter looked at me, made a hell of a sour face expression, and said, "Damn, Tex, what happened to you?"

"Tide came in and a big-assed wave turned the shithouse over on top of me. Trapped me inside. Had a helluva time gettin' out. I'd really rather not talk about it."

He got scared then because he didn't know how to swim and was worried about the water coming up to where the track was. Guess that's the reason he never laughed at me for what happened that night.

McCarter got on top of the track and I stood naked beside it while he poured water on me from the five-gallon jerry cans. I soaped and scrubbed down good from head to toe, even used some sand. He then poured more water on me so I could rinse off. We repeated the same routine until finally I felt thoroughly clean.

I don't believe I ever had a more unpleasant Mother Nature toilet trip or more uncomfortable bathing experience. *In fact I know I haven't.* But I hung in there. Two reasons for that: one, I wasn't about to try and get clean out in those high waves with a strong riptide in force, I'd already had a dose of that. And, two—McCarter told me he wasn't sleeping anywhere within 342 1/2 miles of me cause I stunk like shit—or worse. He did make his thoughts on the matter very clear I thought.

After I was wounded from the land mine on March 10th, I stayed in the field for about three weeks. My left arm started causing me a lot of pain. 1st Lt. Bennie J. Smith, our platoon leader, sent me to Long Binh to have my arm looked at by one of the doctors at the hospital there. When I returned to Recon they put me on light duty at base camp for awhile.

One afternoon, I was sitting on my bunk writing a letter when a guy walks in wearing new fatigues. I figured he was a newbie and asked if he was a replacement troop.

"Nope, I'm just coming back to Recon cause I've been in the hospital for two months. Got wounded on the 16th of February."

"Hmm. That was my first night in the field with Recon. Was a bad night for us, too." Then I made the mistake of asking where he'd been wounded.

"Got shot in the ass."

"Well, I'll be damned!" I said, "let me see." That was another mistake. He promptly turned around, dropped his drawers to his ankles and bent over.

"Goddammit—oh shit!" I yelled. "Pull your pants back up." I'm not real high on looking at another man's ass; I just wanted to see if he was bullshitting me. He for damn sure wasn't. That's the worst scar I've ever seen. It was about 2 1/2 inches wide; went across both cheeks of his ass, turned and went down his left leg to just above his knee. The scar was so fresh that it was still a deep purple, and I could tell it wouldn't take much for it to tear open again. I finally got around to asking him what his name was.

"I'm Larry Nixon."

A few days later I talked to Captain Hector Villarreal. I told him I didn't believe Nixon should be sent back into the field with Recon because of the seriousness of his wound. Nixon stayed with Recon at base camp until sometime in June. He was then transferred to an Engineer Battalion, and I never saw him again until 28 years later. We were and still remain close friends.

I need to say something about heroes. I do not believe that everyone who goes to war or is in combat for our country is a hero. I also need to say something about wounds: there are the physical wounds for which the Purple Heart is awarded. But, there are also the mental and emotional wounds that can't be seen. They are caused by fear. The right-in-your-face kind of fear with seeing the loss of life of some of our country's finest young men and women. The fear of just trying to stay alive and keep your brothers safe, those with whom you've fought side-by-side day in and day out during the horror and confusion of combat. Then comes the reflecting back as to whether or not you made the right decision about having been able to save more lives. All these things will haunt a combat soldier for the rest of his life. The learning to live with all these things is very hard to do, but it is also very important to do.

I searched my memory hard trying to remember the hometowns of the men I served with. I found William (Tiny) Taylor, William Stuart Martin, Larry, and Charles Nixon. We got together 27 years after we got home. Since that first get together we've seen each other several times and call and talk to each other, and it has been a big help in dealing with our memories of war. About five years ago I got a phone call from Lieutenant Lee Alley, a man I saw only three times while I was in Recon. The first time was the morning after the Battle of Fire Base Jaeger. I saw him twice more at our Tactical Operations Command Center. Never spoke to him but for some reason I always remembered his name. He called to tell me he was putting together a 5th/60th Battalion reunion in Denver and asked if I would be willing to show up. I told him I'd be there.

We had another reunion the following year in Charleston, SC. The next summer, Recon had a small reunion at Lt. Alley's home in Wheatland, Wyoming.

About a year prior to our upcoming reunion in Dallas, Texas, I remembered the long-ago conversation I had with Captain Hector Villarreal at our base camp at Binh Phuoc, South Vietnam, as to whether or not I was a Mexican. I remembered he told me he was from San Antonio, Texas. So I looked for all the Villarreals in San Antonio. I got a number of wrong people and had to leave several messages. My phone rang about 10 minutes after I had quit making calls. It was Captain Villarreal. We had a great conversation. I told him we were having a reunion at Dallas in June and asked if he wanted to come. He said, "Yes," and I gave him the phone numbers of some men I had learned were looking for him. We were all happy and thrilled to see him at the reunion.

From that first small reunion in Denver to the reunions we have now, I've witnessed more healing and closure from the internal wounds of war and combat than I could ever have hoped for or thought would be possible.

For all of this, all I can say is, 'Thank You, Lieutenant Lee Alley.' You were a hell of a leader in 'Nam and you still are today. None of us will ever forget you.

I need to finish what I started about heroes. Heroes are men who, in a combat situation, have gone above and beyond the call of duty to save the lives of their fellow soldiers. Men who stood a hair's breath from death and yet stood the ground for everything they hold dear. A songwriter friend of mine, Justin Walker, from Refugio, Texas, penned a line for a song, and with permission from Justin, I'm using it here to describe what I know is burned into the heart of every hero:

"Hanging fragile in the balance of an oncoming wreck,
with no aces up my sleeve, and no room for regret."

Men such as this are: Lt. Lee Alley, Sgt. James Miller, Sgt.

James Simmons, and SSgt. Larry Easter. *These are men with well-earned and deserved* medals pinned on their chests. I proudly salute them. And I give sincere thanks for having had the honor of serving with some of the finest men I've known in my lifetime.

I now know there *is good* that comes from that man-made hell called war.

Chapter 26

We Will Always Be There
for Our Veterans

My name is Dick Prahl, and I knew it was going to be tough, but I had to get my bunker dug before dark, so I was working as hard as I could to get it to the correct depth. Us military guys are like that. I was happy the foliage had grown so much over the past months as this would give me additional cover if we should receive an assault maybe sometime after lunch. Boy, this was tough. I was sweating profusely, and I knew I couldn't remove any part of my military uniform. I couldn't even remove my helmet.

This was hard work for soldiers, but it's just part of what you had to do in your daily routine. I was sweating, deep in my concentration, and didn't see that someone had approached. Then I heard a noise and spun around.

There were two kids watching me. Earlier in the week I had done some recon in the area and observed these same two playing on the other side of the perimeter, but I didn't know their names.

One of them said, "Hey, what're you doing?"

I knew that us soldiers never gave away troop movements or defense position plans so, thinking fast, I answered, "I'm burying a penguin." I just knew that would keep them off the track.

"What happened?" the same kid asked.

"Well, my penguin just up and died."

"Your penguin died. How'd he die?"

Boy, this kid is sharp. "I guess someone was cleaning behind the refrigerator and unplugged it." I didn't want to give away any important additional information.

"You kept a penguin in the refrigerator?"

Doggone, he's good. "Yeah, we kept him in the fridge 'cause it's cool."

"What'd you feed him?"

"Umm . . . we gave him TV dinners."

The same kid asked, "Don't you have to take him to a mortuary or something?"

Damn, this kid is savvy. Musta been trained in interrogation. I responded with what I hoped would be the final answer, "Nope, since he ate TV dinners, he ate the cardboard, too. He was automatically stuffed."

That was my first encounter with Lee Alley. We were both nine years old.

Throughout our lives our paths would cross many times: like high school classmates; the *Playboy Club* in Denver; Central City, Colorado; Fort Benning, Georgia; and the rice paddies of Vietnam.

Proud parents in Laramie, Wyoming raised me. My father served in World War II. He was promoted to the rank of First Sergeant in only 18 months of service due to high attrition in his unit. There was never much discussion about the war in our house, but the presence of my father's service was always recognizable. Whenever special people came to the house, they were treated differently from other guests because there was an undefined relationship with those men that was different. I always knew those gentlemen had ties with my dad from his military experiences.

My mom was a hardworking wife and mother. She traveled from Wyoming to Texas to be with my father before he shipped overseas during World War II. Her travel involved the use of gas, tire, and battery ration stamps. I never tired of the tales my mother told about her journey to Texas to be with Dad.

There was never a question in my mind as to whether or not I would serve in our country's military. I didn't know when, I didn't know where, or why, but I knew it was inevitable.

I was in Vietnam during 1966-1967. When I returned I flew back into Travis AFB, California, and was processed through the receiving center that same evening. Being in the military you understand that due to the large volume of troops, it takes time to do paperwork. Being processed during the night was no unusual event. I later learned that this was a calculated event as antiwar protesters would often line the highway going into and leaving Travis AFB, as well as San Francisco International Airport.

Unfortunately and sadly, it was common knowledge that troops returning through the San Francisco airport from SEA (Southeast Asia) had to "run the gauntlet" during daylight hours. They suffered obscenities shouted and things thrown at them by our caring fellow-Americans in their disgusting attempt to degrade the returning soldiers.

After the living hell and nightmares of Vietnam, what a way this was for our troops, many wounded, bearing both emotional and physical scars, some blind, some in wheelchairs and many needing physical help from fellow veterans to stand and walk; *what a way for these true heroes* to be welcomed home—back home to the country they had daily risked their lives to serve!

As said earlier, my father's war experiences were but rarely mentioned in our home when I was growing up. Once back from 'Nam I tried to follow the same pattern. But one particularly rough day I was sitting alone at the Bum Steer Bar when my father came in and asked, "What's wrong, Dick?"

"Guess I'm curious as to why it isn't obvious that guys like me returning from war in Vietnam are having some difficulty with read-justing to civilian life. Instead of maybe trying to understand that my buddies and I didn't want to go and fight in a war we knew nothing about and didn't want any part of, we are shunned, bad-mouthed, and treated as outcasts. It wears on me, Dad. I remember hearing that you and your Army buddies were treated with respect, and rightly so, when you came home. And then even later on you were shown respect when others learned you were a war veteran."

My father turned and ordered beers for both of us. He put an arm around my shoulders and seemed to look at me in a different light. This was probably the first time my dad realized that being in Vietnam, returning and trying to fit in to the changed attitudes of our country, was seriously affecting me. Hesitantly we began to talk about military life and combat situations; I could tell my father was slowly but surely trying to reach out to me.

Dad died of a massive heart attack in May of 1969.

Later on, well after the funeral, I would find myself visiting his gravesite when I was feeling lonely, missing my father, and wanting to talk to him. As I knelt at the grave beside the small American flag, I looked through tear-dimmed eyes and happened to notice a small, weather-beaten Veterans of Foreign Wars metal emblem. I picked it up and cupped it in the palm of my hand.

I immediately felt a warm comforting and certain knowledge that there are those out there who, despite any civil unrest, disagreement with government, and any or all turmoil—*a brotherhood does exist.* It's a brotherhood of veterans that remains vibrant, stands strong, and very much cares for its comrades.

After leaving my hometown, I ventured off into life. I got married to Kathie and proudly raised my own family. We had two boys, Shane and Hans, and as with all young men, their curiosity would often arise pertaining to my military service for our nation and my time in Vietnam. These innocent young men knew very little of the social fabric of our country during the Vietnam era, but they were blindly supportive of military people who served our country and supported freedom.

I was not surprised when my younger son Hans called one day and said, "I'm at the recruiter's office. What do you think, Dad—the Army or the Marine Corps?"

Seemed like only a short time later Kathie and I were at the MCRD in San Diego watching our son graduate from boot camp. Within a year later we were back there again, this time watching Shane graduate.

Five years passed. Hans returned home and joined a local National Guard Special Forces Unit. Within three months time he was in Afghanistan. Shane was in the Marine Corps Reserve and had served a tour of duty in Iraq.

Thank God, our prayers were answered, and they both returned home safely. Physically they were fine. Like my dad before me, there came an occasion when I was discussing some events with Hans who had served in Afghanistan. I realized that as much as there was an emphasis on us, his family, trying to welcome him home and show gratitude for his service to our country, there was an area within him that needed additional understanding and recognition.

As a parent and a father I knew I had the obligation to try to console and support my son, but on the other hand, there is only a certain amount of information that will be shared with any combat veteran within the father-and-son relationship. I was rather perplexed by the situation—and I knew I needed help; another caring person to extend support in a manner that a parent might not have the ability to do.

I immediately called my lifelong and trusted friend, Lee Alley, and discussed my situation with him. That was a good and most fortuitous call!

"Dick," Lee said in a reassuring tone, "I'm having some members of my Vietnam Recon platoon here at my place in Wheatland, Wyoming. You and your son are most welcome to come spend the weekend with us. Also, there's another member from my old Recon unit, the 9th Infantry, who had a relative in the same outfit as your son. He's going to be here, too."

"Thanks a million, Lee," I responded, "We'll be there." We picked up the additional member en route.

During the weekend there was quite a camaraderie that developed between many of these people who had never met before but were encased in the same brotherhood. The amazing ability of these generations of veterans to enjoy one another's company, and share such good, close fellowship and support, was phenomenal.

I felt like I was back in my parents' house sitting at the kitchen table when my dad's special friends would come by. The companionship and inherent respect for one another was blatantly obvious. There were discussions that lasted for hours on end.

Thankfully, there were also special opportunities taken advantage of for the more needed sensitive and private talks. It was particularly good and heartwarming to see those one-on-one kinds of caring, tender, and specifically set-aside forums take place.

The weekend permitted both veteran groups, the older warriors from Korea and Vietnam who have experienced more than 35 years of suffering with keeping old memories and nightmarish war recollections and fears bottled up—and these recent warriors—our young veterans of today who have fought in countries like Kosovo, Afghanistan, and Iraq to share very personal concerns, fears and troublesome reflections.

These new warriors fought and continue to fight today's battles in far-off lands with state-of-the-art different kinds of weaponry, amazing communications, tools, and electronic equipment that are highly sophisticated. They use battlefield tactics and weapons much more advanced than those of the 1950s, 1960s and 1970s, but the emotional and physical wounds and scars they return home with are, unfortunately, the same as those carried by veterans of all wars.

Different countries, different conflicts, and different eras, but nevertheless *war is war, with life-changing experiences happening in the blink of an eye.* Situations like being under intense fire and exchanging fire with the enemy, being wounded, seeing close friends wounded and killed—the heartbreak, bloodshed, and loss of comrades knows no boundary of time.

I fully realize a casual gathering and short weekend cannot heal all wounds and cannot solve all problems, but the amount of support and the underlying acknowledgment of a duty well done and in support of the sacrifice these veterans have given to their country was truly amazing.

I couldn't help but get choked up seeing the older veterans sitting quietly, listening and speaking from their hearts, caringly putting their arms around the younger veterans, patting them on the back and giving them support, wise counsel, praise and reassurances. It did, most certainly, contribute to a stronger realization that *this brotherhood* is our common bond, and there is an undying respect for each other. It remains steadfast; it is locked and loaded.

And as reflected in that rusty Veterans of Foreign Wars emblem on my father's grave, it remains steadfast. It is poised and confident—ever ready to help anytime, and anywhere.

It—and we—will always be there for our veterans.

CHAPTER 27

MY LIFE TOOK ON NEW MEANING

My name is Ron McCants, and I was with the Delta Company, 5th/60th, 9th Infantry Division from August 1969 to August 1970.

The late afternoon shadows were lengthening as dusk settled in over the thatched roof of the hootch nestled by the small river. The lush green vegetation in the open field, along with the palms and the myriad of other trees lining the riverbank, gave an eerie sense of the uncertainty of what lay beyond them. As the sky grew darker by the minute, I realized it was a night like hundreds of other nights that I had come to hate so passionately. I knew the drill. In just a few minutes, after darkness had settled in, we would be approaching the hootch, sending the inhabitants scurrying to their bunker as we set up a perimeter around the small cluster of dwellings that sat a couple of hundred meters away from the wood line along the river.

Calling in our position to TOC, establishing contact with each position, setting up claymore mines, arranging guard duty, finding a dry spot to lie down for the night, all the things that had become automatic began clicking through my mind like a checklist. I wonder if Charlie has spotted us and knows our position for the night? Did he see us double back just before dark and figure out which hamlet we would occupy? Were we keeping a low enough profile? Is someone trying to get in one final smoke before dark, endangering our location? The blackness of the night, the possibility of what could and often did happen, the emotions of fear, fatigue, loneliness, grief, hatred, all came crashing down in a sudden burst of emotion as the scenery unfolded before me.

But wait! Something was different! My vantage point had changed, instead of seeing the silhouettes of grunts carrying M-16s and machine guns and mortars against the dreary looking sky, the horizon was filled with other sights. I was looking across the Saigon River from the 16th floor of a five star hotel. In less time than it has taken you to read this far, so many of the thoughts and emotions of 35-plus years ago flooded my mind.

Those of you who have been there know exactly what I mean. Although I had planned this trip for months—had landed at Tan Son Nhut—ridden through the streets of Saigon, it still came upon me so violently and unexpectedly that tears began flowing before I even realized it. There is nothing wrong with tears, but I just had not expected the accompanying flashback. Many years have gone by, but certain sights, smells, and sounds will, for a brief moment, put you right back in some jungle, rice paddy, or river that you thought had been forever wiped from your memory. Does the sound of a Huey, or any chopper, still take you back 35-plus years, too? I thought so.

And here I was, looking out the window of a hotel in Saigon, (it's still Saigon to me!) watching as that familiar scene changed to an unfamiliar one. As darkness covered the land a strange new element was being added to the mix. Neon! Neon lights— advertising Heineken, and electronics, and so many other things that I don't recall, made me realize how different, yet how unchanged so many things were. Just the neon, and the ferryboats, and the thousands of motorized bicycles and non-motorized bicycles loading and unloading, as people were headed home for the evening.

So began another chapter in my recovery from my tour of duty in Vietnam. For years, and even to this day, certain sounds and smells—like a bolt of lightning—caused events, places and faces to flash before me in similar fashion. Although I never had serious problems overcoming that event in my life, my return visit revealed that no matter how long ago we were there, the emotion of it is still just beneath the surface. No matter how strong we may be, such a traumatic experience does not just go away with time.

My nature and personality have always been positive and upbeat. I have never been discouraged for a protracted period of time and find it hard to relate to people who have bouts of depression. It's not that I am not compassionate and do not have empathy for them; it's just that I do not understand that mindset. However, no one but the most callused among us who has no conscience can not have some emotional attachment to seeing buddies die or having them die in your arms. Therein lies our difficulty.

Since the Vietnam conflict was considered an unpopular war, the added stigma of having to face a society who was protesting and calling us baby killers and murderers, made our plight unlike any of our predecessors who had fought for our country. The easiest thing to do was just not talk about what we had experienced, and talking about it would be the very therapy we all needed, regardless of our dispositions and personalities.

As someone who had grown up in a Christian home under the influence of Godly parents and a believing community, I had the advantage of a solid foundation, both spiritually and emotionally. However, I had turned away from that as a young teenager and had systematically ruled out God in my life. I became the master of my own destiny, and I didn't need God or anything else to prop me up.

After Vietnam, I followed the path of most of my brothers-in-arms. I came home, got a job, got married, raised a family, and generally got on with my life as if that chapter in my life had never existed. Occasionally, people would ask me about my duties and involvement in the Army. Usually, it consisted of questions like, "Were you on the front lines?" or "Did you have to shoot anyone?" Consequently, the conversations did not last very long.

Soon after getting married I reached a point where things just were not going as planned. I realized that my Christian upbringing was what was missing in my life, so I turned back to God and began a brand new adventure of pursuing my destiny, soon enrolling in Bible College and entering the ministry. I grew as a person and my life definitely took on new meaning.

After 30 years, I had an opportunity to return to Vietnam as well as Thailand and Cambodia as part of a missions trip with several other ministers. Only by being there could I have ever imagined what a chapter in my life that had been. We are all looking for closure, but I believe that is an elusive, if not impossible, pipe dream. If we believe, as I do, that we become a composite of what we have experienced, where we have been, what we have seen, and whom we have met, then that chapter in our lives can never end.

If that sounds like a pessimistic or even futile position to take, let me explain. The chapter, in time and space, has ended, but it will never end as long as we are alive. I believe we can use those types of experiences to build on rather than have them tear us down. It is with gratitude that we are built up rather than torn down by such events in our lives. Although I experienced horrible atrocities and left friends over there that did not make it out alive, I still am grateful for the fact that I made it back, and that I had the honor to serve alongside those men.

There is a fundamental truth that I hold on to every single day: *The way out of your dilemma is to help someone else out of his or hers.* The basis for that is found in the Scriptures. The following passage points this out:

> Luke 6:38 (NIV) *"Give, and it will be given to you…*
> *For with the measure you use, it will be measured to you."*

The true reward that we receive in recovering from our experience in Vietnam is not our own inner healing, but the sheer joy of assisting others in their journey. Once we learn to rejoice with them, and see their inner peace returning, then we are somehow miraculously farther on our own journey than we would be if we struggled and kept to ourselves and never spoke about our experiences.

In 30 years of ministry as pastor, educator, and leader, it seems the greatest joy I have had has been to hang out with other Vietnam veterans at reunions, at coffee shops, and yes, at the bar, discussing the major thing we have in common – one year of duty in the garden spot of the world. I have determined that the grace I have received is worth sharing, and the ones with whom I can identify best are the ones who share that common bond. Thus, Vietnam veterans have become a major mission in my life. Not to force my theology upon them, but to simply show them that there is wholeness and fullness of life after Vietnam. I have found the path to peace. Will you join me?

My encouragement to any veterans who may read this is two-fold. First, find those in your own community or sphere of influence who can relate to what you have experienced and see if you can be of assistance to them. You really only need to learn to listen. (I would also encourage you to find veterans groups, reunions, etc., and attend.) Second, there is another generation of men and women who stand a strong chance of being rejected and perceived as we were, those veterans of the Gulf War in the 1990s and veterans of the Iraqi and Afghanistan wars. Find them and be an encouragement to them.

This is not about politics or religion. The conflicts that are raging within the emotions of the human psyche have no respect to your party affiliation or your faith, or lack thereof. One of the greatest travesties that we could possibly see would be for history to repeat itself among the veterans of these recent wars. Believe me, there are more similarities between them and us than we dare imagine.

Remember when you came back to the world and tried to, just automatically, become a part of society again? There was such radical change in our culture that it was impossible to rejoin it without feeling so different. Even if the societal evolution had not occurred so rapidly, do we really think we could just come home from those experiences and act normally again? When you see one of our recent veterans of war reconnecting to his world, place yourself back 35 to 40 years ago. Imagine his life if someone doesn't reach out and offer encouragement and thanks for a job well done.

So you don't believe in this current war? Irrelevant! That's one of the things that made us withdraw and refuse to talk about our experiences. Obviously, some things are hard to talk about. To express our feelings regarding war experiences is difficult under the best of circumstances. All I am saying is, let's do our part to improve those circumstances. It should not take them 40 years to get where we are. No one likes to hear or read about his or her activities in a critical manner. Take the time to speak encouragement and hope to these young men and women.

It has been said that a person can live three weeks without food, three days without water, three minutes without air, but he cannot live three seconds without hope.

> Matt 12:21 NLT
> *"And His name will be the hope of all the world."*

We have this hope as an anchor of the soul...

Ron McCants

CHAPTER 28

OUR MEDICS, DOCTORS, AND NURSES

As I talk to veterans across the country and conversations including combat situations arise, the discussion always brings me back to those in the medical field, whether it be the young front line medics, or the older, more seasoned doctors in the operating and emergency wards.

In many cases these fine people are the unsung heroes of war. For the soldiers, the medics were always there. Often the first word yelled in the heat of combat was, "Medic!" They became an integral part of every line company's Command Group. Yet when you talk to them today, far too often you hear the self-doubt, "Could I have done more?"

Personally, I admired all I served with. To all our medics, doctors and nurses: Your concern for us, your never failing devotion to duty under fire and in all conditions, and for your life-saving skilled care which was often above and beyond—our heartfelt thanks: you saved us!

— Lee

Chapter 29

The Fates Tied a Knot in My Thread

My name is J.A. Coutant. I was a medic in Vietnam. Most all called me "Doc".

Toward the end of my five years in Vet counseling, I began to look back over my life. I found an interesting thread that began to make sense of the impact of being a medic had had on it. It was a long theme of male associations and bondings.

My dad ran the office of a local lumber mill; his business dress was Pendleton plaid shirts. From the age of three on, I was exposed to life in the lumberyard and the mill workers. It was a conservative mill town. Lumbering is rough, sometimes dangerous work, and done by "real men." This is where I learned about male attitude. To this day, the smell of raw lumber equals "men." Come to think of it, so do wool plaid shirts.

Along with growing up around a lumber mill, I was a Cub Scout, and then a Boy Scout. With Boy Scouts came campouts and summer camp. All male—just guys in the woods. For the rest of the year, in junior high school, I was a coach's assistant for the football, basketball, and track teams. Skinny and uncoordinated, my only participation was running track for one season.

In a nice link to the plain idealism of a nonconformist Protestant upbringing, I was asked to join a boy's Masonic fraternal organization. It was based on Victorian chivalric ideals of love and service to one's fellow man. Its basic tenets were fraternal love and all men are brothers. Hand on a Bible, I swore to that and took it all to heart. It gave an intellectual framework to hang my emotions on. A kind of justification for bewildered, pre-existing feelings. It let my love for another boy be beautiful, if still tormented, and good, as long as it was hands-off. Later, in high school, there were all-male service organizations to belong to, the sports activities were less inclusive, no geeks allowed. It didn't matter; the groundwork had already been laid. A good set-up for what the Army had in store for me a few years later.

Basic training was all men, all the time, 24-7. Now, with two oaths sworn to serve my fellows, they made me a medic. I am taught how to be useful, allowed to be smart, and be of service to those I was most used to being with—men. The job didn't require that I had to shoot anyone, another plus. The life or death thing always took precedence over any military bull, and that helped me to keep a humane perspective. Being the oldest grandchild in my family and an older brother, responsibility for others was already a well-established pattern for me.

All men were my brothers—brothers I had always wanted—and all men were to be loved, and now, to be cared for. I could do that with a quiet, earnest passion. I liked being a medic and worked hard to be a good one. Ft. Sam Houston was full, so I and 19 others found ourselves in Ft. Huachuca, Arizona, the second class to go through ad hoc training that had been established there in a small hospital which served the base and nearby town. Working the wards and outpatient/emergency, in AIT and OJT, allowed me to see the greatest variety of cases and to pick up the odd bits of information and procedures which were not to be found on the wards or taught in class. A few of the doctors took pity on us trainees and helped with our education. The cases came in the double back doors all fresh, usually alive, and I couldn't get enough of it. I had the stomach for the work, curiosity overcoming any shock or disgust; there really wasn't time for either. Handling a hit-and-run fatality, assisting with an autopsy, or holding an Ipecac-vomiting kid who had OD'd on baby aspirin, it was all the same; they needed care and attention.

In Vietnam, the metal met the flesh, my own and others. I received my first Purple Heart one month in-country. I had already seen the panic, shock, torn flesh, and blood in the States. Here it was all larger, more often, and more severe. That was just what came through the Aid Station in base camp. Then my boots hit the mud and the focus narrowed. I was right there, the first man on the spot; it was me against possible death. And there I was with my brother's life literally in my hands. His unique life was now my responsibility.

All my ideals, love, and learning came to that moment. With it came a microsecond view into a horrible void where I could see myself freezing up and unable to do what I needed to do. I knew that if I froze then, I would be a crumpled ruined mess for the rest of my miserable existence. That brief thought was worse than anything that was in front of me and I snapped back. I took charge and anything and anyone was put to service in aid of the man in my care.

Stop the bleeding, clear the airway, treat for shock—the medic's mantra. I could do all that and more. I've rarely felt so confident of my abilities and myself. It was one of life's turning points when I had to declare a man dead. Anything became possible to keep a life. I knew I was a good medic, but there was little to confirm it. The injured men would be taken away, dusted-off, and I would never see them again. Their lives after me forever remaining a mystery. I had no feedback on the job I had done. I saw their damage, their fear, and their agony as they left. The men I worked on I never got to see recovered or whole or as close to whole as they would get.

It didn't stop with the combat work. After a second Purple Heart (minor injury), I transferred to the rear area Clearing Station in 9th Div. Headquarters where the situation was no better. There were the K.P. burns, a suicide (drinking and M-14s don't mix), accidental gunshot wounds, vehicle accidents (I lost a friend to one), messy civilian births, the celebrating new father who drank himself to death, the uncontrollable drunks the MPs would bring us, and the routine stuff. I smoked myself stoned after my shift and showed up for work the next day wearing sunglasses, depressed and wondering about the men I had left behind on the line.

Within a few months of leaving the service, I began to look for medical work in civilian life. This, while my parents had to live with the moody stoner the Army had discharged into their home. I had tried being a prep orderly for one hash-smoking month and was fired for having a bad attitude. It became painfully apparent that there was no place for the kind of skills I had. I applied at the local VA hospital and was told they had openings for full-time college students. I also would have to work three revolving shifts. Somehow working a day shift and taking day classes didn't make a lot of sense, then or now. The training programs for returning medics came years later, when I was already back in college. By then my anatomical knowledge became useful when working with the human figure in art classes. Later on I worked, for a few years, at a nicer hospital, in their laundry, then in central supply. None of those jobs came even close to what I had liked about being a medic. My focus was gone from that aspect of my life. (I am now beyond ever wanting to do medical work again. I've lost both the heart and stomach for it, curiously, in part from having seen too much of my own blood over the years.)

All my giving, and wanting to give, came at a cost. I had gotten very little back in thanks or praise for any effort. I kidded myself I didn't need it. I knew how to look after others but was clueless as how to look after myself. I knew how to get numb and block my experiences out, back then and for years after. The doubts set in, the second-guessing, the what-ifs. The severe depressions came on, the feelings of self-worthlessness, the self-isolation, and displaced anger. With all that, I began to see what I thought I hadn't done, and then thought I didn't deserve to have anything good happening to me.

After all, who had died for what I didn't do? What botched jobs had I never heard about? Who despised me for what I hadn't done for them or when I hadn't been there for them? And there were all the dead I could do nothing for and me, here, still alive. I wondered why I was still living and sometimes thought I'd be better off dead. Looking at my medical training in reverse left me with a lot of options on how to end my life.

Then in the 1980s my brothers started dying again from a slow, incurable disease. I then lost more men to AIDS than I had known killed in Vietnam. These were friends, lovers; men I had known for years and had expected to grow old with. The extended family in my hometown. Having already seen more than I could handle, I could do nothing more but hide. I hid from my own subculture for the next 16 years. My life hurt and, useless medic that I was, I couldn't make it better.

After 30 years of feeling constantly injured and in pain, I got some help. One thing led to another, and I got into a veteran's counseling center. I didn't go to the VA because I didn't then trust them. There I was seen for what I had been in the service and what I had become as a civilian. I was not alone, as a veteran, for the first time in a very long time. I was able to get some perspective on what had happened to me and to others like myself. That there was a pattern to the reactions we had had to combat and how other medics had come out of the experience feeling the same way I did. I wasn't unique; I wasn't bad, or all that odd. All medics carried a package of doubts, guilt, and low self-worth. I am incredibly lucky in that I have a man who has loved and cared for me through it all. He got help for his secondhand PTSD. Trauma can and will fuck anybody up, including those close to us.

Going back through letters, tapes, and what I have previously written of my experiences has helped put things in perspective. I can see again that I was a knowledgeable, well-trained, very well-trained, as it turned out, caring man. I did do the best job I knew how to do and that I was able to do. A big morale boost came when I heard from my line lieutenant. He called out of the blue to tell me that the old unit was having a reunion. During that first conversation I was able to tell him how much I appreciated all the care that he had shown for us, his men. I was able to thank him, something I had wanted to do for years. He told me that he was glad that he had had a good medic with him. I had done a good job. I was someone he and others, my guys, wanted to see again. It was solid confirmation that that part of my life, a critical part, had some worth to it.

To this day, I feel most comfortable when I have with me, or nearby, what I need for First Aid. I carry a good pocketknife, in theory to cut away clothing and to tear cloth into strips for bandages. A small pair of scissors, needles and thread for stitches and tying off bleeders, safety pins, a lighter, and more than one handkerchief. At least two or three Band-Aids are always in my wallet, and I have my more or less personal pharmacopoeia to carry. I can still run emergency what-if scenarios in my head to keep myself in mental preparedness—less often than I used to—they amount to nightmares. And I'm always asking myself if it would be that good for my own well being to get involved with emergency situations in a civilian setting. So far, so good, such a demand has never been made. I don't kid myself; if needed, I know how to respond. Although I still feel love and responsibility for my fellow men, I hope I never have to be a good medic again.

CHAPTER 30

I PULLED MY CHAIR NEXT TO HIS BED AND TOOK HIS HAND

My name is James (Jim) Maves. While a senior in high school, I read a Readers Digest article about the life and duties of a male nurse anesthetist. I looked into the nursing program and found I could enroll for $100.00. I started that program in June of 1958. I entered the Mayo Clinic School of Allied Health Sciences program for nurse anesthetists in Rochester, Minnesota, in July 1962, completed it in 1964, and was then employed at the Marshfield Clinic in Marshfield, Wisconsin. I worked there for eighteen months and then the Vietnam War began to escalate.

My father and two uncles served in World War II. My father-in-law was career Army and I harbor very strong feelings about service to my country. I decided it was time to visit my friendly recruiters. I was soon afterwards commissioned a First Lieutenant, and with my wife and two sons, we were off to Fort Carson, Colorado.

On Good Friday, 1967, I received orders assigning me to Vietnam. I moved my wife and sons back to Marshfield in June and was soon afterwards on my way to the RVN. In Vietnam at the replacement center, I was assigned to the 44th Med Brigade and attached to the 12th Evac hospital in the base camp of the 25th Infantry Division–Tropic Lightning, Cu Chi. Cu Chi is about 50 miles from Cambodia and located on a major infiltration route to Saigon. I arrived there on a hot, dusty day and was assigned to a cot. That evening the boys cooked a little chicken on a charcoal cooker, and about the time I started chewing on a chicken wing, the perimeter opened up. The hospital was located close to the perimeter on the Cu Chi side. It was still daylight and being an old country-boy/hunter who hadn't eaten for a couple of days, I thought I'm not moving to bunkers until I hear a ricochet. So, the new guy started out on the right foot with the old timers, many of whom had promptly hit the bunkers. We did get mortared that night, and the next, which started me to wondering whether a guy could survive there a year.

During one of my first nights I was awakened about 0400 by my cot shaking and the Playmate of the Month pictures, which a lot of the guys had attached to the bamboo matting dividing up the area, that were shaking and blowing away from the bamboo. Next morning I innocently asked if anyone had felt the earthquake. I got a few strange looks then some laughter. It was then I learned about the 'Rolling Thunder' B-52 strikes. I also soon learned about Hanoi Hannah, who mentioned in her radio broadcasts that our unit, the 25th, was receiving horrible damage being delivered on us, and all the boys we were treating in the hospital, on a daily basis by the VC.

The hospital was a scaled down Evac. We had approximately 100 beds.

We had the usual Evac operating room configuration with six operating tables. They were located in Quonset huts with five tables in one Quonset, with 4x6 plywood baffles separating the tables and a common aisle along the side. The sixth table in another hut was reserved for severely wounded soldiers who needed immediate surgery, which means the MASH that we supported had 32 tables. Not really practical in a busy combat area. To staff the operating room we had six nurse anesthetists and one MD anesthetist. The hospital had two orthopedic surgeons, two general surgeons, one thoracic surgeon, one oral surgeon, one ophthalmologist, two radiologists and an internal medicine physician. We had no neurosurgeons so those with head wounds were treated by us and then shipped to the 24th Evac Neuro-Surgical Hospital at Long Binh.

The exterior of the Quonsets was sandbagged to a height of about five feet. During shelling the surgeons and staff would lie on the floor against the outside walls until the shelling stopped. During particularly bad times the surgeons would wear flak jackets and helmets, the jackets with surgical gowns and the helmets with orthopedic gauze. The anesthetists were tied to the patient because most of the time we were breathing for them, so we would wrap around under the OR tables until the detonations ended.

We had a number of patients receive their second or third Purple

Hearts while in the hospital. Very few wanted to linger there after treatment before being sent back to their units because they said they didn't get hit with as much heavy stuff back where they'd come from. The 25th was chronically engaged in exotic places like War Zone C, Hobo Woods, the Saigon River, and the Black Virgin, so we were kept well supplied with plenty of wounded. Our order of priority was GI wounded, ARVN wounded, civilian wounded, and enemy wounded.

The hospital was blessed with extraordinary physicians. I had tremendous admiration for the general, orthopedic, and thoracic surgeons. They, like us, worked until all the work was done. Regular hospital staff worked 12-hour shifts. Most physicians had come from major medical centers and trauma programs. We used the same resources and energy on all the patients. The OR worked seven days a week with Sunday being recognized by an 0830-start time rather than 0800. My longest straight stretch at the table was 68 hours. I remember it because I thought I was functioning well. I carried a litter to the recovery ward at about 0100, and the little sand and dirt piles outside the OR looked white to me.

"Has it snowed, Sarge?" I asked one of the nearby troops. He turned and looked funny at me and said, "Are you okay?"

Apart from our combat war-wounded, we also took care of several troops who were gored by water buffalo. One soldier was on night perimeter guard and a tiger sneaked up and grabbed him by his shoulder and tried to drag him away. Buddies shot the tiger. We had a lot of snakebites. Many of the wounded ended up with plaster casts either on legs or arms or a total lower-body cast, as broken femurs are a very common war injury. After five days we would bring them back to OR to DPC or debride them some more. When the patients were asleep, our cast technicians would saw the casts apart and a characteristic odor would cloud the area. Maggots. The darn flies would get under the cast and lay eggs. If the surgeons had not debrided enough, the maggots would work on the necrotic tissue, so I guess they probably weren't all bad.

I had one patient I'll never forget. It was Thanksgiving Day, 1967, and everyone was anticipating the 1100 opening of the mess hall cause there would be fresh turkey, dressing, and all the holiday dinner stuff. At about 1030 I got a call to report to the OR.

Grumbling all the way about missing my turkey, I entered the OR and saw a black soldier with a very swollen left thigh. "What happened?" I asked.

"Was out on a LRRP, stumbled and fell into a pit on a punji stake. It entered above my left knee and came out by my left hip. We'd made contact early and then had to hide for several days till the chopper could come back for us."

I asked him the standard question, "When did you eat last?"

"What day is this?"

"It's Thursday, Thanksgiving."

"Then I had some crackers on Tuesday."

I don't remember if I got any turkey that day or not. Somehow it suddenly didn't seem that important to me anymore.

When I went to work on my last day in 'Nam I thought, well, I hope I do a 24-hour jobber. I did. Among other things I worked on three boys with heart wounds, two GIs, and one ARVN. I walked out the following morning with head held high. All done! At the replacement depot, SP-4 Danny, our Cu Chi cast technician who was also rotating, and I stepped aboard the plane. The Braniff stewardesses standing at the door of the plane gave us warming smiles and said, "Welcome back to the world." In California I was discharged, said farewell and wished Danny good luck, and called my wife in Wisconsin.

"Grab the boys and head for the O'Hare Inn. I should be there by early afternoon." Around 1400 I was walking down the hallway of the O'Hare Inn accompanied by a young bellhop who wheeled my duffel bag along for me.

"Travel far?" he asked.

"About ten thousand miles."

"Where you been?"

"Vietnam."

When we arrived at the room I gave him a fat tip. He immediately handed it back to me with a smile and said, "No thank you. And, welcome back!" That was my homecoming parade and it was all I needed. I opened the room door and my youngest son, who was standing on the bed, took one look at the suntanned stranger with the handlebar mustache and dove under the bed. The next day I was back at the hospital visiting my old coworkers.

"When are you coming back to work?" they asked. At that point I was only a couple of days from groveling in the Vietnam dirt and sand.

"I'll have to let you know, but it's gonna be awhile."

We packed our car and headed west. I spent the next six weeks reuniting with my wife and sons as we traveled from Arizona to California, to Montana, and finally back to Wisconsin.

My first Monday back to work, about mid-morning, my coworkers said, "We have a case just for you in the emergency room." Seems a young Indian had taken on a Wisconsin state patrolman with a hoe and received a .357 manhole in his femoral artery. In Vietnam any single hole or bullet wound was a relax—take a break—case. Welcome back to the real world.

I thought of my Vietnam experience as tremendously rewarding. Going in I had concerns about my ability to handle certain situations from a professional standpoint. With post-Vietnam, I had the philosophy I could handle anything as long as I wasn't being shot at. I had been exposed to situations that would never, could never happen on the civilian side. I saw the way men handled themselves in stressful situations. I liked and admired the openness and honesty of men who faced death nearly every day. Political correctness is not a real big issue in a combat zone. I thought I had come through the situation with minimal adjustment problems. I tended to smile a lot more after 'Nam. I totally changed my philosophy of life and what is important to me.

Present time: Just last week I interviewed a patient for a surgical procedure. The radiologist was concerned about changes in his chest X-ray as he had a history of a gunshot wound to his chest. I introduced myself and asked, "How did you get the GSW—did a hunting companion shoot you?"

He looked at me and in a quiet voice said, "No. Vietnam."

It all came slamming home to me. I pulled a chair up and sat down. At first I didn't know what was happening, but I realized that after many years, Vietnam had impacted me in ways I did not understand.

I pulled my chair closer to the bed and shook his hand. It was time for me to sit down and talk to this brave man—my brother.

CHAPTER 31

"DUTY, HONOR, COUNTRY...
THE LONG GRAY LINE HAS NEVER FAILED US."
—General Douglas MacArthur

Even though there have been millions of veterans who've served our young nation from Civil War days until this very moment, documented history, current data, and events confirm that among our military services and those serving, there sometimes were, and remain, small fraternities.

The following comments are from a present-day Iraq veteran (from a long, distinguished family line of veterans) who has strong ties going back to my beloved 5th/60th Infantry.

Yet, just one more example of our brotherhood-in-arms connection.

— Lee

CHAPTER 32

IN COMBAT I HAD THE INTUITIVE FEELING OF A PAST CONNECTION

My name is Edmund Christian Scarborough. To many, a person's name serves relatively little service beyond identification. However, mine transcends beyond that to a deep personal awareness steeped in honor and family tradition. I am the nephew of Captain Edmund B. Scarborough. I proudly carry his name. I was born two months after his tragic death on May 10th, 1968, in Vietnam.

My uncle was the Company Commander of C Company, 5th Battalion (Mechanized,) 60th Infantry, 9th Infantry Division when his unit came under heavy fire. Captain Scarborough moved immediately to the head of the column, dismounted from his personnel carrier, and in the face of furious enemy fire, commanded and led his company.

During the battle he lost his life while caring for and leading his men in combat. He paid the highest possible price to serve his country. He did that entirely selflessly and most honorably while displaying the utmost of outstanding courage and bravery.

I find an uncanny familiarity in this writing. I, too, am proudly serving in our US Army, as did my uncle Edmund, my father, and my grandfather, all before me from World War II to the present. I feel a sense of coming around full circle within a family of brothers-in-arms.

When I first arrived at Ft. Bragg, North Carolina, in 1993, I was assigned to the proud 82nd Airborne Division. My commanding general was Major General W. Steele. This is partially where the feeling of coming around full circle comes in: I may be a generation behind the veterans of the Vietnam War, but I have shared the same commander with many of you who served under General Steele when you were in Vietnam. He was then your Battalion Headquarters Commander, Lieutenant Colonel William Steele. I fully believe there are other connections as well.

As a younger soldier I thirsted to taste the experience of combat. That was what I was trained for as a paratrooper. I longed for the experience. I later remembered someone once said, "Combat can be defined as long periods of arduous boredom punctuated by very brief moments of heart-wrenching fear." I soon learned the solid truth of that saying. In February 2003 my brigade deployed to Kuwait in order to position and prepare for the war which would soon ensue in Iraq.

Later, our battalion moved from As-Samawah to Fallujah. Our activity there would set the tone for what would come to pass as one of the most controversial and troubled cities in Iraq. While patrolling the streets of Fallujah, As-Samawah, and Baghdad, I had an intuitive feeling of connections; like a sense that my role model, and mentor, my heroic Uncle Edmund was there, watching over me, helping to guide my decisions and protecting me. I was greatly comforted by those thoughts.

Time passed and I moved from the weapons squad leader position in the Third Platoon to Platoon Sergeant of First Platoon. I was then in Charlie Company 1/325. "Charlie Rock" was chosen as the battalion's main effort on every mission. Much like the Vietnam "Bandido Charlies" of the 5th/60th within Charlie, our first platoon was always the company's main effort. We were at the tip of the spear on every battalion mission in Baghdad—the best—and I was having my experience in combat.

Now as a veteran of Kosovo and Operation Iraqi Freedom, I believe all of us who have been in combat can probably agree on one thing: war and the experience of combat transcends time and generations. It is a universal sharing of hope that those who come behind us will never have to endure those kinds of experiences. From our veterans of WWII, through Vietnam, and on to today's conflicts and wars, I believe that sharing of hope is consistent and constant.

Once I returned home I never felt comfortable with friends and family using my name and the word hero in the same sentence. There just never seemed to be much heroism in the bone-numbing fear for your life that you experience when people are trying to kill you.

What I am slowly coming to realize is that being there for your comrades in the brotherhood, still performing your job, being reliable and trusting your life to someone else, and vice versa are mostly what makes a hero. That kind of being afraid does not make you a coward. It is a natural emotion for anyone in such a circumstance. What you do with that fear is what decides your fate. You must do your job, accomplish the mission, and keep everyone alive to your left and right in the face of that fear. That is what defines the term hero to me.

As with the unpopular Vietnam War, I realize there are many who are not happy with the Iraq war and have reservations and concerns as to whether or not our government was right or wrong in its decision to go to war. Many are not supportive of it politically. But I also realize and am proud and happy that the people of our United States still care about and pray for every one of its soldiers, sailors, airmen and marines who serve our country. They, our families, neighbors, friends, and all of America let us know we are not lost and forgotten in a cause, and they warmly welcome us home as heroes.

I think the American public has realized its mistake of not supporting our troops of the Vietnam War, regardless of the actions of our government back then. They have realized that as individuals we in the military and all veterans are not responsible for the decisions, operations and actions of the government. I believe our nation of caring citizens realizes, as do we who have been in combat, that war in any measure is always a terrible thing to endure—for any generation, for any era.

To our current active-duty military members, to the veterans of Vietnam, and to the veterans of all conflicts and wars: I salute you.

You, truly, are all heroes! Welcome home.

CHAPTER 33

AND THERE HAVE BEEN SOME ROUGH TIMES

Six years ago I had never heard of PTSD, Post Traumatic Stress Disorder. Earlier I'd heard statements of soldiers suffering from shell shock, certain combat-related neuroses and battle fatigue, but never PTSD. I bring this up simply to point out that stress of combat is not new. It has just been given a new name.

It is real and can affect anyone—yeah anyone, myself included. A personal experience: While coaching a girl's fast-pitch softball game, the young dark-haired catcher took a foul tip to the ribs just missing her chest protection. She fell to the ground in pain. To all watching it was of immediate concern, but still just an unfortunate part of the game.

However, instantly, to me the sound of the crack of the bat was a rifle shot, and her grabbing her side and dropping to the ground in agony elicited a far different reaction. I was suddenly thousands of miles away in a different world of war.

"Medic, medic, she's been shot! Where the hell did that round come from? Everybody down! Don't move . . . Secure the area! Goddammit! Where . . ." There was a total silence, surprised stares—and my extreme humiliation.

I left Vietnam and came back to Wyoming and reality. I paused and looked around for a moment then turned and walked from the field, weeping.

PTSD must be recognized and dealt with.

— Lee

Chapter 34

Post Traumatic Stress Disorder
Kevin Robinett, MD

Veterans Administration Medical Clinic
Cheyenne, Wyoming

As a psychiatrist at the Cheyenne VAMC, I have worked with many combat veterans who struggle to improve their quality of life while living with Post Traumatic Stress Disorder (PTSD). I have been with the VA for the past 10 years and know that changes from severe emotional trauma can be enduring and impact other aspects of the lives of those who have been through such experiences. Past experiences including events that are both good and bad become intertwined with our temperament or personality and help to define who we are. But for those who go through the intense fear associated with combat, the changes they are left with can often make their lives more difficult.

People who are exposed to situations where their life is threatened and experience the horror associated with that often have some permanent changes. These include being reminded of the traumatic event in many different ways and finding this to be an unpleasant experience. The natural response is to find ways to avoid these reminders when possible. There are also other changes, which can include living with greater levels of anxiety and having increased difficulty controlling one's emotions. A person's perspective on life can change which can include how they relate to others.

There are other ramifications of PTSD, which are beyond the scope of these remarks.

People who are traumatized often have the greatest difficulty dealing with their problems shortly after they experience these events. Over time these symptoms tend to subside. But they often don't totally go away, and other events later in life can stir them up again. For example, many WWII veterans have had problems with their PTSD symptoms, which suddenly got worse after the loss of a spouse or retirement.

Treatment for PTSD includes talk therapy and psychotropic medications. Medicines can reduce the symptoms which are associated with PTSD, most often anxiety, depression and anger. But people may also have vulnerabilities to other mental disorders that are exacerbated by having PTSD. These could be conditions like bipolar disorder, substance abuse, depression, etc. In such instances medication treatment for these problems can lessen the burden from PSTD.

Talk therapy includes individual and group psychotherapy. This typically starts on an outpatient basis. Sometimes veterans go to a residential program that specializes in treating PTSD. The duration of treatment is usually several weeks and therapy is more intensive. Therapy generally focuses on going back through the traumatic events of the past in order to deal with them and put them into perspective. Another major focus is dealing with today's problems without attempting to relate them to past events.

CHAPTER 35

THE DAY THE REAL WAR BEGAN FOR ME

My name is Samuel E. Bailey. I guess to understand how life has been for me since my return from Vietnam is to start with how I left Vietnam. I call that, "The Day the Real War Began for Me." August 13, 1970, a day that has continued to haunt me for the past 35 years. There has never been a day gone by since then that I haven't had a thought or flashback. No day of rest as I call it. Don't get me wrong, some days are better than others and life has gone on.

My platoon was hit by a Command Detonator 155 round while moving about in the Hobo Woods. Lost, KIA, and several of us WIA. I remember the explosion and disorientation that followed. I still see the body parts, smoke and smell from the same. I won't go into the details. Only those who have experienced such things can relate. It's not a pretty sight. The aftermath was filled with intense emotions. At the time they were normal reactions to just another unfortunate ambush.

Dust-off took place, body bags, body parts, and bodies were loaded on the Huey. No room for me on the inside to lie down. Since I had only wounds to my hands, arms, and legs I could sit next to the door gunner with my legs outside. We arrived at Chu Chi EVAC. I was taken off the Huey so nurses, medics, and others could remove those inside. After that I was put on a stretcher and put back on the same chopper. I was confused, hurting and depressed. Spoke my piece and was told to shut up and enjoy the ride to the EVAC in Long Binh. I would leave my buddies and never see them again until October of 2001.

After a year and several months, several operations and blood transfusions in various hospitals, I was given the option to serve out my enlistment, or be given a medical discharge. I chose to serve out my enlistment with a permanent profile of limited duty and loss of MOS.

While with a medical holding company, I was notified that my stepfather was seriously ill and took emergency leave back to Ft. Ord, California. My stepfather was retired Army in the Korean and Vietnam War. While on leave he passed away so I asked for compassionate reassignment to Ft. Ord to be close to my mom so I could help out since I still had two sisters and a brother in school. This was granted and I was reassigned to HQ Company and given assignment to work in Adjutant General Congressionals as a caseworker. Couldn't ask for better duty.

After 11 months it just wasn't working out. My mother had tried to commit suicide; she just couldn't handle it. Someone needed to be more involved with the siblings. Since I worked with the Adjutant General, I found it very easy to take a compassionate discharge from the army and did so.

I don't know if that was a good thing or not. This gave me plenty of time without structure so to speak, even though I had a day job the day after getting out of the Army as a sales clerk in a drive-through milk and gas stand. I was held up three weeks later. Well, I couldn't just let the guy do this to me. After an argument and two shots fired at me— thank God he had no military background because both shots missed me—I called the police and the store owner. Told the police what happened then turned to the store owner and told him to stick his store where the sun don't shine.

Failed to mention that during this lapse of about two years of being wounded, I was introduced to drugs for pain as well as for my mental state. First year was legal drugs and lots of alcohol. Second year turned to illegal drugs and alcohol. Still feeling both mental and physical pain. Seemed to take the edge off so to speak although I would never be pain-free again.

During my return of compassionate reassignment I would meet my future wife. That would be my Godsend. I would leave the drug and alcohol scene for the most part.

On to marriage, family, and multiple jobs. Never had a problem with getting jobs, just had a problem keeping them. I was never fired from a job, just couldn't get along with people so would walk away. At the beginning of my job career after discharge from the Army, I didn't have a problem telling people I was a veteran of Vietnam, but quickly learned most people had a problem with knowing this. I learned to stay silent and avoid people associations real quick. That would remain the same for the next 30 or so years.

I found I was unable to sleep very much. The nightmares and regularly standing watch at the front window of my home became unbearable. I decided to overcome this by taking two jobs. Eight hours by day and eight hours by night. I would do this for 25 years. I didn't worry too much about sleep then due to exhaustion. When I finished with my rebound job at 0200 I knew I'd be back up at 0700 to return to first job at 0800.

Life went on. After the 25 or so years of two jobs, I would have a heart attack at the ripe age of 42. I would learn to slow down a little. By the way, my doctor said the heart attack was due to stress. Valium, 30 mg a day for one year, would teach me to slow down. Couldn't work two jobs a day like that. So remained as a technician working on sealing systems and point of sale systems for major chain stores. That left me by myself working from my truck through radio dispatch. Proved to be one of the loneliest jobs I would ever have, which was okay with me.

Needless to say going back to only one job left me with a lot of time to think. The nightmares would again return, intensify, and my nightly guard duty at our front window would also begin again.

I had a good day job with the California State Employment Office for many years. I worked various positions there from being the Disabled Veterans Outreach person, State Welfare person to Determination Officer for Unemployment. The job was working out well, then here came the influx of the boat people from Vietnam. The State of California was not prepared for this. I had this office manager who needed help with the situation and since I had worked the welfare side and was a vet of the Vietnam War, she thought I'd be just the right person to put this new program into action. I was put into the position and fought it all the way. But I had no choice in the matter.

I pleaded not to have to work with Vietnam boat people, or veterans. Just didn't think I would be able to handle it. My office manager disagreed, so I was stuck. It didn't take but about 60 days. I flipped out! My office manager tried to get me to go see the state shrink, I told her no! Instead I gave her my 30-day notice and walked away from a perfectly good career. A couple of weeks later I went to my private doctor and was referred to a shrink. By this time I was a mess mentally. I regularly had hallucinations, intensive nightmares and night sweats. My life would never get better; I just couldn't shake Vietnam no matter what I did.

I hoped a career change might be the answer, so I returned to school in 1988 for a solid year, taking a crash course in electronics and microprocessing. I graduated and received a certificate for the same.

I got a job with a company as a calibration technician for various devices including number-sensing equipment. That was going well. I was learning a lot and the job was intense. I still had my night job and the nightmares about Vietnam were still with me.

The company I was working for hired a new engineer—a Vietnamese. I was in a position where I had to work closely with him. After about the second month with this guy I exploded following a heated argument. That happened the first time he spoke to me in Vietnamese. The next thing I knew I was chasing him through the work complex. He found a room and locked himself in it. I left my job and never returned.

There just seemed to be no answers for getting rid of my Vietnam conflict. I have had this thing in my head that the NVA were out to get me because they didn't do their job of killing me the first time. I also had a very disturbing guilt complex about Vietnam and my buddies. I never finished my tour of duty and watched guys killed who had wives and children to go back to. Why them and not me? I had joined the Army and got what I wanted and asked for. A lot of the others were drafted and didn't ask to be sent to war. It just wasn't right.

On August 15, 1994, I had a second heart attack on my oldest of two son's birthday. It was days after my 24th anniversary (Aug. 13th, 1970) of being wounded in Vietnam. After three weeks I returned to work, couldn't bear staying at home.

All was going well with the exception of an angry past and memories I couldn't get rid of. I was now back into the night sweats and nightmares more often.

June of 2001—the first reunion for the 5th Bn. 60th Inf. 3rd Bde 9th Inf. Div. I don't recall too much about how this began for me. I know that during February, March, and April of 2001 I had entered into a new mission for myself. I was bound and determined to find someone I was with in Vietnam. This had become almost an obsession.

Since I have to dwell on Vietnam so much I needed more information. I needed something more than the nightmares and the constant smells, feelings and sounds that were taking their toll on me mentally. I think I found a 9th Inf. web site, left my name as serving with them and Bde, Bn, and company. Lo and behold here came this e-mail from a person by the name of Ernie Saldivar, wanting to correspond with me. He only lives about 150 miles from my home and in the same city I frequently visit because my brother lives there.

Ernie invited me to the reunion. I made him a promise to attend. Figured I'd put this Vietnam thing to rest once and for all.

I remember showing up in Denver. I was scared and feeling guilty about going to begin with. Would I remember anyone, and what would I do when I did meet someone I knew? After arriving I checked into the hotel and sat in my room asking myself, "Do I really want to do this?" I finally went to the bar for some courage. Sitting by myself and looking for anyone I might know or someone who might know me. That was kind of foolish since all of us have changed in our growth of 30-odd years. This to no avail. I didn't know anyone and was afraid to start a conversation. I finally went upstairs to register with 5th/60th. I met a few guys, introduced myself and felt very out of place. When I told a few people I was there in 1970 I felt everyone was just staring at me dumbfounded. Most people there had been with Charlie Bandidos—a Mech unit from 1966 to 1969. Who the heck were Charlie Bandidos? Never heard of them. I knew I was in the wrong place.

I left and went back to my room. I was already checking for a flight out and back home where it was safe and sane. There was a knock at my door. It was a short guy who introduced himself as Alan and said he wanted to talk with me. I went with him to another room and he began to grill me with questions. I answered the best I could about my time in the RVN and the areas I operated out of. He really seemed amazed. He had maps of RVN. I started to remember more than I cared to know. It seems no one at the reunion had known about Charlie Rangers and the Cambodian campaign in

1970. He filled me in on Charlie Bandidos and the history of the
Battalion. Alan, nicknamed Shorty, was the historian of the reunion
and was just as surprised about Charlie Rangers as I was about Charlie
Bandidos. What a mess I was in now! I couldn't really handle this.

No one I knew was there, not anyone from my time period or
Company. I remember going back to my room, locking the door and
weeping like a baby. After very little sleep, I decided to once again
try to make contact with someone familiar. It didn't happen. I had
another one-on-one with Alan and tried communicating with some
of the others. I felt so out of place.

This just wasn't for me. I went off on my own for awhile, and
came back during the Friday evening session and was sitting around
the bar. I overheard different conversations which reassured me this
was not for me and didn't even include my era with 5th/60th.
Someone came in the area by the name of Hair. I remembered the
name Hair. He had left RVN several weeks before I got there. I went
over and introduced myself. He invited me to sit at his table and
finally I was having a conversation that made me feel a little more
comfortable. The drinks I was putting away made me more relaxed.

Next thing to happen was John would yell out Ernie's name. I
remembered Ernie as the person I corresponded with via e-mail and
whom I promised I would attend this reunion. Ernie and his wife
would sit at the table and we would all have good conversation. I
told Ernie and others about those I had served with and area of operations. Ernie made me feel comfortable and good that I showed up.

Well another sleepless night and some more weeping would
ensue. I still hadn't met anyone I knew and felt kind of left out.

Next day, Saturday, we had time to visit a room with memorabilia
after which we were all to meet together. I remember going in and
seeing post articles and stuff guys had brought back from RVN. I
never made it through the room, I can't explain the feelings that
overcame me, but it sure did make the past seem so damn real. I was
feeling, smelling, hearing, and seeing Vietnam all over again. So in
tune with the bush. I was there and scared shitless. I left and went
outside ready for flight. I stayed out there for the longest time. I just
couldn't handle it. I was ready to get back on the plane. It would cost
me over $100 to reschedule. So I decided to make the most of it,
found a bus stop and went downtown. I found myself just walking

aimlessly. I walked all day.

I returned that evening, and remained outside. Ernie came out and got me. He said they found someone I might know. I reluctantly went back inside and was introduced to Toby. I remembered that name almost immediately. He was a lieutenant with the 2nd Platoon. I recalled Toby because of what took place between him, my platoon leader and my squad leader in RVN, during stand down after Cambodia. I won't go into the story although it was a good comedy show on its own.

After some old war stories and laughter, things seem to get serious. I had a buddy in my squad that I thought had been killed on our last ambush. Toby reassured me this person was still alive and he would forward his e-mail to me. What a shock! Jim was still alive! After all this time of remembering what took place the last day with my squad, I couldn't believe it.

I was glad I went and stayed at the reunion. Toby and his wife Betsy have become close friends to my wife and me. We see each other at least twice a year now.

Toby and I would talk back and forth via e-mail and phone. I needed more than that for I had to see Jim in person to make a face-to-face apology. During that ambush I had tagged Jim for dead. He was a double amputee, extreme blood loss and no pulse that I could feel. It seems I lost it during the ambush, and I was no medic. What a mess that day was. I remember my Lt. giving me Jim's legs as I was sitting on that dust-off, to accompany him back home. It remains one of my worst nightmares!

I made plans to meet with Jim. My flight tickets for September 12, 2001 were in hand. Jim was to pick me up at the Indy Airport on that afternoon. Little did we know that on 9/11 there would be such a tremendous disaster it would immediately and devastatingly change our nation—in fact—the entire world!

Jim's and my plans were put on hold.

On September 11, 2001, I became a different person. I grieved over the terrible tragedy for the loss of so many lives. My mind would go back to Vietnam in so many ways. I had continuous flashbacks that I couldn't cancel out, more so than ever before. I became so selfish and reckless with my thoughts. One of which I'm ashamed to share. I couldn't help but think now the people of the

U.S. might understand how it was for me as a Vietnam Vet to lose so many friends. I would no longer be alone. I would also think to myself and a couple of times out loud: 'The gooks have done it to me again!' That seems to be my favorite thought when things go wrong for me. Plans for Jim and me would come to life in late October 2001. We would finally meet.

What a reunion between two people who haven't seen each other in over 30 years. What a difference to be able to talk with each other without a war all around us. It was too good to be true. I made my apology to Jim. He looked me straight in the eye and said, "No apology needed. I'm alive and I wouldn't have my life any other way." With that said and out of the way he wanted to take me down to Kentucky to see Nick's gravesite. Nick was my squad leader in Vietnam who had been killed in the same ambush August 13, 1970. I agreed, and we set out for the visit.

After an overnight trip we came to the town where Nick was buried. We were at the gravesite paying our respects when all of a sudden we both alerted on an old familiar sound, and simultaneously looked in the same direction. For those who have experienced combat and the pulsating feeling of helicopter rotor blades, you will understand. You feel it before you see or hear it. There were two Cobra helicopter gunships that came out of nowhere. We both knew this was a signal. A sign. Nick was acknowledging us being there. What a feeling! When we were ready to leave, a Red-tailed Hawk made an appearance, screeching and flying directly over us. This Jim would understand, as he is of Indian ancestry and spends several weeks a year on the reservation.

It was now time for us to put Nick to rest. We went to Nick's brother's house and were invited in. Nick's brother and sister were uneasy regarding the explanation of Nick's death. I didn't want to explain the circumstances and Jim didn't either. We both tried to comfort them as best we could but they were persistent in wanting to know how Nicky had died. Finally I came out and told them the truth. Without going into graphic details, they now know Nick was killed in that ambush and they know how his life ended. It wasn't from a bullet to the head, but from an explosion from close proximity to a 155 howitzer round which had been laid out as a booby trap. We also told them about Nick's leadership quality and how well he led his squad. Without Nick, more of our squad would be KIA or WIA.

After returning home I became more agitated and more aware of my declining state of mind. I made an appointment with my private physician. I could no longer sleep and the nightmares and sweats became overwhelming. So much anger. I could no longer communicate with my own family.

I spilled my guts to my doctor. I couldn't hold it in any longer. I would hear the words PTSD for the second time in my life. The first time was with Ernie at the reunion. I had no clue what PTSD meant. When my doctor explained it to me I told her she was full of it. I had come home from Vietnam and had made a life for myself and a good home for my wife and children. I wasn't a Vietnam vet on the corner of a road asking for money or a handout from anyone. She again tried to explain and I refused to listen.

Doc gave me a prescription for Prozac and recommended I seek counseling. I refused the counseling and flushed the Prozac.

Nightmares, sounds, smells, and pulling perimeter guard at my home during the nights seemed normal. I always kept two dogs, both trained and obedient. One for the front door and one for the back door. I always kept loaded weapons at hand just in case.

Comes the 2002 reunion for 5th/60th and I was eager to go this time, feeling the need of the company of those I felt would understand me. Maybe meet someone else I knew in Vietnam. I would meet a couple of other guys who served during my time and knew of the same area of operations. Today we still stay in contact via e-mail. After this second reunion I would slide even more toward the deep end, so much so I returned to my doctor and took the referral to counseling. I was in private counseling for approximately four months, going nowhere. I couldn't bring out what really needed to be said. I guess the counselor and I just didn't click. Things were still getting worse and I had no way to vent. I had given up on communicating with my sons who lived nearby. They wouldn't understand because I had never talked with them about Vietnam. They had seen my old uniform, citations and medals, but I never explained any of that except the Purple Hearts. All they knew was I served in Vietnam and I was wounded there, but I never told them how or why. My wife knew to leave well enough alone, because I had told her in the past I never wanted to talk about it. Married 30 years and we no more often spoke of Vietnam than a person could count the fingers of on one hand.

One morning, after again pulling guard duty at my front window until sunrise, I got dressed and went to work. I stayed about 30 minutes or so then left and never returned as an employee. I went home and locked myself in my room. I stayed there for two weeks. My wife got me back to my doctor who made some phone calls then gave me a name of a VA counselor. I was desperate for help so I went to see her.

Talk about shedding some tears—I just let it happen. I finally found someone who really cared and really understood.

I was put into an anger management group where it took me about six weeks to speak. I would meet some Vietnam vets who were in the same state of mind as I was. I was no longer alone. I would become close friends with some, and we remain close friends today. We seemed to have bonded and trusted each other so much so that we formed our own little group and met every second Thursday without VA interference or supervision.

My counselor and VA psychiatrist recommended me to the VA's new Horizon Group at Menlo Park, CA, which was 80 miles north of my home. They said I would acquire tools to help me with anger management as well as communication skills.

I arrived and attended several days of class. I felt out of place, with mostly drug abusers and alcoholics there. I wasn't having problems with either. I really felt out of place when I learned only three out of the 30 of us were Vietnam vets. I did meet a couple of guys with the same issues as me—communication problems. I would benefit from this eight-week course. I was able to come home on weekends so I stuck it out.

While at New Horizons I was put on medication. Every couple of days I would see a psychiatrist who was interested in my dilemma. I had heard of a program called the PTSD program and talked with the psychiatrist about it. They usually don't make referrals to the program, that was up to your counselor and regular VA psychiatrist. But they made an exception in my case. I would be given an interview with the Menlo Park PTSD staff and was accepted. I took a week off after the New Horizons program was completed and reported back at former Fort Ord. I was extremely upset and stated I wasn't ready for this. Without my wife's blessing, I went anyway.

Once I was at the PTSD program I called my wife the second night and told her to come pick me up. I wasn't going to do this. For the first time in our marriage she refused me. Told me to stick it out a week then we would talk about coming home. I was extremely upset. Several of the guys in the group knew I was disturbed and wanted to leave. They all introduced themselves and we huddled. They told me they had the same feelings when they first arrived.

They talked me into staying and didn't leave any unanswered questions.

This program was an inpatient hospital setting. The program staff consisted of nurses, medical doctors, including psychiatrists, counselors and clergy.

You are given a complete physical including mental. Extensive testing is done including your combat-related stress. It was a community of various types of military veterans, those who had seen combat to those who didn't see combat in the military.

The one part that didn't set well with me was those military vets who had not seen combat. Some of those guys supposedly suffered from PTSD resulting from military duty. I won't go into details.

This PTSD program was a learning center. A place to learn various techniques for dealing with your affliction of PTSD. I was made to understand there is no cure for PTSD, but there are skills you can learn to cope with PTSD. Medication and coping skills (tools) to help change your thinking like your cognizant distortions. Ways to improve your living habits, ways to improve your health, both physically and mentally.

Focus was where you were put together with three others in a small group, revealing the trauma you had encountered during your military tour. Some people had noncombat trauma-related PTSD. Mine was combat-related.

Due to my depressed state of mind, I made plans to hang myself and let it be known during one of my psychiatric sessions. With this the staff was so concerned that even after spending 84 days in this PTSD program, I was committed to a lockdown psychiatric facility in the Palo Alto Hospital. I was no longer in control. I had been held against my wishes by the medical staff for 14 days on a psychiatric hold. The medical staff communicated with my wife and had her remove all of my weapons from my home and made me sign some papers stating by law I couldn't own or purchase any weapons for five years. I was then released and given follow-up appointments with my local counselor and psychiatrist at the old Ft. Ord VA facility. This was late June of 2003.

That summer after being released, my wife and I took off in our car traveling the United States for 45 days. It was one of the best times my wife and I would ever have with each other. During our travel we stopped in Washington, D.C., and planned on spending two days sightseeing. My mistake there was I visited the Vietnam Wall Memorial. I spent approximately 45 minutes there, then got my wife into our car and didn't stop until we reached my sister's home in Ohio. We visited awhile and then set off toward home.

If the PTSD center did any good for me it was that I met and made friends with some Vietnam vets, and that still today we are friends and call each other in our time of need. That's okay with me.

I did make it to the 5th/60th Bn's reunion in 2004 where I would meet eight others from Charlie Rangers Company. What a blessing. It was a good time to have met my former company commander and others. My buddy Jim was there and I would learn a lot about so much I had forgotten, both good and bad.

These days, I mostly spend my days alone in my backyard with my two dogs. I try not to think about the past. But that in itself is a never-ending battle. It's a constant in my life. I have days of loneliness and guilt. If it were not for my group of nine PTSD members I visit with in mutual respect every Thursday afternoon, I would feel far worse.

When life seems to get unbearable in my backyard, I leave for a friend's house in Texas. He lives out in the country near a lake, and he understands where I'm at in my life. It's okay to be there. Far from anyone, fishing on a lake. But now and then I think about career soldiers. Maybe if I had stayed in the Army, maybe with some of them we would have had each other to be with. Help one another. I'm sure we could have told each other war stories, then looked at one another and said: "Hey, it's okay now. Life is good." I'll never know.

May God bless those who have served! And may God bless those who continue to serve. I pray each of you will find peace in your life.

CHAPTER 36

I'LL NEVER FORGET
THE LOOK IN THEIR EYES

My name is Delmer "Buck" Dopp. I served in Vietnam as a Squad Leader, with A Company, 1st Amtrac Battalion, and 3rd Marine Division during 1967-1968. Our Battalion's A and B Companies were grunts, thus we dubbed ourselves AM-Grunts. We were stationed at the mouth of the Cau Viet River in the far north-eastern section of South Vietnam.

Our Battalion area was fairly primitive. The closest town was Dong Ha, about 25 miles southwest straight down the Cau Viet River. Our Grunt companies were unique in that we were all trained Amtrackers who were converted into Infantrymen.

On March 31st, 1968 we were on a sizeable hunt out in the bush looking for our enemy. We primarily fought the North Vietnam Army, better known as the NVA. These were hard core, well-trained, uniformed soldiers who stood and fought, or almost always attacked in large numbers.

Our A and B companies were on a sweep mission along with other Grunts from the 2nd Battalion, 4th Marines and a tank company. Someone asked for a volunteer out of my squad to go north on a recon mission to find and mark a trail that would be suitable for tanks to maneuver over. I volunteered and left with a lieutenant, a mine sweeper and two other Grunts. I didn't know any of these guys so it was kind of an eerie feeling being on a mission with complete strangers.

We marked the trail with white strips of cloth every 20 to 50 feet depending on the conditions of the bush. After a couple hours into our recon, we unexpectedly came upon four NVA soldiers who were buck-naked, taking a bath in a B-52 bomb crater. For a moment I didn't know if they were friendlies or NVA, but a quick glance at their piles of uniforms and weapons gave me the answer. They were an NVA scout team taking advantage of what they thought was a safe place to wash off no telling how many days of dirt and grime.

I'll never forget the look of shock on two of the soldiers looking directly at me as I silently appeared about 20 feet from them. One of them screamed something and they all started scrambling for their rifles that lay a few feet from their reach. The lieutenant and I both opened fire at the same time, killing all four of them before they touched their weapons. We made sure they were all dead, and after taking all the documents they had on them for Intelligence purposes, we continued on our mission.

Shortly after the bomb-hole incident, we came to a wide-open clearing about as big as a football field. The lieutenant told us to hold up at the edge of the clearing while he radioed for the main force, tanks first, as usual, to move to our position.

About 30 minutes later I could hear the noise of the tanks coming our way. When the lead tank passed by where I was kneeling— about 10 to 15 feet to my left—*wham!* There was an instant flash of red-orange hot light accompanied by a powerful force of concussion. A moment of silence was followed by faint voices I was able to detect despite my loudly ringing ears; "Anyone hurt?"

I quickly checked my body. I had been blown a good distance by the concussion. I felt pain in my left arm and leg. I saw black gunpowder, ripped clothing, and blood on my arm and leg. I became immediately aware that I was seriously wounded.

The minesweeper had missed the antitank mine. I was the only one wounded and due to the seriousness, I was transported back to the rear-area medical station in a good old Amtrack that came rumbling up the trail to collect me.

This would be my last mission. I would soon be leaving Vietnam as I had just received my third Purple Heart. There was a rule: three hearts and you're out of the game. There were many, many Marines in my outfit who left 'Nam that way, some not nearly as lucky as me. I was happy as hell to be heading out. I had seen more than enough action. The Tet offensive in January and February of '68 was really hell. I'd had my share of facing the grim reaper in the eye and coming out of it alive.

Within a few days I was in Okinawa, Japan. I spent a couple of weeks laying around doing nothing in a Casualty Company and was then assigned to a unit that was in charge of security for a hush-hush building out in the boonies. Loved it! Turned out to be Have Party & Get Rowdy Time, and I got drunk damn near every night I was off. Also got into two or three fights a week. This was a sudden change and a totally out of character thing for me. I figured somewhere along the line I had somehow become overly sensitive about things, and if I thought someone looked or seemed threatening or disrespectful to me, I would start throwing punches. Seemed like I got to where I really enjoyed the fights. Felt like some sort of a needed release for me, and I had absolutely no fear of other men no matter their size or number. Seemed suddenly there was a different and wild side of me becoming apparent. For sure it was a wild time.

I arrived back in the states in December '68. I didn't experience any of the jeering that I heard so many other returning guys had to deal with at airports. It was all rather uneventful in that area for me.

I landed at the small airport near my home of Scott City, Missouri. I remember it was about midnight. My dad, the greatest guy I ever knew, picked me up and we drove the short distance to my grandmother's house where my grandma, mother, and three sisters were all waiting to give me a warm reception. Whew! I'd made it.

I had joined the Marine Corps shortly after high school in 1965. I spent three years in the Marines, been to nearly a dozen foreign countries, been to war and now I was back home and a civilian again.

The next day I went to town and bought me some civvies, put all my military stuff in a few boxes that I soon afterwards threw away.

I didn't face the usual situation most 'Nam vets did when they had to go straight from the bush and a week later found themselves back home. I had been in Okinawa for several months. There I had escaped the horrors of war long enough for me to reacclimatize to a noncombat environment. It seemed to me at the time that I had done my bit—Vietnam was now a part of my past—a place I would never have to deal with again.

I didn't have the slightest inkling that 15 years later Vietnam would return to haunt me on a daily basis. Turns out Vietnam would have a profound influence on me for the rest of my life.

I've been told it was probably always with me from my first

exposure to combat. I didn't realize it just then nor did I recognize what an important influence 'Nam had made in my life.

Now, after years of therapy I can look back and see what combat did to shape my life all the way along to today. It has been an interesting, sometimes horrifying, sometimes dangerous journey, but today at age 57 I can still hear the sounds, smell the odors, taste the tastes, but most of all, feel the feelings of the 20-year-old Marine squad leader who is lucky enough now to at least recognize and understand the handicaps I received from serving my country in Vietnam. My road back home has taken some unusual twists.

The first couple of years after my return continued to be mostly party time for me. I attended college on the GI Bill, drank a lot of booze, still got into fights, but basically I thought everything was okay.

I very seldom spoke about Vietnam. There seemed to be a collective mindset among 'Nam vets. *Don't talk about your experiences. Keep everything inside. Forget about it.* Given the fact that so many of our contemporaries viewed the war in a variety of negative ways, swayed by the slant given by the mainstream media, I believe that the majority of us just tried to quietly assimilate back into society.

Plus the government started to retreat on the war and the warriors. Fuck it! Maybe our service wasn't honorable or worthy of praise. Maybe it had just been a big mistake. I still felt proud of myself but didn't want to share my thoughts of Vietnam. I tried to pretend it didn't matter—but it did.

After a couple of years in college, I married, had two kids, a good work record as an engineer on the railroad, had stopped fighting and drank a lot less. Hell, I was living the American dream and was strong emotionally. There were some signs of depression at times, but I was always able to regain my optimism by recalling what I had told myself dozens of times in Vietnam when in life-threatening situations. "If I ever get back to the real world alive and well—I'll never bitch about anything, unless someone is again trying to kill me." This credo has helped and continues to help me cope with adversities in life.

I don't remember exactly when, but I remember how I started experiencing PTSD. I was reading an article in one of those Playboy-type magazines which had to do with an assault on a village in Vietnam. It was from the grunts' perspective and well written. It roiled feelings in me that overwhelmed the stoic, strong but silent type person I had been for several years now. As I continued to read, tears suddenly came flooding and adrenaline began pumping. By the time I finished the article I was totally exhausted. Afterwards my thoughts on 'Nam increased, and I discovered I was entering a new world—a world of deep depression, pervasive thoughts of Vietnam, hyperalertness, nightmares, flashbacks, anger, manic stints and more.

Slowly over the next few years the symptoms began to surface more and more. I divorced after 11 years of marriage, bought me a Harley, and began to hang out with crowds I should have avoided. I found myself back in very dangerous situations. Got shot at, was in knife fights, had about a dozen car wrecks, two motorcycle accidents, a head-on collision between two trains and other problems.

A fellow Vietnam veteran friend of mine told me about PTSD. It was the first I'd heard of it. He told me I showed definite signs of having it. I shrugged it off. Hell, I was too tough for something like that. No way could I succumb to any emotional or mental problems. I was in complete denial.

I remarried for the second time. My wife worked in the psyche ward at the local hospital, and recognizing that I needed help, she talked me into seeing a shrink. I couldn't believe I was actually sitting in a psychiatric office talking about my depression. I was diagnosed as bipolar, manic-depressive and started taking some pills, which helped me to feel better. In the meantime my wife and I separated after only four months of marriage and were divorced two months later. I began to feel much better and decided I didn't need the medication anymore. Stopped my pills and visits to the doctor.

I got involved in Vietnam Veterans' movements. I met important players on the local, state, and national political levels. I put myself a hundred percent into doing all I could do to fight the fight—and help the veterans. Correct the wrongs! Although I was a dedicated activist, my skills at being politically correct were poor. I could put on the correct suit, and smile for the cameras, but I made enemies here and there with my manic-depressive cycles. During some of those times I became nearly impossible to get along with. I felt as if I were a squad leader again back in 'Nam. I didn't need to be concerned about anything but getting the job done. I finally realized that for me to do what I'd set out to do, it would be necessary to kiss some ass and at times sleep with the devil. I couldn't do either one. I'm glad that some of the brothers could. I still helped when and where I could, and there were some gains made. In fact, over time, many goals have been achieved.

Where once the government denied that Agent Orange caused harm to anyone, millions of dollars have now been paid to ailing veterans who had been exposed to it. Mission accomplished. Also, the need to search for the POWs and MIAs is now a well-funded program that even today is still finding our military personnel's remains and finally bringing them home so families can have closure. The historical importance of the Vietnam War, which once could hardly be found in textbooks, is now offered as credited college and university courses. We turned the tide of public opinion about us from shamed losers to revered and honorable warriors who did a superb job on the battlefield.

We came home to no glory, but we now stand proudly alongside the veterans of all wars, past and present. We lobbied not only the politicians, but also the media, the academic world, and have worked our way to the top of society. We are now recognized as successful lawyers, doctors, business executives, professors, congressmen, senators, and vice presidents of the U.S. and undoubtedly, someday one of us will become President and Commander-In-Chief. We have memorials erected in every state honoring the Vietnam Veteran. There are finally dozens of good books and movies to promote our image in a more positive manner.

However there are still more initiatives that need to be addressed. We should rotate troops in war zones, not as individuals, but as units. When they return home we should shower them with gratitude and give those who need it counseling and ID early any symptoms of PTSD.

I was proud to be a part of some of these successes, however small, but I again crashed. I went through more manic-depressive cycles and once more decided I needed some help. I went back to the doctor and for years religiously attended individual and group counseling sessions and slowly came to realize some of my symptoms would probably last a lifetime. Nightmares, hypervigilance, acute reaction to loud noises, and other reminders of 'Nam such as smells, tastes, visual images—both real and imagined in my mind's eye—bouts of depression, feelings of survivor's guilt, reluctance to form close relationships, inability to cope well under stressful situations, throw in and totally from out of nowhere a flashback now and then and you've got yourself a good old dose of PTSD.

This discovery tweaked the hell out of my system. For the first time in my life I was talking in detail about things I had been through in Vietnam. It was a surreal journey back to remembering details I had blacked out over the years. I started to realize how 'Nam had made me numb to the fact of death and mayhem.

After seven years of VA therapy, I felt like I didn't need to continue anymore with the sessions. I've pretty well come to grips with my disorders. I still visit my shrink every six months and take my prescribed meds. I'm classified 100 percent disabled—PTSD—so I have enough money to live on. I lay kind of low and am about to get married for the fourth time. I try to avoid stress and stay out of trouble.

All in all I'm glad I served my country as a Marine in Vietnam. I regret that PTSD has stunted my participation and productivity in society, but those are the cards I've been dealt. I smile when I can and try to keep it all in proper perspective. "If someone's not trying to kill you—it don't mean nothing."

Semper Fi, and may God bless all of you my brothers-and-sisters-in-arms!

CHAPTER 37

THERE IS NO END

In reading rough drafts of the book, and sharing my thoughts with others, I often heard comments like, "What's the conclusion? To what end is the book written?" In an immediate gratification society, we always want instant answers; "Where's the beef?" In *Finding Hope & Understanding In Life After Combat* there is no simple answer. I do know, however, there is a common thread that weaves itself through all veterans. They feel there is no one to talk to; there is no one who will understand. So, they remain silent, bottling up their memories and emotions. This book has mentioned several things that will help, such as unit reunions. What works for one may not work for another. As a nation, we must understand war affects all it touches. For many veterans, there is no conclusion, there is no end. It was best said in a book by James Bradley *Flags of our Fathers* as the marines stormed the beach for the battle for Iwo Jima, Private Tex Stanton stated, "Life was never regular again. We were changed from the day we put our feet in that sand."

I hope everyone will understand.

— Lee

P.S. If there is a key, it is most often held by those closest to your heart. For me, there has always been one person who understood; one person who never wavered in her support. It is my wife of 34 years, Ellen. Her story follows.

CHAPTER 38

IT'S ONLY A MOVIE

Ellen Alley

I was 20 years old. The war in Vietnam was winding down. I never paid much attention to war. Born after WWII, I'd only heard about Vietnam in school. Wrapped up in being me, my world revolved around my immediate life and those around me. I was like most of us were at that age. War was not real to me.

I met Lee Alley during the fall semester of 1971 at the University of Wyoming. I'm not quite sure when I became aware that Lee had been a soldier and was now a veteran of the Vietnam War. We never talked about it. No one in his family ever mentioned it. He never said. I never asked. We were married in late 1972.

My new husband struggled with nightmares, but he never said what the nightmares were about. I shook him once to wake him from one of his frequent bad dreams, and he leapt from bed, crouched to the floor and looked around wild-eyed. After he quickly recovered his senses, he said, "Don't do that again." I didn't.

He startled easily, especially at loud banging noises: sonic booms, gun shots, and firecrackers. It was a part of him I came to accept. I stopped laughing after the first few times because of the brief look of terror I saw in his eyes. Others who didn't look that closely never ceased to be amused when Lee would throw himself to the ground at the crackle and pop of the first firecracker on the 4th of July.

Why didn't I ask him about his nightmares? Why didn't I ask about his service? The truth: It wasn't real to me. These days, two conflicting questions puzzle me: How could I have asked about something that I didn't relate to or even understand to be real? How could I have been so naïve and insensitive?

Over the last several years, as Lee slowly emerged from his silent suffering, people have thanked me for caring for Lee all these years and for what I've done for him. They don't know that I never did anything. Until a few years ago, I had not even thanked him for his service in the military.

Lee is what he is because of his personal strength and will, not mine. He has been the backbone of our family, the strong one, the solid one. Other than the occasional jumpiness and persistent nightmares, Lee hid his scars and internal struggles from me, the children, and the world.

People sometimes ask, "What's it like being married to a war hero?" My answer is that when you don't know they're a war hero, it's like being married to anyone else. I've been blessed because Lee is an extraordinary individual. He is compassionate, caring, and even-tempered. He did a thorough job of hiding the memories of war deep inside. I asked him once about his time in the Army, he responded, "A few years after Vietnam, I decided the only way to live in *this* world was to leave that one behind." To his credit, he tried to do that; but, his mind betrayed him. War haunts Lee, as it does many veterans. Candidly, he quit drinking heavily after we met, but became a work-a-holic instead. Lee would do just about anything to try and exhaust himself so the ghosts would stay at bay.

Knowing what I know now, I have realized many things. Lee wasn't just being a gentleman when he pulled my chair out to seat me with *my* back to the door, and he took his seat with his back to the wall. He wasn't ignoring me when he marched ahead of me as we walked down the street and not beside me. He wasn't searching the room for friends as he took a quick recon of his surroundings at a public gathering.

I was married for 30 years to a veteran and a war hero and I didn't even know it. How could I have been so unaware? I have wrestled the last few years with this question. You see, it was a phone call about six years ago that brought the box of war memorabilia off the shelf and out of the closet. These last couple of years have been an emotional roller-coaster ride for both Lee and me.

It was the first reunion in Denver, Colorado, 2001, when it hit me. Over a shared life of 30 years, I had been given glimpses into Lee's year in Vietnam. His pain had become my pain; his secrets had become my secrets; his past had become a part of me. When I met his comrades-in-arms, they were instantly family. The flood-

LEE ALLEY & WADE STEVENSON

gates of emotion opened for them, and for me. I wept and still weep with them and for them. My heart breaks for all veterans and for what they carry inside.

America is blind to what we've done to our veterans. We have ignored them and have expected them to just go on with life. We do not stop to value the price they've paid. I can't believe that I, a wife of 30-plus years, did not see the pain. Could I have done something? Are there other moms, dads, brothers, sisters, wives, kids, and friends who do not acknowledge the veterans in their lives and their service? Why do we not say a simple "Thank you" or "Welcome home," or teach our fellow Americans to do the same? It is time we Americans recognize the changes war brings about in every person who has ever served. We can help. We can do something.

During the last year, I've gained a better understanding of our collective ignorance and apathy. For most of us, it's just not real. It's only a movie. Most of us have only seen the TV shows, the movies, and photos of war. We weren't there. The unfortunate fact is: We will never fully understand. We, as a society, have been conditioned to deal with the unknowns and tragedies of life by living by the following sayings: "Out of sight out of mind." "Ignore it and it will go away." "Don't think about bad things." "Change the subject and let's talk about something fun." "Don't talk to survivors about the loss of a loved one." "Pretend it never happened."

What can we do? As non-veterans we can start by saying, "Thank You." You can begin to understand that the soldier is changed and will never be the same. You can accept that you will never fully comprehend what they have experienced. Introduce them to a fellow veteran. Any veteran. It doesn't matter what war a veteran fought in, their emotions, memories, and scars are similar. They all share similar feelings. Love them. Honor them as the heroes they all are. Thank them for their service and the sacrifices they've made for our country. Never pass up a veteran of any age without telling them you are proud of them and you appreciate their military service.

Despite your thoughts and feelings on war, never, ever condemn the soldier. They honor each of us and our nation by their service. It's OK to hate war. It's not OK to disrespect our soldiers. If you didn't like the curriculum in a school, would you attack the students? Our nation is on the brink of facing some major problems.

Soldiers with pain and guilt are returning from our current war and will not initially be able to grasp why they can't just get back to a normal life. It won't help that some Americans will not be able to grasp why our veterans just can't get back to a normal life. It seems neither of us know what to do.

My prayer is that this book could be read by every American. My message is: America, we need to open our eyes. If we are going to continue to send our most valuable resource, the young men and women of our country, off to war to fight on foreign soils, then we must also begin to see that they will come back from war forever changed. War changes everyone it touches. Johnny will never be Johnny again and we need to accept that and accept him. It's time that we Americans stand up and show respect for, honor, and acknowledge our veterans. They have all paid a price for freedom in a way that we will never fully comprehend.

Lee says: "The down payment for the price of freedom is paid for with the sacrifice and blood of our fallen soldiers; the balance is paid for by the lifetime mortgage that is taken out on the lives of our surviving veterans."

In closing, if you are a veteran, you are not alone. The feelings that you have are common and shared by other veterans. Don't let phrases like these prevent you from seeking out the camaraderie of your brotherhood: "No one will understand." "No one wants to hear about my experiences." "I don't want anyone to know what I did over there." "If my family or friends knew what I did, they would be ashamed." "Why did I live and my comrade die?" "I should have been the one to die."

To family members and friends of veterans, I compassionately pass along this to you: Be gentle. In addition to thanking them, acknowledge the fact that they have been at war. Let them know you want to listen if they want to talk; but, don't be surprised if they don't. If they do, just listen. Don't judge. You can't even truly empathize because *you weren't there*. And, I've learned that they don't want our sympathy. Connect them with a fellow veteran. Educate yourself with what is available in the form of medical and mental assistance for veterans. If they do decide to get help, it will most likely come from the insistence of a fellow veteran. That's OK. They are not shutting you out, they're just afraid to let you in…right now.

To all veterans of all wars, I say "Thank You and Welcome Home." I appreciate the sacrifices you have made for me and our country. To our new veterans, I urge you: Do not spend 30 or more years alone with your memories. Recognize now, instead of later, that you are going to have struggles because you are changed forever. Ask for help. To the older veterans of past wars, find a way to let it out. You, too, may need some help. To every soldier, search out other veterans and go to reunions of your unit. What you have done was done in the name of honor and freedom for our great nation. Nothing you did or didn't do is shameful. Each and every one of you is a hero. Be proud. You are a part of our past and part of our future. Tell your story. And finally, seek those you served with and see if *they* need help. You fought for them and with them in war, fight for them and with them now, in life.

God Bless America and the American soldier.

PART FOUR

SECURE THE AREA
& CLOSE DOWN

EPILOGUE

I believe that within every person who has had a traumatic experience in combat there is a story, or possibly a book. It just needs the right set of circumstances to come to fruition. It's taken me several years and only after much repeated, gentle nudging from a man I greatly admire, Hector Villarreal, did I actually force myself to begin to put some of my memories down on paper. My reluctance has always been based on the feeling that, *in actual fact, I really don't see anything heroic in what I did.* Rather, I've seen myself simply as a 21-year-old from Laramie, Wyoming who happened to be thrown into what turned out to be our nation's least popular war. A sudden real-life situation where the sights, sounds, and stench of war instantly became a harsh reality.

Although I am very proud of my service and would go back in a heartbeat, I had hoped war would skip this generation. My feelings, I'm sure, are not uncommon among fathers. "Take me, don't take my son." This prayer was not answered as the blood of our American young is once again being spilled on foreign soil. I am not writing this to argue the policies of our government, but rather to reinforce the idea *we must learn from our mistakes.* Let's bring our veterans home in a celebration of pride of their service to our great country! War, any part or parcel of it, is difficult enough—to the extreme—without compounding the problems our young warriors will experience when returning home.

If we as a nation are willing to send our armed forces to the far corners of the world in defense of freedom, why is it so difficult to look those same soldiers, sailors, marines and airmen in the eye when they, by the grace of God, return home to us as veterans? I often hear, "Johnny has changed. He's not the same person we knew when he went away."

I respond, "Of course he has changed! The arms of the eighteen or twenty-year-old who not long ago held his prom date or some other special friend or loved one are the same arms which some twelve months later are holding or carrying a wounded or dying soldier.

Another special someone of whom he has grown fond and cares for as a close friend and comrade. Of course he's changed. If he has been blessed and is lucky enough to return home from war, how could he not change under those conditions?"

We, if we care for our loved ones, must show it, accept and acknowledge those changes. We owe it to them, and it's the least we can do. These veterans are the today and tomorrow's walking, breathing history of our great and proud nation. Look history (any veteran) in the eye, embrace the occasion, be proud of it, and learn from it.

Let them know we care! Give him and her a warm smile, an encouraging pat on the back, a high-five!

Please, let them know we care.

The VA Claims Process

Getting Help Early:
How To Do It Right

My name is Robert Craft. I have been the VFW's Department Service Officer for Wyoming since June 1994. I am a member of the VFW's National Legislative Committee. Prior to retiring from the U.S. Army, I was a helicopter pilot and aviation maintenance officer. My assignments include serving overseas with the 4th Infantry Division, the 2nd Infantry Division, the 8th Infantry Division, 5th Corps, and 8th U.S. Army Headquarters.

The Army aircraft I flew were the UH-1 Huey, the AH-1 Cobra, and the OH-58 Kiowa. I was involved in the operational tests of the AH-64 Apache prior to its acceptance into the Army inventory.

In recognition and appreciation of faithful military service, the United States government provides health care, disability compensation, pension, rehabilitation, and other veteran's benefits to eligible veterans, their families, and survivors. The Department of Veterans Affairs (VA) administers these programs through their network of VA Medical Centers, outpatient clinics, and Regional Offices located throughout the country.

Veterans service organizations, such as the American Legion, Disabled American Veterans, and the Veterans of Foreign Wars have dedicated themselves to the mission of assisting veterans and their families in obtaining those entitlements earned and justly deserved by serving in the Armed Forces. Numerous veterans service organizations, most states, and many counties have veterans service offices that are dedicated to easing the anxiety and reducing the confusion of those seeking assistance from the VA. Veterans service officers are a vital link in a complex and highly technical VA claims processing system that can become quite lengthy.

Veterans Service Officers assist veterans, their dependants, or survivors with their VA claim. Services are provided at no charge and without regard to membership in the veterans service organization and are located throughout the country at VA Regional Offices and some VA Medical Centers. Many states and counties have Veterans Service Officers who assist with VA claims processing.

Veterans Service Officers can assist with the filing of your VA claim and will help identify evidence or other records necessary to support your claim. If your claim is denied, professional Veterans Service Officers can assist with an Appeal to the Board of Veterans Appeals.

One of the keys to a successful VA claim is to get help early. Seek out an advocate who will assist you with your claim and will protect your interests. Search for an advocate who knows the VA's rules and regulations and understands the complexities of claims development. Thank you for your service to your country and good luck!

OTHER SOURCES TO CONTACT FOR HELP

With the Internet one can access many resources for help. Below is a listing that we're aware of at this time. Remember there's constant changing and updating of this type of information. Make sure you have a good, reputable site when seeking trustworthy information.

www.military.com
8 million members – Connects service members, military families & veterans to all benefits of Service; government benefits, scholarships, discounts, friends, mentors, stories of life/missions.
Click on Veterans Report

http://grunt.space.swri.edu/armylf.htm
U.S. Army Lost and Found Locator
To locate lost comrades

www.no-quarter.org
Vietnam Casualty Search
This is the best of the search engines for Vietnam KIAs

http://cybersarges.tripod.com/casualties.html
Statistics on Vietnam War Casualties

www.sdit.org
Sons and Daughters in Touch (SDIT)
Children of KIA Veterans

http://9thinfdivsociety.org
9th Infantry Division information, reunions, photos and history

www.oldreliable.org
Helps find 9th Division Veterans

www.mrfa.org
Mobile Riverine Force information

www.va.gov
> U.S. Department of Veterans Affairs
> Veterans Administration

www.bigredone.org
> Division information

www.tommyfranks.com
> Commander of Operation Enduring Freedom/Afghanistan and
> Operation Iraqi Freedom

www.fortunecity.com/underworld/defender/153/al1.htm
> 5th Battalion Headquarters Company – Mechanized

www.angelfire.com/gundam/vietnam/
> Alpha Company – Mechanized

www.angelfire.com/gundam/vietnam/bcomp1.html
> Bravo Company - Mechanized

www.vfw.org
> Veterans of Foreign Wars Official site

www.vva.org
> Vietnam Veterans of America
> Non profit, congressionally chartered. Founding Principle:
> "Never again will one generation of veterans abandon another."

http://etext.lib.virginia.edu/kjv.browse.html
> International Ministries
> Complete Bible; King James Version with Revised Standard
> Comparison

www.archives.gov/veterans/
> U.S. National. Archives & Records Administration
> Military services records

www.crsc.army.mil
"Combat Related Special Compensation"
Links to Wounded Warrior Project

www.ssa.gov
U.S. Social Security Administration Official site

www.firstgov.gov
Interagency portal to government agencies and services administered by U.S. General Services Administration's Office of Citizen Services & Communications

www.govbenefits.gov
Federal site which provides access to government assistance programs

www.defenselink.mil
Department of Defense official site
Links to the Pentagon Channel

www.tricare.osd.mil
Official site for tricare beneficiaries & military staff

www.dod.mil/dfas/
Defense Finance & Accounting Service
Civilian workforce who provide financial and accounting services for the Department of Defense military services - Army, Navy, Air Force, Marine Corps - and other Defense agencies

www.usmc.mil
Marine Corps

www.uscg.mil
Coast Guard

www.defendamerica.mil
News about the troops on the frontlines in the Global War on Terrorism

www.senate.gov
>Session schedules, legislation, senators list, history, etc.

www.house.gov
>U.S. House of Representatives

www.ready.gov
>U.S. Homeland Security
>Emergency preparedness for citizens, businesses, and kids

www.medicare.gov
>U.S. Department of Health and Human Services
>Official site for Medicare recipients

http://www.nmfa.org
>National Military Family Association

www.operationpurple.org
>NMFA's Operation Purple Summer Camps
>A free program helping military children of deployed
>service members

http://www1.va.gov/directory/guide/home.asp
>VA Facilities Locator and Directory

Telephone & Yellow Page Office Contacts

Department of Veterans Affairs..............1-800-827-1000

Veterans Administration
Benefits & Assistance 1-800-827-1000

VFW Helpline 1-800-VFW-1899

VA Office of Inspector General Hotline ..1-800-488-8244

Disabled Veterans National HQ (DAV).....1-859-441-7300

DAV National Svc Foundation 1-859-441-7300

The American Legion, Washington, DC ..1-202-861-2700

Veteran's Special Issue Helpline 1-800-749-8387

National Military Family Association 1-800-260-0218

Dos & Don'ts

I am neither a psychiatrist nor a psychologist and certainly don't have a lock on the Secrets of Life. However, from my own experiences and talking with other veterans, I have compiled a simple list of dos and don'ts that perhaps may help some readers. I hope one clicks for you.

Don't

1. **Don't sit on a barstool and tell everyone what a war hero you are.** First of all you are talking to the wrong crowd. Ninety percent of the bar patrons could not care less, plus they have their own agenda. Second, most of the bar stories have huge credibility problems, and anyone present who's "been there, done that" can spot the half-truths instantly. The answers aren't in the bottle, I've looked. Please, my brother, don't do it!

2. **Don't buy into or pick up on the warmonger, baby killer, psycho, misfit label** given to the veterans by the antiwar and Hollywood activists. You, like me, are just an average American young man or woman who sincerely felt they were answering the call of our great nation. Not everyone is willing to do that. You are now a member of an elite group. Stand and walk tall. Be proud! You've earned the privilege many times over.

3. **Don't ever apologize for your MOS—a role while in a combat zone.** I have talked to countless veterans who have said, "I was just a truck driver." "I was just a mechanic." "I was just a routine repairman." When I hear this I immediately grab the individual, hug them, and thank them for my life. When you are pinned down, can't move, taking casualties, grab a radio, and call for medevac, or artillery gunships, the most important people at that moment in time are the routine repairman, mechanic, etc. Whether I get out of this situation largely depends on everything coming together as a team, how each person does his or her job.

4. Don't beat yourself up for surviving war. This may sound strange but, in reality, it is an emotional roller coaster many veterans ride. The horrors of war play strange games with our minds. Far too often the Purple Heart, for physical wounds, and the emotional wounds for which there is no medal come with a price. For many it is the guild of survivorship. *Why did I survive and my best friend not? Could I have done more? It should have been me, not him!* I don't know. I don't have the answer. I can only say I truly believe if you are given a second, sometimes third and fourth chance at life, there is a reason. With survivorship comes a duty for you to carry on. Set an example, your purpose, the reason for your living will come.

Do

1. Get registered with the VA medical center. As a veteran you have earned this right; it is not welfare. Once in the system I was shocked not only by the amount of services available, but also by the true caring individuals I have come in contact with. **Do it!**

2. If you have problems i.e. medical, emotional, getting your questions answered - **get yourself a caseworker.** The VFW, American Legion, Purple Heart Association all have paid staffs eager to help. **Do it!**

3. Let it be known within your community you are a returning veteran and are willing to speak to civic groups. All groups, i.e. Lions Club, Kiwanis, Rotary, have guest speakers on their programs. You don't have to be an eloquent speaker. You are the living history of our nation. Speak from the heart. These short talks are not only information to an unknowing public but, equally important, voicing your feelings, concerns and experiences is very therapeutic. **Do it!**

4. Do let your local schools know you are willing to be interviewed by students. At some point in all history and civics classes your war will be covered. Teachers and students alike are always looking for up-close and personal experiences. You have them. Show it. The students love it—and it helps all when you share. **Do it!**

5. Do stay in contact with your war buddies. Your war experiences will tie you together forever. When the consequences of decisions and actions can be the difference between life and death, a bond develops that time and distance will never erase. I often hear, "I'm not ready," or "I just need to get away." I understand completely. However, I must recommend at the very least, *please* write down names and addresses, and phone numbers of your comrades while they are fresh. There will come a time when it feels right. **Do it!**

6. Join local VFW and American Legion units; the fellowship is great. It's not just a bunch of old veterans sitting at the bar telling war stories. Projects vary, such as putting out flags on Veterans and Memorial Day. Sponsor patriotic speech and writing contests in public schools. Contact them. Find the right one for you. **Do it!**

7. Do help set up and attend military reunions. These reunions can vary from Division 5th/60th, i.e. 9th Infantry, 1st Infantry | to Squadron 512. Get together. I feel the better reunions are the smaller more personal ones, Company to Squadron size. These are where your real attachments are. However, it is important to attend the large ones—Battalion-size or Company—because this is where the connections are made. From the large reunions the more personal ones seem to spin off. **Do it!**

8. Do look in the top of the closet or the trunk in the attic. The memories you buried are there. Get them out. Look at them, show them. I am proud of you. I thank you, and I love you.

Welcome home my brothers and sisters!

— *Lee*

SAMPLE REUNION AGENDA

Putting on and attending a military reunion is something I highly recommend. These reunions give both veterans and family members a setting where we can deal with the issues of having no one to talk to or no one who understands.

In planning the reunion there are very few must dos, as each unit is different. However, we insist on three items:

1) **Location must be near a major airline hub.** Cost and frequency of flights are important.

2) **Major hotel close to airport with complimentary shuttle service.** Surrounding tourist sites and activities are not as important as we find most attendees never leave the hotel.

3) **Must have a local coordinator.** We have always picked locations where we have an Association member as our point man in finding hotels and handling local arrangements, such as finding a local dignitary to speak to our veterans.

Hotels should offer free meeting rooms, banquet rooms, and one to two suites in return for number of rooms/nights reserved.

THE AGENDA

It is the feeling of our Association that a fairly structured agenda is necessary. People like to know what is going on at all times. Having said that, make sure time is available for small group discussion and for individuals to reconnect.

We've found this type of sample agenda to be effective:

Wednesday: Officers of our Association fly into a location to go over agenda and meet hotel staff in order to discuss room sizes, conference areas, menus, etc.

Thursday: 1-5 pm. Registration room opens.

5-7 pm. Ice Breaker: Hosted by the Association.

7 pm- . Dinner on your own.

Friday: **8-9 am.** Continental breakfast in large meeting hall.

9-10 am. Official welcome is usually by a local dignitary. Welcome by Association President. Review agenda with group.

10 am-12 pm. Begin "Group Talk Around". We pass a cordless mic around and allow each veteran to introduce themselves, tell where they were and when, and just talk about whatever is on their minds or hearts. This may take all day, but the dividends are huge. Some have not talked about their war experience for many years, i.e. for Vietnam Veterans, it's the first time in 30+ years.

12-1:30 pm. Lunch break.

12-1:30 pm. "Others Luncheon" This is a luncheon for non-veterans: wives, partners, children, parents, etc. We encourage a talk around for these folks where family members tell each other what their life is like living with or around a veteran. Once again, it is a place where people understand each other and can relate. We've seen some good healing go on in these luncheons.

1:30-4:30 pm. Continue "Group Talk Around".

6-7 pm. Cocktail party, usually pool side.

7 pm- . Dinner on your own.

Saturday: **9-10 am.** Continental breakfast.

10 am-12 pm. History of Association presentation. We have a historian who has compiled the history of the unit from our deployment from Ft Riley, Kansas, through the years in Vietnam and to the retiring of the colors back in the states. His presentation also includes first hand reflections from others in attendance. This section is consistently powerful, interesting and well received.

12-1:30 pm. Lunch break.

1:30 pm. Group pictures. We always hire a professional photographer who not only takes group pictures, but also puts together a memory book usually costing around $20-$22.

2-5 pm. Small Groups Discussions. Small groups can be done by Company, Platoon, years of service, significant battles or campaigns. Each group should be assigned a leader. As with all activities, we encourage family members to participate.

6-7 pm. Cocktail hour in banquet room.

7-10 pm. Association Banquet. Evening will include presentations and special recognition of individuals, plus two or three speakers. Speakers a) are always chosen from within the association (all units have interesting or talented people) and b) should limit their speeches to 10-15 minutes.

Sunday: **9-10 am.** Association membership meeting for the purposes of general business, election of officers, preliminary discussions of future reunions, etc.

10 am- . Memorial Service for our Fallen Brothers. Representatives are picked from each company to read the names, not only of those who sacrificed their lives in war, but also those who have passed on since the conflict. A brief inspiration message can be included and delivered by a "minister-type" veteran, preferably one who is a member of your association. We've found this to be a very emotional time.

For additional information on the 5th/60th Association, please visit: http://5thbattalion.tripod.com/alpha.html.

ABOUT THE AUTHOR
LEE ALLEY

Lee Alley was born into a Wyoming ranching family in 1946 and is one of seven children. Lee always felt he was just a country boy from Wyoming, but within the ranks and archives of the US Army's 5th/60th Infantry Division, he became a legend to all who knew and served with him. He is also described as Wyoming's Audie Murphy in author Keith Nolan's best-selling novel, *Playing the Enemy's Game.* Lee was one of the Division's highest acclaimed and decorated Vietnam-era soldiers. He was then, and even more importantly remains today, highly admired and respected by all of his former brothers-in-arms—his superiors, equals and subordinates alike. He was tough, demanding, yet boyish and immediately likeable all at the same time. Most significantly, he stood out as a tried, tested, and true leader of men.

During his many combat encounters and some of Vietnam's documented most dangerous and embattled operations, he was a steadfast, caring commander of his unit and men. He seemed cut from the original and genuine mold of a soldier's soldier.

Lee earned and carried a true hero's reputation by always placing his men's safety and well-being above all else. At the infamous Battle of Fire Base Cudgel when his unit of 35 men was being overrun by a Vietnamese force of from 150 to 200 enemies, he ordered his men to retreat and made a singular defensive final stand in his bunker using every possible weapon available.

He, alone, guarded and protected his men against that over-whelming enemy force until his men were able to reach safety across a river. He was wounded in the process, but miraculously also escaped from the enemy and resumed command of his unit.

For those actions and for his many other acts of courage during his service to his country, he was nominated for the nation's highest military award, the Congressional Medal of Honor. Awards he received include the U.S. Army's highly coveted Distinguished Service Cross for honor and for valor, the Silver Star, Bronze Star, two Purple Hearts, the Soldier's Medal, two Air Medals, National Defense Service Medal, the Vietnamese Cross of Gallantry, and Combat Infantry Man Badge. Lieutenant Alley attended the Army's

Airborne Jump School and earned his Jump Wings at Fort Benning, Georgia, and from the Jungle Warfare School in Panama, he proudly wore his Jungle Expert Badge. On Veterans Day 2004, the Daughters of the American Revolution honored Lee with their most prestigious Medal of Honor for his "leadership, trustworthiness, service and patriotism."

Most recently Lee has been selected and honored by the Governor of Wyoming to serve on the State Veterans Council. The local VFW Post in Wheatland honored him in 2004 for providing Outstanding Service to Veterans of the Community. Lee is the featured veteran on the Victnam War portion of the memorial in Veterans Park, Casper, Wyoming. His hometown of Wheatland presented him with a Certificate of Civic Achievement in 1997.

Lee has traveled all around the country (coast to coast and in between) giving speeches, attending reunions, formal military cere-monies/awards and other functions. He is specifically sought out and always responds positively to help with special military functions, holidays and any event honoring our veterans. He routinely accepts invitations to speak at schools and civic organizations. *He is always there for our veterans and whenever asked to help our troops.*

Upon his return from 'Nam he, like many of his fellow veterans, struggled with overcoming the horrific memories of warfare and the many negatives associated with that unpopular conflict. He had his own dark haunting moments of fear—his own unwanted reflections, memories of the guns, the sounds, the sights and smells of war.

Indeed he had his own struggles, but once again he became con-cerned for his many comrades-in-arms who, he was sadly beginning to learn, also had big problems and were suffering tremendously. He challenged himself to help them.

He tracked down and made contact with as many of his comrades as possible and constantly continues in that search. He is most active in and extremely proud of his role as President of the 5th/60th Association.

In summary, Lee has continued his lifelong quest to champion returning war veterans whether they are wounded physically, men-tally, or unscathed from their unselfish and valorous service to their country, and all of its people.

He resides today with his wife of 35 years, Ellen, and their chil-dren, a daughter Kresta, and son, Bo.

About the Author
Wade A. Stevenson

Wade Anthon Stevenson is a retired Special Agent from the U.S. Department of Defense (DoD) Investigative Service, a Federal Law Enforcement and Investigative Agency. His 35 year plus career with the U.S. Government ranged from performing duty as an armed guard and courier with the Armed Forces Courier Service in Europe, to serving as a U.S. Intelligence Officer. He has worked on counterespionage/espionage cases involving offenders such as Boyce and Lee (the infamous Falcon and Snowman team), James Durward Harper, William H. Bell, the Navy Walker family and others.

He held an executive position with Presidential and other Departmental Top Secret-level clearances in the most secret of all Pentagon operations—the Black World Special Access Programs Office—Office of the Secretary of Defense.

Stevenson is the author of numerous government articles, directives, manuals, regulations, pamphlets, bulletins and classified reports. His unclassified publications have been distributed worldwide to all U.S. military services and branches; to our embassies, as well as each U.S. cleared DoD contractor, i.e. RCA, TRW, Martin-Marietta, and others.

His classified writings have reached the U.S. Congress, Senate, and the White House. His short story, *A Special Cup of Coffee*, was published in the *Rocking Chair Reader Anthology* by Adams Media Corporation and distributed on a global scale in September 2004. He is the author of two thriller genre novels: *The Salzdorf Wellspring*, and *Mountains Prime Evil;* he has interrupted work on the final novel in the trilogy tentatively titled, *The Salzdorf Legacy,* to assist in this writing. He also has written under the pseudonym of Seth Aidan.

Worldwide assignments and travels have involved Mr. Stevenson in working closely with the National Security Agency, the Central Intelligence Agency, the Federal Bureau of Investigation, the Secret Service, the National Aeronautics and Space Administration, and other agencies, both foreign and domestic, on government high-level classified projects.

Mr. Stevenson was born in Gillette, Arkansas. His undergraduate and some graduate level studies were completed in the U.S., Europe, and the Pacific. He resides with his wife of 47 years, Dorothy Jane, in Wheatland, Wyoming. Their children are: a daughter Cynthia Jane Palm who resides in Longmont, Colorado; a son Mark Anthon Stevenson (a Naval Veteran of the Desert Storm war in Iraq) in Van Buren, Indiana; and a daughter Dawn Marie Stevenson in Lusby, Maryland.

Editor's Note: Sadly, Mr. Stevenson passed away in December of 2005 before this book went to press.

AUTHOR NOTES
LEE ALLEY

When I started *Back From War: Finding Hope & Understanding In Life After Combat* seemed to me to be the perfect title. I am convinced that when a combat veteran returns home, his or her most basic and strongest driven desire is to get back to a normal life. Life as it was before war. A catch phrase in seeking this life has piped up. We have all heard it. Maybe even said it ourselves many times: "We need to find closure." I hope this book will help with that seeking.

In the middle of my writing, I took a week off to fly to Texas and participated in a mini reunion with several members of the Recon Platoon I hold in highest reverence. During three days of hugs, tears, and belly laughs, the term Closure came up with *stout convictions.*

Sergeant Larry Easter, one of my Recon Sergeants, with obvious emotion said, *"I do not want closure—as long as I live, there will never be closure for me!* To me closure means to forget. I can never, will never forget what we did. I will never forget the great soldiers, close buddies, the many brothers we lost. I will never let our country forget the Vietnam War!"

I was stunned. Caught completely off guard. Had I in fact been writing a book to find *that kind* of closure? How could I, in any sense, dishonor my slain comrades by forgetting them? *I couldn't, and would never!*

Two days later as I relaxed with my wife Ellen, in a quiet, and peaceful area of the River Walk in San Antonio, I remained troubled with my thought about the term Closure and its strict interpretation by Larry. Later, alone, I walked over to the location of the famous battle site, the Alamo. At the entrance I paused to read the letter written by the Commander, Lieutenant Colonel William Barret Travis, on February 24th, 1836, which reads, in part:

> . . . *I am besieged by a thousand or more of the Mexicans under Santa Anna. I have sustained a continual bombardment & cannonade for 24 hours . . . I am determined to sustain myself as long as possible & die like a soldier who never forgets what is due to his own honor & that of his country—Victory or Death.*
>
> *William Barret Travis, Lt. Col. Comdt.*

My hands suddenly began to tremble. I felt like I knew Colonel Travis and his men. I, too, have experienced the horror yet fierce determination in facing and fighting overwhelming numbers. I most certainly have seen the face of death—too many times.

Guided to the amphitheater I sat in reverent silence as the guide told the history of the Alamo and the extreme bravery of the 183 who gave their lives for freedom there.

After the presentation ended I sat alone with tears evident. Forced to move, I approached the speaker.

"I try and give a great presentation in honor of these men," he told me. "But I don't think I'm that eloquent."

"To me, sir, you were talking about my men, my soldiers. You were talking about Fire Base Cudgel in Vietnam where only eight of thirty-five men were able to return and fight the next day. You did a fine job, and I thank you."

I thought when he ended his talk with the somber words, "Remember the Alamo," *what about remembering the 58,245 whose names are cut into the stone of a black granite wall in our nation's capital?* Each and every one of them, just as much a hero as the 183 men who fought so gloriously here for those 13 days of the Alamo Battle. *I shall always remember them, too!*

The term Closure means different things to different people, but I will never use that word again in the sense of forgetting, of closing a door, tightly shut for once and for all, never to bring to mind again.

Indeed, we must remember the Alamo. You bet. But in all remembrances I pray at the same time we will remember every soldier, each of our military members, who shed his or her blood and gave their lives with their personal cry and brave showing for freedom.

If needed, I hope this book will help you in finding hope and understanding in life after combat—but never—please, never forget!

My thoughts, every best wish and prayers are with you.

— Lee

To share your stories or provide feedback to Lee, please email him at lee@leealley.us.

AUTHOR NOTES
WADE STEVENSON

In the late 1960s I was with the U.S. Air Force and had occasion to travel to Hawaii's Headquarters Pacific Air Forces at Hickam Air Force Base on Oahu. On the first leg of my trip, I left Scott AFB, Illinois, near St. Louis, Missouri, aboard one of the Air Force Mobility Command's newest Aeromedical Evacuation aircraft, a C-9A/C Nightingale.

The Nightingale had the capability to carry 40 litter patients, 40 ambulatory patients, or various combinations thereof. There was a mixture of litter and ambulatory Vietnam veteran patients aboard that flight and three empty seats. I sat in one of those empty seats beside a young man who was missing his left arm from just below his shoulder. During our initial takeoff, I tried talking to him and he responded, but feebly and, thankfully, he was soon in a deep, comfortable sleep aided by his medication.

Other passengers on that flight were missing fingers, hands, arms, feet and legs. Some had been blinded; some had very serious head and body wounds. Probably close to 80 plastic IV bottles swung freely, seemingly in cadence from ceiling receptacles during the frequent takeoffs and landings at both military and civilian airports near hospitals en route to Travis AFB in California. It was a quiet flight except for the two flight nurses and three Aeromedical technicians who stayed busy checking their patients. The wounded mostly suffered in silence during the bumpy landings or air turbulence.

The wounded veterans all seemed to have a similar look—not of a total abandonment of hope, but certainly beyond easy consolation. It was heartbreaking to look at their scarred faces, with crooked, broken and missing facial features. That was a flight and an experience I will never forget. I continue to pray for these veterans and for all of our service members.

During my more than 35 years service to our country I was also in a war zone, but I never experienced anything like the daily actions our military forces lived through on a 24-hour basis during some of their tours of duty. Unfortunately I have, however, seen the horror of death the instant it was delivered in the form of ghastly head wounds, terribly mangled, broken, and dismembered bodies.

Those memories remain with me today as vivid as they were then. I don't believe the sight of such carnage is ever erased from one's memory.

I have known many comrades, closest veteran friends who proudly wore the uniform of our country. They were in Vietnam and other war zones, and sadly, too many of them are no longer with us. I remember them daily, and shall always remember and miss them. Whether in uniform or in civilian attire, they were true heroes and patriots. They offered their lives in their service to our nation. They could not have done or given more.

It has been my distinct honor and privilege to work with Lee on this book. There've been many occasions during its writing and preparation when I could sense that some of the more gripping passages, and the reliving of these painful memories, were particularly difficult for Lee.

There were also times when we both felt so deeply moved by what we were working on that we turned away from the computer and unashamedly reached for Kleenex to dry our eyes. I am fortunate to have been privy to a side of Lee that perhaps only his closest family members and very few others have seen.

In closing I'd like to thank Lee and all of our brave veterans who have throughout their lifetimes in many of our nation's conflicts placed our flag, their country, and the safety and well-being of their fellow service men and women—above all else.

A distinguished relative of mine, the former Governor of Illinois, the American Ambassador to the United Nations and twice Democratic presidential nominee, Adlai E. Stevenson II, asked and answered the following question, which I believe aptly describes a true patriot's devotion and patriotism to our country:

"What do we mean by patriotism in the context of our times?

I venture to suggest that what we mean is a sense of national responsibility—a patriotism which is not short, frenzied outbursts of emotion, but the tranquil and steady dedication of a lifetime."

Lee and many of our fellow veterans have not only dedicated their active-duty service, but also their lifetimes to the patriotism they feel for our country. I salute them and extend my heartfelt

thanks to all veterans past, present and future. To every blessed soul—
every mother and father's son and daughter of our great nation.

May God bless and keep them,

— Wade

Glossary of Terms

ACR – Armored Cavalry Regiment.
AFB – Air Force Base.
AFN – Armed Forces Network.
AIDS – Acquired Immune Deficiency Syndrome.
AIT – Advanced Infantry Training.
AK-47 – Russian made machine gun – VC favorite.
APC – Armed Personnel Carrier M113.
ARTY – Artillery.
ARVN – Army Republic Vietnam.
ASAP – As soon as possible.
Bag-Drag – Rolling up sleeping bag from a night's rest.
BDE – Brigade.
Beehives – Artillery shell containing 8,000 tiny metal arrows.
    Fired slightly above intended target(s). Devastating to
    life and denuding to all foliage.
BFD – Big fuckin' deal.
Bn – Battalion.
BI – Branding Iron, University of Wyoming paper.
Boom-Boom – Short time visit with a prostitute.
Camon Ty – Halt or stop.
C-Rats – Canned meals.
Caca Dau – Vietnamese term meaning "I'll kill you!"
Cam On – Thank you.
CAS – Close Air Support.
Choi Oi – Vietnamese term meaning "What the hell?"
Chotto Mottie – Wait a minute.
Civvies – Civilian clothing.
Clap – Caused by a bacteria called Neisseria gonorrhea. A
    relatively common venereal disease.
CO – Commanding Officer.
Deuce and a half – Two and one-half ton truck.
Di Wee – Vietnamese term for Lieutenant.
Dinky Dow – Vietnamese term for "You're crazy!"
Div – Division.
Di Di Mau – Move fast!
Du Mi Ami – The F-word with maternal overtones.

Dust-Off – Nickname for a Medevac helicopter or mission.

Dung Lai – Vietnamese term for 'stop!'

DVD – Digital Versatile Discs that provide video, audio data storage.

Eagle-type operations – Quick helicopter drop/retrieval of troops in search of enemy.

EM – Enlisted Men.

ER – Emergency Room.

Evac – Evacuate/Evacuation.

Flak Jacket – Heavy fiberglass-filled vest for protection VS shrapnel.

FNG – Fuckin' New Guy.

Foopy-Tan – Very fast.

Forty-Five – Automatic pistol famous for large shell 'knock down' quality.

Frag – To intentionally kill or wound one's superior officer, especially with a hand grenade.

FS – Fire Support Base.

Ga Mug – Vietnamese term for 'thank you.'

GI – Government Issue.

Grunt – Infantryman. Originally slang for a Marine fighting in Vietnam, but later applied to any soldier fighting: a boonierat. Also 'Pounder', or 'Crunchie.'

HHC – Headquarters & Headquarters Command.

Hootch – A house, living quarters or a native hut.

HQ – Headquarters.

ID – Identification.

Inf – Infantry.

KIA – Killed in Action.

KP – Kitchen Police, detail duty as helper, dishwasher, etc., in mess hall.

LT – Lieutenant.

LTC – Lieutenant Colonel.

LP – Listening Post. Provides early warning.

LRRP – Long Range Recon Patrol.

LZ – Landing Zone. Drop off point with Air Mobile Operations.

M-1 – Thirty-caliber semi-automatic rifle.

M-16 – Fires 650 – 700 rounds per minute, carries 20 rounds.

M-60 – Fires 500 – 650 rounds per minute, holds 3,000 rounds.

MASH – Mobile Army Surgical Hospital.

Maulen Dung Lai – Fast.

MCRD – Marine Corps Recruit Depot.

MD – Medical Doctor.

MECH – Mechanized Unit.

Medevac – Medical Evacuation/Helicopters with medical personnel.

Mg – Milligrams.

MIA – Missing In Action.

MOS – Military Occupational Speciality.

MP – Military Police.

MPH – Miles per hour.

NCO – Non-Commissioned Officer.

Nuoc Mam – Fermented fish sauce. Also called Armpit Sauce.

NIV – New International Version. Holy Bible.

NKJV – New King James Version. Holy Bible.

NLT – New Living Testament. Holy Bible.

NVA – North Vietnamese Army.

OD – Overdose (medical), – Officer of the day.

OJT – On the Job Training.

OPCON – Attached to for a specific operation.

OR – Operating Room.

PC – Personal Computer.

Piasters – Dollars.

Pop Smoke – To direct intense artillery fire or Air Force ordinance on enemy positions.

POW – Prisoner of War.

PRC-25 – A major field radio, commonly called 'Prick.'

RCN – Reconnaissance/Recon.

Recon – Reconnaissance.

Romeo 6 – Lieutenant Alley's Recon Call Sign.

RPG – Rocket Propelled Grenade.

RTO – Radio Transmitting Operator.
S-3 – Army Plans and Operations Activity.
SEA – Southeast Asia.
Semper Fi – Latin motto term meaning 'Always faithful.'
Sgt – Sergeant.
SSgt – Staff Sergeant.
Short Timer – One nearing his end of tour.
SITREP – Situation Report.
So Mudi – Number 10, the worst!
SOP – Standard Operating Procedures.
SP-4 – Specialist Fourth Class.
Spooky – C47 Gunship with 3 7.62 Gatling miniguns
    mounted in side windows. They could fire 16,5000
    rounds of ammunition. From '64 to '69 Spooky fired
    over 97 million rounds and killed over 53,000 enemy
    soldiers.
Sq. or Sqdn – Squadron.
Swamp Devil – Small patch(es) of fog hovering over
    ponds, canals or swamps which quickly evaporates at
    sunrise.
Syph – Syphilis. An infectious venereal disease transmit-
    ted by sexual intercourse or acquired congenitally.
Tet – Vietnamese Lunar New Year holiday period. Also
    refers to the NVA-VC offensive that began during Tet,
    1968.
Ti Ti – Little bit.
Tin Tù – Fast.
TOC – Tactical Operation Center.
Toss One's Cookies – Vomit.
Tracks – Armored vehicles that move on tracks rather than
    wheels.
Trung Wee – Sergeant.
USAF – United States Air Force.
VAMC – Veterans Administration Medical Center.
VFW – Veterans of Foreign War.
WIA – Wounded in Action.
WU – Wyoming University.
XO – Executive Office/Executive Officer.

VA – Veterans Administration.
VC – Officially: Vietnam Cong San (Vietnamese
    Communists)

INDEX